MW01137775

"Beautiful, visceral, and powerful writing that speaks from the heart and to the heart. I could feel every word: the frustration, the confusion and the joy. *Foreign Fruit* is a raw and fascinating book that delves into the important meaning of fruit that we take for granted every day, as well as the history of fruit in Asian cultures. I absolutely adored it."

—**Angela Hui**,
author of *Takeaway*

"*Foreign Fruit* offers one of the strongest openings of a nonfiction book I've read in a long time, refusing history to stay at a distance and the trade wealth is built on to remain elusive, subverting the popular genre of the 'history of things' in elegant ways. Katie Goh writes with as admirable a preciseness about self-othering as she does about botanical history. What's more, she injects her memoir writing with an essential critique and awareness of what it means to turn your own pain into a commodity as a person of colour in a white-dominated media landscape, and as a writer of mixed belongings in a market that seeks to routinely label."

—**Jessica Gaitán Johannesson**,
author of *The Nerves and Their Endings*

"*Foreign Fruit* is an encounter not only with the orange, but with the reality of diasporic life in hostile environments. Goh patiently and skillfully reinvents the orange as a means of inventing her identity, finding ways to grow and claim a story beyond which she'd first thought was hers to take. And what we're given is a story more surprising, potent, and various than we could ever have imagined."

—**Amy Key**,
author of *Arrangements in Blue*

FOREIGN FRUIT

FOREIGN FRUIT

A Personal History of the Orange

Katie Goh

TIN HOUSE / PORTLAND, OREGON

Copyright © 2025 by Katie Goh

First US Edition 2025
Printed in the United States of America

Manufacturing by Lake Book Manufacturing
Interior design by Beth Steidle

Library of Congress Cataloging-in-Publication Data

Names: Goh, Katie, author.
Title: Foreign fruit : a personal history of the orange / Katie Goh.
Other titles: Personal history of the orange
Description: First US edition. | Portland, Oregon : Tin House, 2025.
Identifiers: LCCN 2024051345 | ISBN 9781963108231 |
ISBN 9781963108316 (ebook)
Subjects: LCSH: Oranges—History. | Fruit-culture—History. |
Citrus fruits—History. | Citrus fruits--Historiography. | Goh,
Katie—Travel—China—Longyan Shi. | Goh, Katie—Travel—Malaysia. |
Chinese—Malaysia—Biography. | Women authors—Biography. | Goh family.
Classification: LCC SB369 .G594 2025 | DDC 634/.304—dc23/eng/20250110
LC record available at https://lccn.loc.gov/2024051345

Tin House
2617 NW Thurman Street, Portland, OR 97210
www.tinhouse.com

DISTRIBUTED BY W. W. NORTON & COMPANY

1 2 3 4 5 6 7 8 9 0

For my parents

CONTENTS

CONTENTS

●●●●●●●●●●●●●●●●●●●●

PROLOGUE

PROLOGUE

• • • • • • • • • • • • • • • • • • • •

THE MORNING AFTER A WHITE MAN MURDERED SIX ASIAN women, I ate five oranges. They were not dainty tangerines or pretty satsumas or festive clementines. These were unwieldy, bulging oranges, pockmarked and rind-covered fistfuls of flesh. I ate them all until my body ached.

Inside a blue-and-white porcelain bowl, the oranges had been waiting for me. My father had read recently that processed orange juice contains as much sugar as a glass of Coke. This, his newspaper explained, is due to the concentration process, which adds sugar, eliminates pulp, and shreds the fruit's fibre to release fructose into the bloodstream. Bottles of juice had since become contraband in my parents' house. Now, if I wanted the satisfaction of orange juice, I had to labour over a dingy plastic juicer, each twist of the wrist releasing a thimbleful of nectar. I soon learned that it takes more than five oranges to fill a glass. My frequent juicing had become an extravagance during lockdown, and soon our household was buying a ridiculous quantity of citrus. But these oranges were not the sort to be carefully peeled and savoured one segment at a time. This was fruit cultivated, exported, and sold to be split open, crushed, and ruined.

Resting in the bowl beside bruised apple pinks and mottled pear greens, the oranges stood out as something foreign; it was

1

their skin that gave them away. Surely nothing that bright could have been raised from Irish soil. This was a fruit that began its life a plane journey—or two—away, growing like golden ornaments on boughs, bloating under blue skies along the Iberian Peninsula. The sight of Spanish oranges sitting in an Irish kitchen, bought in a British supermarket stocked with fresh fruit cultivated across the continents of Africa, North and South America, Oceania, and Asia, is as close a thing as we have to a modern miracle—as well as a perfectly banal picture of domesticity.

Most days I breezed past this bowl of fruit, paying it little attention. But that morning I studied it. I picked up one of the oranges and set it in the palm of my hand. A white sticker declared its place of origin to be across the ocean. I peeled it off with my thumbnail. Now naked, the orange offered no information. Unlike delicate strawberries or nectarines, oranges give little away by their skin. The fruit's rind holds the flesh's secrets. I wondered: If I were to cut into the orange, would it be dry or juicy? Bitter or sweet? Tough or tender? Disappointing or rewarding? Would it be unbroken on the outside and rotten on the inside?

I set the orange down, picked up a kitchen knife, and sliced through its skin. Juice bled down the blade. Inside I found no true seeds—the fruit's genome had been meticulously selected to avoid this inconvenience—and yet nature had still found a way for vesicles, those tiny translucent teardrops, to form around the occasional pip. As I divided the orange into segments on a white dinner plate, the flesh shone like silken jewels glistening in the morning sun. I paused to look at them. And then I started to eat.

ORANGES ARE GLEEFULLY ANTISOCIAL. Juice sprays across the table and runs down wrists to spoil shirtsleeves. Pith gathers under fingernails. Segments explode in the mouth. Fibres catch between teeth.

In Victorian Britain, oranges were a vulgar fruit. Manners books of the period sternly advised young ladies never to consume the slippery, staining, spraying orange at the dinner table. "The difficulty of eating this fruit daintily is a heavy weight on its popularity," laments an article in The Girl's Own Paper in 1897.[1] The eating of oranges, particularly by women, particularly in public, was an affront to good manners. In Elizabeth Gaskell's 1853 novel Cranford, two characters retire to their private chambers to consume oranges: "When oranges came in, a curious proceeding was gone through. Miss Jenkyns did not like to cut the fruit; for, as she observed, the juice all ran out nobody knew where; sucking (only I think she used some more recondite word) was in fact the only way of enjoying oranges . . . and so, after dessert, in orange season, Miss Jenkyns and Miss Matty used to rise up, possess themselves each of an orange in silence, and withdraw to the privacy of their own rooms to indulge in sucking oranges."[2]

Even today, the potential for social embarrassment from eating oranges remains. On a family holiday to London as a child, my appetite for the fruit became the trip's running joke. Presented with wedges of oranges at the end of meals in Chinatown restaurants, I ripped wet flesh from white pith with my teeth, possessed with the same vigour as when I tore meat from ribs. My uncles chuckled and called me a wee beast as I tossed triangles of rind on the table. As I grew older, I learned that eating food with savage gluttony quickly ages out of being cute. With the self-preservation of a Victorian lady, I restricted my orange eating to a meal for one, a private pleasure to relish behind closed doors.

THE MORNING AFTER a white man murdered six Asian women, I sat alone at the kitchen table and ate one orange after another. As I had done those years ago as a child in a Chinese restaurant,

I picked up each pyramid of flesh and tore it clean off the rind with my incisors. Juice ran from my mouth and splattered the white plate.

Earlier that morning, a thread of messages had broken—and decided—my day.

"Such sad news," a friend had written to me. Squinting at my phone's blue light, I tapped on a news app and found the source of her sorrow, described in a single sentence. Eight people, six of whom were women of East Asian heritage, had been murdered by a white man in Atlanta. I scrolled for more information. The man: twenty-one, Christian, with an alleged sex addiction. The women: mothers, aunties, workers, immigrants, Asian. The man had taken a gun and opened fire in three massage parlours where the women worked. The Cherokee County Sheriff's Office had already commented that these places were, to the man, a "temptation for him that he wanted to eliminate."[3] The sheriff's captain added at a press conference that the white man who had murdered eight people, six of whom were Asian women, was having "a really bad day."[4] In the days following the shooting, a photograph posted by the captain would circulate online. Its subject was a T-shirt that read, "Covid 19 imported virus from Chy-na." With it, a caption: "Place your order while they last."[5]

I agreed with my friend's message; this news was indisputably sad. It was horrifying. But I wasn't shocked by its violence. Since the beginning of the Covid-19 pandemic, news media had run articles about the spread of the disease illustrated with photographs of Asian people wearing face masks. The president of the United States had called the virus "kung flu," while people of East Asian heritage were being abused, beaten, and murdered in the streets.[6] For over a year, my mornings had been mangled by reports of violence that targeted people who looked like my family, my friends, myself. Most of the time the people harmed were strangers. Occasionally they weren't. Clicking, sharing, and consuming accounts of bodies hurt, humanity disregarded, and blame cast had become habit. I spent my days getting lost down rabbit warrens of hyperlinks. When I thought I had found the worst testimony of pain, I always managed to find something deadlier. My daily scrolls through this bombardment of violence, coupled with the isolation of lockdown, had begun to gnaw at my insides.

ALL VEINS IN the north of Ireland pump history through the body. The weight of family lineage is carried by blood, but, as a child, my ancestry wasn't so easily hidden beneath my skin. I grew up mixed race, Chinese and white, in the north of Ireland, a place that was 99 percent white when I attended primary school.[7] Within that 1 percent, there were so few Asian people that if the census were to round its decimal points, we would have made up 0 percent of the population. The number of non-white students in my school could be counted on one hand. There were so few of us that survival meant an assimilation into a sea of whiteness. To be separated out from the pack was a social death sentence.

As a child, I learned that visible difference was something shameful, something to hide. As I grew taller, I shrank farther into myself. I became quiet and self-conscious, forever stressed that my body would betray me. I rounded myself down to zero.

When I left the north of Ireland and moved to Scotland for university, I began to write about myself. Or, rather, my identity. It was the early 2010s and people who suffered systemic, political, cultural violence—namely, people of colour, women, queer people—were being encouraged to write their pain away. The simultaneous boom of the personal essay and internet identity politics was presented as an opportunity to break into journalism and to cauterise the past; a chance to capitalise on scar tissue. I leapt at the chance.

I learned there was pleasure in writing about pain, like pushing a finger down, hard, on a yellowing bruise, before letting go
and watching the numbness bleed back into the skin. I discovered I was good at wielding vulnerability and empowerment: the
persona I presented was convenient; the narrative arc neat. I told
myself that this was healing. I was taking control of my story. I
was writing myself out of the shadows of the 0 percent. But the
more I wrote, the more I ripped at the wounds of the past. There
is only so much pain you can exchange for capital until each trans-
action is violence in itself. By the time I reached my mid-twenties,
my skin was peeled and what remained was a bundle of exposed
nerves. I no longer knew what was story and what was memory.
I had measured my existence in the narratives I could fulfil for
other people, and now I feared I had left nothing for myself.

The morning after a white man murdered six Asian women,
I got out of bed and commuted two steps to work. I logged on
and tried to summon the motivation to answer emails and not
refresh pandemic death counts. And then—an email jumped into
my inbox. "Asian hate crimes?" read the subject line. I opened it.
An editor wanted to know if I could write eight hundred words
on the murders of six Asian women by midday. "Write it from
your perspective," she told me.

I stared at the words on the screen for so long that my laptop
switched off its display to save power. My reflection stared back
at me. *Write it from your perspective.* I had done that before. I left
my laptop and walked into the kitchen. And there, waiting for
me, were five oranges.

As I ate the fruit, I lifted my phone with my free hand and
began scrolling through the news again. The families of the
murdered women were gathering outside their workplaces,
now crime scenes. Their children held each other and wailed.
Juice stung my tongue, my gums, my lips. I cut the third orange
in one swift movement, from top to bottom, and then ripped
the two halves apart with my thumbs. My jaw was beginning

to ache. I scrolled past statistics and headlines and talking heads who were parsing meaning from the murders. To call it a hate crime or not to call it a hate crime? I opened the email on my phone and looked down at the screen that was now sticky from sprayed fruit juice. *Write it from your perspective.* I could no longer taste the fruit, but I ate until my body was hot and heavy and full. When there were no more oranges left to eat, I slumped back in my chair to reckon with the damage. Each white rind faced up to me like a taut knuckle of bone.

PLANT AN ORANGE SEED. If the constellations of climate, chemistry, and good fortune arrange themselves just right, the seed will sprout. And if the young sapling can weather frost, drought, and blight, an adult tree will grow tall and straight, its leaves unfurling in waxy dark greens, its blossoms erupting in perfect white stars. An orange tree is self-fertile and can reproduce by itself or with the help of insects pollinating its flowers. Once fertilised, the blossom falls away as a knot swells into an unripe fruit. As the weather cools, the skin colour turns russet and then one day, years after the seed was first planted, a tree comes to bear ripe fruit. A hand reaches through the leaves and pulls down from the branches, not an awaited orange but instead a lemon. Or a grapefruit. Or perhaps even a squat yellow yuzu.

Citrus is fruit that freely betrays. Plant a seed from an orange and any of the fifteen hundred species of the Rutaceae family, commonly called the citrus family, could grow from its burial place. Citrus trees have a promiscuous tendency to breed across varieties—both spontaneously, through cross-pollination in the grove, and by design, in the laboratory. In 1997, the British botanist David Mabberley traced the convoluted lineage of all commercial edible fruits in the *Citrus* genus back to three "original" species: *Citrus medica*, the citron; *Citrus maxima*, the pomelo; and *Citrus reticulata*, the mandarin orange.[8] Beyond those three fruiting trees, every other citrus is a hybrid: sour orange from mandarin orange and pomelo, lemon from citron and sour orange, and grapefruit from pomelo and sweet orange.[9] In Mabberley's family classification, citrus is wanton; hybrids spawn further hybrids, new species (known as sports) spontaneously erupt in the wild, and trees endlessly reproduce themselves with their own self-pollinating flowers.

The genomic spontaneity of citrus makes it a risky harvest. Few farmers would dare to grow its fruit from seed. Instead, grafting—the common horticultural technique which joins the tissues of plants together—is how citrus is cultivated, in both commercial farming and amateur groves. The grafted plant consists of two ends: the rootstock—an already rooted host tree chosen for its resilience to soil-borne disease—and the scion—a slip of budwood from the fruiting tree that is to be replicated. A sharp knife slices these two edges of bark, and thin twine binds the wounds together. In time, the cuts heal and the bark merges to form a perfect clone of the bud's original tree, but now with steady roots. Only a faint scab tracing the trunk will bear the memory of two plants that were once foreign to each other.

Grafting provides growers with a consistent stock of trees. Fruit trees from the same families are often paired together for the strongest graft connection: apples with pears, apricots and plums. Citrus, a genus with seemingly endless offspring, are grafted together: pomelo to lime to blood orange to lemon, so that a single tree could host pink, green, orange, and yellow fruit—all different species and all thriving together.

The branching tree has become our model for tracing family lineage and bloodlines, yet grafting complicates the myth of a single stable tree, a single consistent species, and a single extractable fruit. The grafted citrus branch with its hanging oranges, lemons, and limes is an amusing—and astounding—sight, but it also offers a cornucopia of endless possibilities, a tribute to the variousness of nature.

Paul the Apostle, author of the New Testament's Epistle to the Romans, recognised the poetic opportunity of the grafted fruit tree, which, in his time too, was how fruit trees were cultivated. In Romans, he uses the propagation technique as a metaphor for religious survival, addressed to Christians: "But if some of the branches were broken off, and you, a wild olive shoot, were grafted in their place to share the rich root of the olive tree, do not boast over the branches. If you do boast, remember that it is not you that support the root, but the root that supports you."[10]

Paul offers God's holy tree as rootstock for "wild" Gentiles. If this new religion can only graft itself to a more ancient and stable creed, Christianity might flourish. Grafting has always offered a ripe opportunity for adaptation and survival.

IN A MODERN, commercial orange farm, neat rows of grafted trees run for miles. An orange tree can live for over a century and bear abundant fruit for eighty years. Most supermarkets in northern Europe import Spanish oranges, from groves in Andalucía and Valencia, where oranges have been cultivated since Arab armies first carried citrus to Europe's western coast. Every March since the eleventh century, white blossoms have filled the Iberian groves with their sweet fragrance. Once a tree's last flower wilts under the sun, thousands of tiny, tough clusters appear along its branches. Most will follow the blossoms to the ground, but the hundreds remaining will ripen into oranges over nine months. One tree yields a single harvest each year. In small traditional groves, the fruit is picked by hand and collected in crates. On sprawling commercial farms, mechanical shakers replace the work of many hands. A metallic claw with bristles is attached to a tractor and driven down avenues of trees to untangle their knotty canopies. Shaken from their branches, oranges are collected in large metal cages. In less than fifteen minutes, a machine can work through one hundred trees, collecting thirty-six thousand pounds of fruit—what would have been a day's work for four labourers.[11] The demand for oranges, year-round, has increased employment for the canopy claws, making their slower human counterparts increasingly redundant.

Once harvested, the fruit is driven in refrigerated lorries to processing factories. Unlike climacteric apples, pears, and bananas, oranges do not continue to ripen once they leave their tree—nor do they bruise so easily or rot so quickly as more tender fruit. The production cycle is less a race against time to beat decay and more a contest to get produce onto supermarket shelves as fresh and as fast as possible. On conveyer belts, oranges are sorted by hand. They are checked and culled—any misshapen or pierced fruit is removed to be juiced—and the remaining, perfect orbs are loaded into boxes. While each piece of fruit is of a similar size and weight, no two oranges will ever be exactly the same. Each fruit is unique in flavour, texture, and aroma, even those that grow on the same grafted branch. A sunburnt orange grown in direct light, near the outside of its tree, will weigh less, hold less juice, and taste sweeter than fruit ripening in the shade.[12] Each orange is individual, consisting of its own distinctive quantities of acid, sugar, vitamin C, and water. Despite laboured attempts by farmers, botanists, and corporations, perfect consistency is impossible to achieve with the orange. It is a fruit born with inherit divergence in its genes.

From processing factories, boxes of oranges are transported in climate-controlled trains, lorries, and ships across Europe. The fruit arrives at border controls with the correct paperwork. Once granted entry, the oranges are taken to factories where they are checked again, labelled, and bundled into netting that is dyed red, a marketing ploy to make the peel appear a livelier shade of orange to the human eye. Loaded once more into crates, the nets of fruit are driven along the arteries of countries, up motorways, and down lanes until they reach supermarkets in cities, towns, and villages. Per person, oranges are the most consumed fruit in the world.[13] No matter how remote or cold or incongruous a climate might be, oranges will be there.

EVEN DURING THE PANDEMIC, when global supply chains broke down and countries went into lockdown, oranges kept arriving. For a moment, I was flummoxed by how the citrus fruit could journey across land, sea, and sky to end up in the big Tesco, a ten-minute drive from my parents' house, during what felt like the end of the world. Perhaps I shouldn't have been so surprised by the reliability of the fruit; citriculture has a long history of endurance, often buoyed by waves of crises. Globalisation is often considered a modern phenomenon, but widespread networks of goods, ideas, and cultures have existed for as long as there have been roads for them to travel along. Bitter oranges arrived in Europe with Arab armies, but even before then, the fruit was carried in the hands of religious zealots, ambitious traders, and weary soldiers along the Silk Roads from East Asia. Since sweet oranges began to be imported into Western Europe in the sixteenth century, they have flowed along the world's trade routes, from east to west and back again, desired as an exotic food, a cherished luxury, and a religious emblem. A twenty-first-century pandemic was not about to hinder the lucrative, and resilient, orange industry.

Armed with a face mask, surgical gloves, and hand sanitiser, I set out on a weekly quest for oranges during the pandemic. No matter the state of the world outside the chilled supermarket walls, I always encountered aisle upon aisle of fruit under fluorescent lights. Small white stickers charted an exotic map of modern food production—Morocco, Spain, Cameroon, Brazil, South Africa, New Zealand—places that may as well have been on different planets, they were so physically and psychologically removed from my everyday life during lockdown. As I browsed the fruit, I felt a tug of guilt at my complicity in its carbon foot-print. And yet, insatiable desire for fresh juice on my mind, I picked up two nets of oranges, dropped them into my trolley, and rattled on. After I carried them home, I tore apart the red plastic mesh and out tumbled a blazing cascade. In a bowl the fruit waited, until, one morning, a shadow fell over them and a hand reached out to consider an orange.

AFTER AN ORANGE IS EATEN, its peel is discarded. The tough, bitter ribbons are left to wither and shrivel, their edges curling back in on themselves. They are tossed over hedges, dropped onto compost heaps, or, as my family has always done in win-ter, scattered into the hearth, so that fire blackens the skin to ash and the smell of singed citrus rises with smoke. But in the orange business, the peel is a prized part of the fruit. Tiny glands, their openings only 0.3 micrometres in diameter, give an orange's rind its porous texture, and inside each of those pinpricks is a chemical treasure trove. A single gland contains over one hundred different molecules of essential oils that are coveted by fragrance companies and perfumeries.[14] As each orange is unique, so too is the chemical composition of each peel. The climate a tree grows in, the water its roots absorb, the insects that gorge upon its flowers, the sea-son its fruit ripens in: all this history determines what an orange expresses in its skin. Before pulping, industrial orange juice fac-tories set aside the peel to extract its oils. These essences are either sold to fragrance companies or reinjected into pasteurised juice during the final stage of processing to improve its diluted flavour.

The process by which discarded peel is squeezed in presses and its oils are siphoned off is called expression. Citrus is the only family of fruit that undergoes expression, an endeavour to extract what lies hidden within the skin. The noun "expression" is rooted in the Latin verb *exprimere*, meaning "to press out." The word's more modern meaning—the external manifestation of innermost feelings—came later, in the seventeenth century. This squeezing, this extraction, this *expression*, was a process I knew intimately from my writing. I often wondered if the final commodity—palatable, homogenous, exploitable—was worth the exhausting labour.

The morning after a white man murdered six Asian women, I stared down at the white rinds of five oranges. I knew I was going to write more than eight hundred words about this. As I wiped stinging juice from the corners of my mouth, I knew I was going to stop crushing myself to tell a convenient story. As I ran my stained fingers under cold water, I knew I needed a new means of expression. Peel might be valuable to an orange tycoon, but I had gotten all I needed from it. I tipped the plate of rind, pip, and pith into the compost bin.

I AM NOT THE FIRST person to discover meaning in the eating of an orange—or five. Emperors and artists, slaves and kings have interpreted the fruit ever since sports of orange trees first pushed through the Tibetan Plateau. As the Silk Roads connected continents, Chinese horticulturists grew mandarin oranges on an industrial scale, and the fruit became so beloved for its beauty that during the Han dynasty, a minister of oranges was responsible for presenting the fruit at court.[15]

Carried by hand, beak, and gale, oranges moved west as the sprawl of the Silk Roads traversed Asia, Europe, and Africa. Passing through constantly shifting borders, the fruit was traded and turned into a product with monetary value. The orange tree became revered by followers of Islam and Judaism, who found spiritual, artistic, and medicinal purpose in its fruit, flowers, and branches. When oranges first arrived on Italian shores, the Romans called the fruit a "gift from the gods," and citrus was adopted by Christian iconography as Renaissance artists painted Florentine oranges into religious frescos. Alboin, king of the

Lombards, invaded Italy after being sent a basket of oranges from Byzantine Rome.[16] Christopher Columbus delivered the first orange seeds to the New World.[17] William Shakespeare debuted his plays to an orange-munching audience—the fruit was the popcorn of Elizabethan London and was lobbed at the heads of actors who forgot their lines.[18] King Louis XIV loved oranges so much he built the world's grandest orangery at Versailles, where he could walk under the blooming boughs of orange trees in every season.[19] The cardinal Thomas Wolsey held an orange stuffed with a vinegar-soaked sponge beneath his nose as he strode the streets of London, to cover the stench of poverty.[20] During Carnival, the fruit was pelted through northern Italian towns, so that orange gore squelched between foot and shoe for days.[21] The First Fleet that set sail from Britain to Australia carried both convicts and orange tree saplings.[22] Enslaved African people ate oranges as they toiled in Europe's Caribbean plantation colonies.[23] Queen Victoria wore a wreath of orange blossoms on her wedding day, a fashion choice that incited such a frenzied fad that bouquets had to be shipped in salt barrels to England from the groves of Provence.[24] California and Florida became the citrus industries of the US; gardens of paradise where immigrants could seek their fortunes. During the Depression, this American dream went up in flames when golden mountains of fruit were sprayed with kerosene in a desperate bid to stabilise the stock market. Disgusted by the waste, the author John Steinbeck called these pyres of oranges "a failure . . . that topples all our success" in his great denouncement of American capitalism, *The Grapes of Wrath*.[25]

The orange is a souvenir of history. Across time, its appearance has been a harbinger of God and doom, fortune and failure, pleasure and suffering. It is a fruit containing metaphors, dreams, mythologies, superstitions, parables, and histories, all held within its tough rind. So what happens, then, when the fruit is peeled and each segment—each moment of history, each meaning across time—is pulled apart? Seemingly everything, according to the Irish poet Louis MacNeice, who eats a tangerine in his poem "Snow." He describes peeling and dissecting the fruit, experiencing a "drunkenness" of plurality.[26] It is the exhilarating intensity of taking a tangerine apart that gets closest to expressing just how strange, how varied, how intoxicating it is to be a person existing in our world. Unlike the apple with its wholeness of the flesh, the orange can be taken apart and put back together again, segment by segment, skin over skin. It can be remade.

I wished to be remade. I wished to hold variousness in my own skin and exist as all the incorrigible things I am at once—not peeled and portioned out and made palatable for someone else's appetite. I sought my own meaning, expressed how I see fit.

Sometime after a white man murdered six Asian women, I sat at the table where I had eaten five oranges. The fruit was gone, and in its place I set down a blank page. I am not the first person to discover meaning in an orange, and I am not the first person to seek refuge from a hostile climate, one that seeks to divide us. As I would soon discover, the orange's history is entangled with the story of migration, of exile, and of invasion.

I have felt a kinship with the orange's story ever since I discovered that its origins parallel my own: ancestral roots in China that venture towards the equator, and then traverse the long roads from east to west to reach Europe. I decided I would retread the history of the orange, to discover what role it has played in different lands across time. What stories could I unravel from the orange's long, ribboning peel? What new meanings could I find in its variousness, as it moves from east to west and from familiar to foreign?

ONE

LONGYAN

ONE

· · · · · · · · · · ·

LONGYAN

ALONG THE HIMALAYAN MASSIF, THE REMNANT STRAGGLES of ancient citrus groves sprawl. It is here, where the plains of Central, Eastern, and Southern Asia erupt into mountains, where the orange begins its journey eight million years ago.[27] Citrus is unpredictable. The speed and ease with which interspecific hybridisation can happen means that the genus is perplexing for scientists to trace back in time, never quite maintaining a straight chronology. DNA is unable to offer neat distinctions among indigenous, naturalised, and mutated species, and history is uncertain of the impact ancient civilisations had in cultivating the fruit. Yet a cryptic past indulges mythmaking, and the first orange warrants an origin story.

In the shadow of a mountain, an insect hurries through a grove. From the mouths of pomelo blossoms, it collects golden pollen. Dazed and a little dozy from the morning's labour, the creature withdraws; its stained wings weigh its body down on the flight home. All it desires is to deliver its yield back to the hive and rest. And then—a sweet scent in the air; a ripe, mellow stickiness that lacerates the insect's drowsy fog. Thrown into a frenzy, it darts to the source: a mandarin tree's pale flower. Yellow dust brushes off its wings and onto the stigma as the insect sucks nectar from the blossom. Jade leaves quiver in the breeze. Satisfied, with a belly full of sugar, the insect drifts out of the grove, its part in this story concluded.

A week later, a spring wind rushes through branches and the fertilised flower collapses. In its place, fruit begins to swell. A mandarin grows, ripens, and disappears into the mouth of an animal that spits the pips, and presses each of the seeds into the earth with a heavy paw. Genomic endlessness offers a sport of a new strain of citrus. Part pomelo, part mandarin, a hybrid grows. Years pass, until the first wild orange falls from the tree.

Fruit spawn trees spawn seeds spawn life. Carried, blown, and dropped by beasts and wind, each orange begins its own journey, taken away from its homeland. Some move south, drawn to the heat of India. Others go east, spreading across the Yunnan province of China, which has subtropical highlands that are so fertile, future scientists will nickname it "the Kingdom of Plants."[28] Monsoons from the Tibetan Plateau splinter Yunnan's earth, and the rivers Mekong, Yangtze, and Salween burst forth to permeate Southeast Asia. Into rushing water, seed-stuffed fruit falls, floating for miles until it washes up on new muddy shores. Across centuries, oranges traverse rivers, forests, and mountains until, one day, a person chances upon a tree.

Sour and tangy, glossy and bright, oranges become beloved in China for the pleasure they bear. Odes to the fruit are composed. One of the earliest mentions of oranges in literature is in the *Shūjīng*, documents of Chinese antiquity and a record of the divided nation's past carried from dynasty to dynasty, first compiled by Confucius.[29] In "Tribute of Yu," a chapter written about the mythical leader of ancient China in the third century BCE,[30] oranges and pomelos are carried in the bundles of island people, offered as tributes in eastern China, along with precious metals, bamboo canes, and elephant teeth.[31] Oranges appear again in etiquette books, instructing the reader on the most courteous ways to peel the fruit while attending a royal court.[32] Ribbons of bitter peel are added to honey, wine, and tea for flavour, while the whole fruit is placed around temples and homes, its brightness evoking sunshine, flames, and life itself. The orange becomes as much ornament as food, treasured for its beauty and for what it symbolises by its skin. During festivities such as Mid-Autumn Festival and Lunar New Year, bright fruit are portents for hope. Oranges and pomelos are left for ancestors and presented to gods in exchange for fertility, joy, and luck.

Oranges beguile early botanists, who become obsessed with cultivating hybrid species. Written in 1178 CE by Han Yen-Chih, the *Chü Lu* is the oldest known document dedicated to the orange and describes twenty-eight varieties of the fruit.[33] By this time, the wild orange's bitterness has been cultivated into something more palatable. Groves flourish across China and turn the orange into a product of commerce. Soon, the fruit is an industry unto itself, sold at markets and taken out of China to leave for new lands.

In 1646, Giovanni Baptista Ferrari, an Italian botanist, devoted Jesuit, and translator, publishes his masterpiece *Hesperides, sive de malorum aureorum cultura et usu*, a study of citrus. In between sketches of gardens, citrus cross-sections, and strange hybrids, Ferrari gives the orange his own meaning: "So I bestow upon this little rounded fruit the merited name of an ornament of the world, for in its golden dress it seems a decoration for the earth."[34]

When does a fruit become more than a creation of nature? When do the borders of skin become an ornament, a commodity, a mythology, a world? Across history, the orange has been cultivated until its origins have been lost. It has taken on new meanings, found new homes, and now the modern orange is a fruit designed in a laboratory to appeal to our senses, mass-produced to maximise profit, flown in planes to every corner of the world, marketed as wellness in waxy peel. It is a fruit continually mythologised anew by capitalism, religion, art, and history as it moves forward in time. Its future possibilities seem endless. And yet, it cannot return to its authentic state or its original home. An exile of its first garden, the orange moves where the world takes it, always a stranger who must assimilate to a new home. Would the modern fruit even recognise its own ancestor, that first wild orange that bent its bough to fall to earth and begin its journey?

LINE BY LINE, it came to life. First a bowl—arched, effortless, a crescent moon—supported by three squat legs that raised its belly off the table. A confusion of orbs followed, none of them in full view. Piled on top of one another, the imperfect spheres were re-formed as other shapes—triangles, squares, hexagons— cut with sharp edges. And, here and there, a waxing gibbous, half buried in the yawning mouth of the bowl. Pencil held loose between finger and thumb, my hand guided graphite to line, mark, and shade. As the sketch emerged from the white haze of the paper, I was no longer conscious of my drifting wrist. My focus was settled on the centre of a table where a bowl of unstable citrus sat. I studied each fruit like my life depended on it.

Inside the bowl were kumquats, oranges, and a pomelo. As I sketched the fruit, my eyes flitted between object and sketch, original and creation, absolute and attempt, always returning to settle back on the real bowl. And yet, the more I sketched, the more unsatisfied I was with my subject. The ceramic's glaze and the fruit's skin shone glossy and cosmetic under the kitchen's spotlights. The scene lacked depth. I took one of the oranges, sliced it open, and arranged three of its quarters in front of the bowl. The fourth slice I ate. Drying juice from my page, I returned to the still life and surrendered to the work. Schooled instinct guided the grey of my pencil. For the next thirty minutes, nothing existed beyond bowl, citrus, and paper.

The sun rose. My grandparents' alarm clock let out a shrill ring from across my Auntie Sian's apartment. I finished my sketch.

For the first time since I'd arranged the orange, I sat back to inspect the paper. My errors were immediately obvious. The pomelo's proportions were all wrong; its edges curved down too soon, its bulky globe diminished to the size of an orange. Or perhaps it was the oranges that were wrong, magnified to be the same size as the pomelo. The spot-the-difference continued. Occasionally I had simply invented fruit, adding a kumquat into the sketch where I thought one would make a pretty addition. Brow pinching, I turned my attention to the bowl. The sketched ceramic had such a cavernous mouth that it was no wonder I had invented fruit to fill it. Only the orange wedges were a perfect match to the ones that lay an arm's reach away.

I drummed my pencil against the table. I had been awake since the middle of the night, my brain foggy with jet lag and my body still running on European time. As I inspected the page, my head throbbed. I was sleep-deprived. No one can be expected to perfectly replicate reality on three hours of sleep. Still, as my eyes darted from sketch to citrus, I was disappointed. In my sketchbook was a pale, smudged representation of what sat in front of me. Still life; dead art for dead nature.

I pushed back my chair and left behind real and imagined fruit. Stretching stiff muscles, I stepped out onto the balcony. It was the summer of 2010, and Kuala Lumpur was waking up. In the city's business centre, cleaners filed out with bursting bags of shredded paperwork. At the open-air market where Ah Ma, my grandmother, bartered with Malay and Chinese sellers, stalls were being set out for the morning rush. Drivers stuck in traffic skipped through radio stations. Children walked to school. In the patch of rainforest that I could glimpse from my aunt's apartment block, monkeys screeched to one another as they woke. And twenty floors below where I leaned over the balcony railing, Ah Kong, my grandfather, would soon commence his morning qi gong.

My father and I had arrived in KL two evenings ago. We were staying in the apartment of his sister, my Auntie Sian, along with

Ah Kong and Ah Ma, and that night we would all be leaving together. My grandparents were visiting the city of Longyan in southern China, where both their families were from. They hadn't been back in a few years, and neither my father nor I had ever made the homegoing journey before. My father had grown up in Malaysia, and though I had often come to Malaysia as a child to visit my grandparents, I had never been to China. Some of my uncles and aunts had decided to join as well, so we would be a party of ten. That night we would fly, first to Shanghai and then onwards to Xiamen, before driving to Longyan in the coastal province of Fujian, which lies across the water from Taiwan. There, we would be hosted by my grandmother's cousin and his family. But the true purpose of the visit was to leave the city and travel to the small, rural village where my grandfather's parents had come from: our family's place of origin.

My school exams had finished weeks before the trip, and I had devoted my summer to researching Fujian on the internet. The province is famous for its tulou buildings: contained, circular structures that once housed entire villages, built by the Hakka people as long ago as the fifteenth century and as recently as the twentieth century.[35] I scrolled through photographs of these grand buildings, which were fortresses unto themselves, several storeys high and perfectly symmetrical. *Tulou* translates into English as "earthen building."[36] They were designed with feng shui precision for and by their inhabitants to exist in harmony with their surrounding rural landscape. Now heritage sites, most of Fujian's clusters of tulous are no longer occupied—in the twentieth century, most families left their fortified homes and relocated to modern buildings. But the images of these old, grand ring structures thrilled me. I knew our village would not be a tulou, but still, I let the fantasy run away from reality. As I clicked through photographs, I imagined my ancestors in their open-roofed tulou, where they lived under rain, sun, and stars. I saw them throw open the gates and cross the threshold into neighbouring groves and fields to tend the earth. Their hands pressed to the hard ground and warped trees. I could feel their kinship to their homeland, how it pulsed through the body. There was nothing I desired more than an affinity like that: to a place, to a history, to a sense of belonging.

I was seventeen, a teenager on the cusp of adulthood who was fixated on finding authenticity. Everywhere I looked I saw people who seemed certain of the skin they were in, who claimed their beliefs in a place that was home to them. I was frequently shocked by my classmates, who revealed their desires, miseries, and apathies, and who expressed them out of their bodies and into the world without hesitation.

In hindsight, I doubt all my classmates were quite as certain of themselves as I saw them then. Our school prized success—in academia, sports, and religious dedication—above all else, and the pressure—from teachers, parents, and peers—crushed children. Some students cried in toilet cubicles. Others turned to oblivion to escape the stress, lighting up rollies and swallowing pills. Life beyond our school gates offered little relief from scrutiny. A Unionist, Protestant stronghold in the northeast of Ireland, our town was the living legacy of centuries of British colonial occupation. Here, religion was wielded in the community with an iron fist. In July, Orangemen—named for the Protestant King William, not the fruit—marched under red, white, and blue bunting, and on the month's eleventh night, effigies of Sinn Féin politicians, racist placards, and Irish flags hung from bonfires. After the bank holiday, the politicians who'd joined in with these festivities returned to Stormont to ensure abortion access and same-sex marriage remained criminalised.

Growing up in my corner of northeast Ireland, I saw how bodies that could not assimilate into the majority white, patriarchal, Protestant social order were deemed to be a threat. People who were non-white, queer, Catholic, immigrants— were openly demonised as foreign invaders. I would see local news reports about Anna Lo, an Alliance Party politician and the only East Asian public figure in the north at the time. I listened to newscasters recount the abuse Lo faced every day: how she was chased in car parks, abused online, hounded as she walked the streets of Belfast. When she decided not to stand for re-election, I was glad. I was convinced that one morning I would wake up to the news of her murder.

I understood that the curtailment of self was paramount for survival. I was privileged—I could pass for white from afar—and so, if I remained vigilant about how I presented myself in public, I could fade into the background. I learned to quiet down, to avoid being recognised as different. I became secretive, refusing to give myself up to even my closest friends. I had seen how even the nicest people could succumb to hatred if provoked. I existed in a limbo between truth and fabrication, part person and part shadow. And so, as I aged and I saw my classmates articulate themselves as individuals in our small corner of the world with reckless disregard, I was stunned. Now, as an adult, I recognise that it was only my classmates born into the social majority who embodied the freedom of expression I so admired as a teenager. It was those with bodies which could move through our world without fear, who could afford authenticity.

But always inside my body blazed a yearning to belong. I wanted to inhabit a body that could move recklessly, like those of my classmates. Surely if I reached there—wherever this fantastical place might be—I would also discover my own authentic way of existing in the world. So, when my father suggested we join my grandparents on their homegoing trip, I leapt at the opportunity. As I looked through photographs of Fujian's tulou dwellings and imagined my ancestors living in communal harmony, I had already decided that this was where I needed to go.

Before we finished school for the year, my art teacher had suggested we use the summer to gather inspiration for the coming autumn term.

"You'll hit the ground running in September," she warned our class. "Take a sketchbook and a camera out into the world with you."

This trip was the perfect subject for a project: there would be a wealth of new sights that I could explore. And more slyly, I was convinced that with China as my muse, my art would stand out from that of my classmates, with their dreary landscapes, pet portraiture, and yellow Harland & Wolff cranes. I could already imagine my teacher moved to tears while reading my essays about how finally feeling a sense of belonging had inspired a pastel sketch of a Fujian mountain. I would document my homecoming. I would make art from it.

The second morning after I arrived in Kuala Lumpur, I had begun this endeavour with the still life of the fruit bowl. I left the balcony and wandered back into the kitchen. My failed sketch faced up to me on the table. I flipped the page over. And then, in front of the fruit bowl, I noticed a slice of orange squirming. I leaned in to take a closer look and leapt back in disgust. Ants crawled over it. High on sugar, they hurried across the fruit, their bodies swollen with juice, teeth devouring flesh. They had marched across the floor and up the table in single file, lured by the scent of an orange, ripe and rotting in the heat.

FROM THE PLANE touching down at Xiamen's airport, to Ah Ma's cousin driving us the two-hour journey to Longyan, to dropping our bags at his house which was as tiered and marbled as a wedding cake, to our first morning on the city's streets: my first impressions of China were a series of disorientations. My grandmother's cousin was the patriarch of his family, and in his house lived every generation of his lineage. After the evening meal on our arrival day, still jet-lagged, I left the adults to their beers and conversations and crawled into the bed I was sharing with my aunt.

The drive to the village would take several hours, so we woke with the sun. With renewed energy I threw myself out of the bed, slipped my palm-sized digital camera into a pocket, and headed downstairs. Morning in the house had begun long before the sun—or I—had risen, and a clangour of ringing metal, shuffling slippers, and women's voices was already emanating from the kitchen. Steam poured through the grates of the windows as boiling water sloshed out of steel pots to smack the sink. One of the aunties stirred a vat of simmering congee, while my great-aunt severed muscle from bone with a cleaver so polished she could have applied lipstick in its mirror. In the scullery doorway, a younger auntie squatted to wring out wet clothes over a drain. Hands supporting stiff knees, she rose to peg the limp shapes to lines of cord that ran across the balcony. As the women went about their morning tasks, they spoke over one another, tongues racing to shape the words that tumbled from their mouths, their chorus rising with the kitchen's smoke, steam, and smell into the rest of the house.

I watched them from the doorway. My stomach growled for breakfast, but I was too shy to intrude into the noisy domestic space. My great-aunt spotted me first. Cleaver still raised in one hand, she wrapped her fingers around my wrist and pulled me from the shadows into the light, laughing at the sheepish expression on my face as we went. I was passed to another woman, her niece perhaps, by the stove. We had no shared language, so she came forward to pat my arm and back with affection. Hot, sticky rice was ladled into a small bowl and placed into one of my hands. Into the other went a spoon. With a final, firm pat, I was pushed back through the door to join the rest of my family at the round table.

Ah Ma's cousin had arranged for a driver to take us to the village, and the white minivan pulled up to the house after breakfast. Bellies full, we waved farewell through the kitchen door to the aunties, who were already mincing garlic and chilli for the meal we would eat on our return. On the way out, I passed a wooden

Buddha in the living room, and gave it a tap with my knuckle for some last-minute luck. Then I set about untangling my sandals from the pile by the front door.

As soon as the minivan pulled away from the house and the air-conditioning clamoured into life, I regretted my bare feet. The driver was an elderly man and conversed with my uncle in the front seat.

"He says you must be uncomfortable here," my uncle said, half turning his torso in the seat. "The humidity must be difficult for you."

I returned the driver's smile in the mirror and hoped he wouldn't see me shiver.

For the first hour on the road, it seemed like we would never leave Longyan. Broad streets lined with every kind of store, cafés with queues of morning commuters, and restaurants already full for the breakfast rush gave way to roaring construction sites and enclosed condominium blocks, only to return to tarp-covered markets and glass-walled skyscrapers. When our driver begrudgingly braked at stoplight junctions, crowds surged forward to cross the intersections. Old men with newspapers tucked underarm spat as they waddled past cars, while young women in pencil skirts strode past them, one eye on their phones, the other alert for drains that might catch their heels. Children screamed in prams, pensioners opened pastel umbrellas, and businessmen charged forward to make the crossing before the lights flashed green. At last, the van turned a corner to join a highway. Cutting through the city's sprawl, the road was so straight I imagined Longyan's city planner had slapped a ruler down on a map, drawn a line, and called it a day.

As we drove, I soon grew bored of staring at motorbikes, cement, and lorries, and I sat back in my seat to try to doze. Each time the van's vibrations lulled me to sleep, a fresh blast of frigid air blew strands of my own hair across my face, each prickly end irking me awake.

And then the city fell away, so suddenly that I missed the exact moment when concrete turned to fields, and we were driving through Fujian's countryside. Now I was wide awake, trying to take in the view from every side of the vehicle at once. From each window, I saw only green: rows of sweet potato, groundnuts, and sugarcane running one after another until domed hills carried them away into the distance. The recent monsoon season had soaked the pastures, and months of hot relentless rain had coaxed sprouting seeds to race towards the light, stems growing tall and true in the summer humidity. As we drove farther away from Longyan's polluted haze, outlines of mountain peaks erupted in the distance to meet the pale blue sky. I rubbed goose bumps out of my arms. The snow-dusted range on the horizon felt closer to me than the muggy heat that smeared its breath on the minivan's cold windows.

So this was China beyond its hectic cities. I was shocked by how similar the country's southern rural landscape was to Ireland's, how recognisable the fields seemed to me. But then the occasional building tucked my imagination back inside my body. There was no mistaking the sculpted eaves, the wooden balconies, and the colourful shutters as anything familiar to me.

After another hour, our driver turned off the highway, down a winding road that brought us deeper into the fields and closer to the hills. Concrete buildings became more frequent, as did spotted dogs that chased us down dusty paths, catching up to us each time the minivan slowed to roll across a cragged pothole. Through the windows, their panting pink tongues greeted us and then they were off again, tearing across parched ditches and through tall grass. At the end of the road, we caught up with the dogs as we reached a cluster of buildings. The driver pulled into a short, concrete driveway. We had arrived.

As my family clambered out of the van, a host of people hurried from one of the buildings to meet us with waves and shouts. My grandparents greeted them, changing between Mandarin and Longyan dialects, tones rising and falling as both parties rushed to meet the other in a common tongue. I waited and patted the dogs weaving between our legs.

This was it then. This was where I was from. As busy tails thumped against my bare shins, I turned to take in the village. Backdropped by foothills, the buildings on the outskirts were like the ones we had passed on the road: squat, solid, and concrete, with walls that had become speckled over time by smoky fires and acid rain. Tiles sloped down to split into hip roofs, finished with the only extravagant flourish in sight: eaves that curled like lapping flames caught in clay by the sculptor. Other buildings were more modern—flat-roofed, double-glazed, multi-storied—completed as the village's families expanded and demanded electricity. Short stone walls marked the borders of the homestead. Beyond them lay fields of crops and occasionally a lone tree with splintered grey bark.

"They want to show us around lah." My auntie Suan nodded towards the crowd.

On our trip, I had stuck close to her, an aunt not by blood but by intimacy. She was a family friend who had grown up with my father and his siblings, and she was closer to me than some of my blood relatives. Auntie Suan's family came from the same village, in a house just down the road. Our families had been so close that when they arrived in Malaysia in the twentieth century, both took the surname Goh as a transliteration of our Fujian family name. A Mandarin and Longyan speaker, Auntie Suan had been acting as my translator on our trip.

I turned my gaze back to the villagers. "Are they all related to us?"

"Some of them. Ah Kong's father, your great-grandfather, was born in this village before he migrated to Malaya. See that lady?" Auntie Suan pointed towards the crowd. Peeking through gaps left between bodies, I glimpsed a figure so small I had missed her when we had first disembarked from the minivan. Her face was wizened and lovely, with wrinkled skin that folded down and gathered around a plump chin. Her small mouth frowned in a permanent downturn, and her gaze never left the earth. Despite her age, the woman had a shock of thick white hair that was neatly combed and tucked behind her ears with two pink clips. Wearing a navy felt jacket and belted apron, she was dressed more traditionally than the other villagers, who wore starched jeans or loose dresses. She held my grandmother's hands tight in her own.

"She married Ah Kong's uncle," Auntie Suan said, beside me. "He's dead now but she still lives in the same old outbuilding by herself. She won't move into one of the new buildings with her family. Imagine that! Aiyo . . . this lady in one of those outbuildings." My aunt gave a dramatic shudder. "She's the oldest person in the village now."

The lady led our group while the dogs lapped us. When we reached the single-storey concrete buildings, I noticed that most of them were derelict storehouses. None of the windows had glass panes but instead were filled with vertical bars to keep out farm animals and nosy neighbours. Cracks ruptured the walls, and vines tumbled from gaps under the eaves.

"No one lives in these buildings anymore," my aunt translated from the conversation happening around us. "These are all used for animals and storage now. Well, apart from the old lady's room."

"How long has Ah Kong's family lived here?"

My aunt rubbed her chin. "Forever lah. Your great-grandfather left the village to go to Malaya when the English were still there, but his brother, Ah Kong's uncle, stayed here."

My feet were starting to sweat in my sandals, and small pebble shards caught between my toes. When we reached one of the modern buildings, I kicked off my shoes at the door, grateful for the cool tiles underfoot. Women hurried through an inner doorway, pushing back its beaded curtain, and returned with trays of steaming teapots and clinking cups, cans of beer and Pepsi and crystal bowls of monkey nuts still in their hard shells. They waved us over to sit at a table. Cans hissed open and tea was poured. As the adults talked around me in the Longyan dialect, I watched a tea leaf whirlpool around the bottom of my cup. It slowed and sank, and unfurled its edges, releasing its bitter flavour and staining the hot water yellow.

"They're amazed we still know their dialect." My uncle Bob nudged me with his elbow. "They think we would have forgotten it by now."

He chuckled and cracked a shell between his finger and thumb. He threw his head back and the peanuts followed and then he rejoined the conversation with relish.

My father's generation will be the last of our Malaysian family to speak Longyan. Uncle Boon's sons, my cousins, had been raised in Singapore and learned mandatory Mandarin in school. My brothers and I knew no Chinese languages. When our father and aunts and uncles died, there would be no one left who remembered Longyan. Our family's connection to the language and the village would sever as future generations branched farther and farther away from this place that we came from. And even beyond our own family, in the thicket that connects a nation's generations, Longyan would also falter. Under the Chinese Communist Party, regional languages and dialects were dying out as the government united a new generation in homogenous Mandarin. One language for one nation of one billion people. As I looked around at the faces of my family, who sipped beer and roared with laughter, I was struck by a sudden wave of panic. I set my teacup down. This was our family's last generation to live and think and remember in Longyan. Not only would a language disappear, but so too would a history. In forty years, I would be unable to return to this village. Without an aunt or an uncle or a father, I would have no one to guide me or translate for me or explain to me where the roots and the branches of our family's tree meet. Alone, I wouldn't even be able to find the village. Around this table, I was unable to converse with the women who poured my tea in their own language. I was a stranger. No more than a guest in someone else's home and a memory that would fade as soon as I left.

My father broke my stupor. "Let's go, Kate. The lady wants to show us her home." Leaving behind rings of condensation and broken shells on the table, we rose and collected our shoes from the doorway. A small group of relatives led us across paths of concrete towards the older outbuildings I trailed behind, tripping over cracks in the pavement as I twisted my neck from side to side, trying to take everything in at once. Lining the paths were ditches filled with the lush green heads of string beans knotted to wooden canes with fraying rope. Women shook out wet clothes on their porches and threw sheets and shirts across cables that bridged building to building. A small boy sat on one of the walls and watched us pass. I smiled at him, and he stared back with wide eyes as he chewed on the foot of a khaki toy soldier.

The path left the homestead and ended in a conclave of old buildings.

"That's the lady's room." My aunt pointed towards an entrance.

I left the group and stepped across the threshold. The door frame was so low, I had to bow my head to avoid smacking it on the wooden beam. The floor sank down farther than I had anticipated, and my stomach gave out a horrible jolt as my foot met air where it expected solid ground. Startled, I leaned a hand on the wall to save my balance. The room's fading wallpaper was cool after the midday sun and felt damp to touch with the heat of my hand. As I lifted my palm off the shedding paper, a ribbon of peel came with it and dropped to the floor. My eyes took a moment to adjust to the darkness. A four-poster bed swallowed most of the room. Pale netted sheets hung across its posts. I imagined this old woman at night, pulling them across her body to protect her skin from mosquito bites. I wondered if she ever woke from a dream and, for just a moment before she was back in her body, saw phantoms in the curtains billowing above her in the night breeze.

Other than the door, the only source of light in the room was a small window. A dusty slab of wood waited on a hinge, ready to be closed over when the weather turned cool in the winter months. By the window, a straw broom bound in twine rested against the wall, cobwebs still caught in its bristles. The woman brushed past me. To reach her bed she stepped on a low bench, and then the four columns devoured her tiny form. Face still turned to the ground, she patted the covers beside her. I sat down and the mattress sank. From our perch, she guided me around the room, murmuring a little. Her finger roamed through the air across stained wooden trunks and the dark insides of cupboards that held folds of cloth, rusting tins, and plastic trays. Fading ceramic vases rested in a corner. Everything had its place. Amongst the room's browns and greys, the only bright spot was a lemon-coloured handbag hanging from a hook. I pointed to the bag and said I liked it in a voice too loud for the quiet room. She rose from the bed, took a wobbling step off the bench, and shuffled across the floor. I followed her, my legs taking few steps for her many. Sewn into the bag's yellow cotton, a cat's whiskered face smiled at us. The woman reached up to touch the cat's face.

As I watched her, I wanted to ask if her life had been everything she had hoped for. Was she satisfied with her origins? Did she know who we were to her? I wanted to know if she felt lonely or content, and if her memories were failing her, and if the past was slipping away. But we had no common tongue, and my mouth remained closed. We stayed there together, as silent as the cat, until one of the aunties called for us through the bars in the window. We left then and stepped up and out of the room to join our family of strangers.

OVER AN ANCIENT GATEWAY, a pair of crimson dragons danced in the breeze. Their long balloon bodies shimmered like goldfish scales and contorted under the hot sun. The dragons perched atop a larger balloon arch, the blood-red plastic hitting against the stone of the tulou. The walled village was even bigger than I had imagined when I had scrolled through photographs. One of Fujian's most visited tourist spots, the Chuxi tulou cluster was designated as a World Heritage Site by UNESCO in 2008 as an example of an exceptional preservation of tulou architecture. Centuries ago, it would have stood amongst groves and fields. Now, tour buses and black tarmac waited outside. Head tilted back, I watched the dragons fly as we waited for our guide to meet us at the entrance of the tulou. I raised my camera to my eye and took a dutiful photograph.

We were nearing the end of our trip, and our family had encouraged us to visit the pride of Fujian before we flew back to Malaysia.

"You'll get plenty of inspiration for your project," an auntie told me through Auntie Suan's translation after I mentioned my art class. "Lots for you to sketch."

The tour guide appeared at the gateway. He was a young local man, who gripped his clipboard and laughed a little too manically at my uncle's jokes. "Call me Jason," he told us, his English flawless.

We were ushered over the threshold and into a crowded cobblestone courtyard. Groups of tourists, most of them from other Chinese provinces, gathered around stalls selling souvenirs and hot snacks, shiny cheongsams and paper fans.

"This way." Jason delivered us to the first stop on the tour: a tea ceremony. We sat cross-legged on pillows, facing a woman who poured scalding water from pot to pot and cup to cup. I stopped listening to Jason's whistle-stop history of Chinese tea, instead fixated on the water flowing from spouts to splash into porcelain. The woman was precise, never spilling a drop as she filled and emptied vessels. She finished her ceremony with eight small cups and presented them to her audience. I took my share and drank the tea in a single swallow. Fragments of leaves caught in my mouth as the bitter liquid washed over my tongue.

We followed Jason for the rest of the tour as he told us about the community that had lived in this round village, almost two hundred people, many related by blood. Most of the residents had moved on or died in the late twentieth century, but there were still some people living in the upper levels of the tulou. Looking up, I could see some lines of washing floating above our heads. In the past, most of the residents would have farmed the land outside the tulou, but now they made their living through tourism, selling souvenirs, performing tea ceremonies, and hosting homestays, Jason explained as he led us through a curving corridor. A television blasted a Cantonese drama somewhere above us, while our group moved through other tourists. Life in the tulou had adapted in order to survive, and the building held both the present and the past in its round clay walls. I enjoyed hearing about the history of Fujian's tulous, which went back as far as the fifteenth century, but I was, without question, a tourist here.

Jason's tour ended where it had begun, in the courtyard. It was quiet now that the other tour groups had filed back onto their buses. I browsed the stalls. One sold charms in the shape of lucky cats, each tiny statue painted with a hanzi, a Chinese character.

"Name?" the seller asked. She laid one of her charms in my palm. Three cats were linked together by fine pink thread and finished with a decorative knot.

"Ah!" Jason appeared beside me. "Each cat has a character on it, see? She attaches them together to create a personal charm out of your name." He pointed to the stall. "Do you have a Chinese name?"

I looked down at the hundreds of ceramic cats in cardboard boxes, each with its own inky character painted on its belly. I had never seen my Chinese name, the name bestowed on me by my grandparents, written down as characters before. I only knew the pinyin, the romanised system for teaching Chinese pronunciation. I had no idea what my name looked like in its native language.

"Um, let me ask my ah ma."

I hurried over to where my grandmother was inspecting the fabric of a dress, rubbing the teal silk between her finger and thumb.

"Ah Ma, can you help me?"

We returned to the charms stall. She read each character aloud to me as she found my name in the stall's clutter and set them down, one by one, in my hand.

Three cats, one name. I handed them over to the stall's owner and she threaded them together with red string. I paid for the charm and sat on a stone bench by the exit to wait for the rest of my family. I let the cats run through my fingers, the ceramic cool and smooth. I didn't even know my own name. I had come to Longyan with a fantasy of finding the place where I would belong, where I could be an authentic version of myself, and I couldn't even pick out three ceramic cats from a stall. I looked around the tulou then, at the cheap souvenirs and the plastic antiquity and the balloon dragons, all held inside a reconstructed version of the past. In Ireland, the lure of true assimilation had eluded me. I had convinced myself that if I could just stand in history, if I could just go to the place where I was from, I could find myself in it. But in the tulou I was a tourist, and in the village, I was a stranger.

Jason left us by the tulou gate, and we crossed the tarmac to meet the van that would take us back to the house for our final night in Longyan. Tomorrow we would return to Kuala Lumpur, and then my father and I would leave once again to fly back to Europe. I let my family walk on without me while I stopped to face the tulou one last time. The dragons still flew. I took a final photograph, and then I turned and hurried to catch up.

IN THE NINETEENTH CENTURY, a boy is born near the French country commune of Chambon-sur-Dolore. When he is old enough to attend school, he crosses a bridge each morning to be educated by priests who teach him the alphabet, the Bible, and the map of France's territories. In neat calligraphy, he copies letters, stories, and borders over and over again until his hands are slick with black ink. A visiting priest arrives and tells the boys stories of faraway places. A daguerreotype print is passed around the class. When it is his turn to look, the boy rests the film on his open palm. It is the first time he has seen a photograph. It is cloudy but there, unmistakable even in the chemical haze, is a sun-bleached house. Fruit trees sway beside the sea in the background. In front of the building stand light-skinned officers and dark-skinned servants. During his lessons, the boy daydreams about the faraway land in the picture. He sets the biblical stories he is reading in the photograph, amongst the fruit trees and by the water. He begins to dream about gardens growing in the hot sun. One afternoon, the boy's father brings home a bag from the town market. From the rustling paper, he unearths half a dozen small, bright oranges. When the boy bites into the fruit, he can taste that faraway place, that holy land, that photograph.

Leaving boyhood behind, he joins the Brothers of the Annunciation, a Christian missionary group based in France's new colony of Algeria. When he arrives in the dusty city of Misserghin, at the house of the religious order, he is asked for his name. Here is a chance for reinvention. He offers a name that is not an inheritance but a creation. He becomes Brother Marie-Clément Rodier. In an Algerian orphanage, Brother Rodier finds his purpose caring for lost boys and spreading God's word. The garden becomes an important metaphor for his teachings. It is a paradise gained, then lost; a secret refuge; a place of anguish and a site of spiritual revelation. The brother holds his lessons on the orphanage's grounds, in the shade of trees. Between classes he tends the land.

On a visit back to France, Brother Rodier notices the beauty of his homeland, how the trees grow fragrant, flowering, fruiting. He returns to Algeria with cases of saplings and buds snipped from the South of France. The orphanage's estate fills with vines, shrubs, and flowers that are not native to northern Africa. Studying his Bible, Brother Rodier reads a paragraph on grafting, Paul the Apostle's metaphor for spiritual survival. The next morning, he takes a kitchen knife to a tree, slicing off budding bark and grafting it to an old rootstock. The stem takes to the foreign plant. The wound heals.

Years pass. The brother is now an ordained father, who still holds his Bible lessons in the open air. Above the heads of the father and the boys, a tree bears fruit. Its branches sag heavy with produce that is unlike anything else in the father's garden. It is neither mandarin nor orange; its skin is too thin, its colour too red. When the fruit ripens, Father Rodier pulls one from the tree. He pushes his thumb through the peel. There is no thick white pith. Juice runs down his hands and catches in his sleeve. He brings his wrist to his mouth. It is as sweet as honey. The father recognises a gift from God when he tastes one.

Now, when a boy graduates from the orphanage, Father Rodier bestows on him a graft from the tree. Slips of bark are carried in the pockets of young men who cross Algeria into Morocco, leave on ships bound for Spain and Portugal, and trek east along the roads to the Holy Land. The boys in the orphanage name this new fruit after their beloved father. They call it a clementine. An invented name for an invented fruit.

Or, the story goes like this. Brother Marie-Clément Rodier is resting in the garden after delivering a successful sermon to his students. His eyes follow a bee that is busying itself, flitting from a bitter orange tree to a mandarin tree, burying itself in mounds of pollen. The brother notices a smear of yellow painted across a blossom's white petals. His mind begins to wonder as the bee crosses from flower to flower, leaving behind golden dust as it buzzes indiscriminately from tree to tree. Curious about what effect this cross-pollination might have, the brother ties a red ribbon to the flowering bud of a mandarin tree that is now empty of nectar and coated in pollen. Over a humid Algerian spring, the petals fall from the ribbon and a mandarin grows. When the fruit is ripe, the brother peels the skin, eats the flesh, and buries the seeds in the garden's earth. Weeks pass until, one day, a sapling pushes its green head through the clay and a tree bursts forth. Years pass until a French botanist notices the branches of strange orange fruit that hang over the orphanage's garden walls. He suggests the name 'clementine' after the beloved brother.

Or, it goes like this. As a father, as a brother, as a boy, Marie-Clément Rodier hates oranges. He despises the mess of their juice, the sting of their spray, the bitter taste of their peel. In Algeria, Rodier shuns the outdoors, choosing instead to educate the orphaned boys in the sweltering heat of the closed classroom. He hates the garden, hates dirt catching under his nails, hates the whine of insects around his ears, hates this foreign sun burning the nape of his neck. When Rodier dies, a clementine tree appears outside the orphanage. The boys nickname the tree's fruit after their dead father in jest. But the name sticks. As the fruit makes its way from northern Africa into southern Europe, and across the Atlantic to Florida and California at the turn of the twentieth century, the clementine's glossy peel comes to symbolise the sun. For a century after its namesake's death, the original hybrid tree stands in the garden and witnesses history: the orphanage abandoned during guerrilla warfare, millions of citizens made homeless by violence, Christianity ousted after France loses its colony, crude oil discovered, crude oil lost, the rise of military rule, the protests that ripple like waves across the country. And every year, the tree blooms, fruit falls, and the cycle begins again. Once tended to by the dead, a living clementine tree standing in the present is a reminder of history—its fruit a legacy. Who will eat next year's harvest?

I read accounts of the clementine's origins and I dream up stories in the gaps between facts.[37] I wonder which version of this tale is best to employ; which is the most powerful, the most allegorical, the most illuminating. We are constantly choosing the best tale to tell: at job interviews, around dinner tables, on first dates, to nosy strangers on aeroplanes. We make our origin stories neat, linear, satisfying—yet, when we live them, they are rarely so immaculate. The past is a mess of false starts and way-ward decisions, never-ending journeys and regrettable choices. It is impossible to tell it authentically. History is chosen, a selection of stories dependent on both fact and contemporary circum-stance. Like so many second-generation immigrant children of empire, I am a relic of a past that many people would prefer to forget. As the British Empire fades, a decision, conscious and unconscious, has been made to represent its past as innocuous, proud, and disconnected from the present moment. When I was taught British history as a child, my teachers did not mention the nation's legacy in our own island, fearful of reigniting sectarian-ism in a post-Troubles generation. My understanding of history is warped by the false optimism of post-colonial and post-racial Britain, a country that reckons with its bloody past by installing statues in memory of it. When I visited Malaysia as a child, my connection to my father's country did not go further than a fort-night's holiday in the sun. I was ignorant of its history and never once questioned why so many of its places bore British names.

"It is only when you are stranded in a hostile country that you need a romance of origins," writes the author Saidiya Hartman.[38] Mythology is born from a desire for belonging. The history that I inherited as a child left me desperate for an origin story, something that could redeem my foreignness, my attempted assimilation, my un-belonging. I thought that journeying to my family's ancestral village in Fujian would give me a story, one that was neat and arching, that could show me a way to move forward. But my attempt to graft past and future failed. As I left

Longyan, I couldn't skirt my disappointment in finding myself a stranger in my ancestors' land. The story I had told myself—one of a fantasy, one of a tulou, one of an authentic self—fell away as southern China disappeared out the window. As the plane carrying me home levelled out at thirty-six thousand feet and dimmed its cabin lights to meet the night sky, the estrangement that I had been feeling since leaving the tulou surged through my body. From my window seat, I watched as a constellation of electricity was extinguished in the churning black night, and in its place a ghostly reflection of my own face emerged in the darkness. It was not simply language or geographical distance that made me a stranger in the village. History had been severed somewhere. I had thought the roots would be waiting for me, but time passes, wounds heal over, weeds grow. My dream of a homecoming was a mythology I had inherited from the remnants of empire.

I returned to school in September. Over a desk stained from years of students expressing themselves, I spread out photographs from my trip to China. There was the wet market that one of the Longyan uncles had insisted we visit; close-up shots of yellow chicken legs dangled from red string, sacks of rice piled high, tendon residue sliding off cleavers, bouquets of leafy bok choy, and baffled turtles caught in nets. There was the procession of lilac, peach, and teal umbrellas that had opened when a sudden storm split the sky and raindrops the size of marbles fell. There was the temple we had visited, with its sacred stone lions that guarded the gate, the burning joss sticks that glowed red despite the rain, and the bowls of oranges offered at the altar. And there was the tulou with its plastic dioramas of ancient Fujian. From my sketchbook, I pulled out the still life of the fruit bowl and placed it among the photographs. On the classroom computer, I had been researching the history of the foreign fruit in my drawing and I was startled to discover that oranges originated in Asia and not Spain like I had assumed.

"Oh, that's interesting!" My art teacher picked up one of the photographs taken in the temple. She tapped the paper "Look at those funny lions. Maybe you could create one in clay?"

She let the print flutter back down to the table. In the mess of paper in front of me, I recognised an opportunity for creation. I had gone searching for origins and now found myself even more estranged from the past. The story I had desired— of bloodlines and homecomings—had proved fruitless. But no matter, here was the possibility of something new. Instead of being stuck like an insect in amber, frozen by the past, I could go forward and discover other mythologies. Immigrants are inventors, after all, tasked with making themselves up, remembering and forgetting in order to assimilate. Perhaps that would be my inheritance.

The orange, with its lost origins, liberates itself from being fixed to a single moment in time or a myopic meaning. It dances through history, appearing and disappearing in the texts that survive, out of China and along the Silk Roads. The orange migrates from east to west, where it finds that there are new myths to be created.

TWO
....
THE SILK ROADS

ON ANY ORDINARY AFTERNOON DURING THE TANG DYNASTY, Chang'an's Western Market is the centre of the world. Running from wall to wall, lanes divide the market into nine sections, each designating a trade: butchery and fish mongering, apothecaries and goldsmiths.[39] When the Western Market's two sets of gates open at midday, crowds surge from seller to seller, to argue and gamble, plead and purchase, win and lose. The market sprawls: two hundred merchant guilds are present within its walls and three thousand shops line its lanes.[40] Traders travel from across China to reach the central city, but many of the Western Market's merchants have journeyed from beyond the Tang dynasty's borders. Turks, Persians, Indians, and Sogdians of Iran arrive in the city with wares to flog at the end of the Silk Roads. Spices and gems are exchanged for porcelain and silk. Tea and rice grown in the fields of nearby provinces are delivered by China's waterway trade routes. Citrus arrives from the river, too, shipped by growers in the south who, over centuries, have specialised in growing fruit which ripens in the heat. The provinces of Guangdong and Fujian have built their economies on the art of cultivating fruit, and the provinces' farmers devote their lives to growing oranges, lychees, and kumquats to export far and wide.[41] Golden shrines of fruit illuminate the shadows of the Western Market.

A breeze rises, and with it come fistfuls of petals shaken loose from magnolia trees. Pink confetti scatters over the recently executed, who rot and hang from the walls. The dead watch over the living as Chang'an's shoppers file out of the market gates to the beating of a drum that brings the day's trading to a close. The final strike is delivered and fades along the market's empty lanes. The young drummer slips through the closing gates and becomes one more face lost in a crowd of thousands. The sun is setting on the seventh century. In a millennium, historians will proclaim that this moment was the golden age of imperial China, but right now, it is time to leave.

Chang'an is the world's marketplace, where the Silk Roads begin and end and where they begin anew. It is the gate through which China's produce leaves, loaded onto carts and animals, checked by market officials, and delivered to the world. And it is a symposium for ambition and appetite that turns on an axis of life and death, where criminals are put to death and merchants deliver new commerce, new ideas, and new gods.

In the morning, visiting merchants will depart the city in caravans and take with them Chinese goods which will transform from local to foreign as they move along the western roads, farther and farther away from where they came from: bolts of silks; scrolls of paper; dried and fresh fruit and fish; robust jade and fragile porcelain; gourd bottles containing greasy medicines; and miscellaneous, misshapen ironwork and goldware. But before the exportation can commence, there is one last night to spend in the cosmopolitan city. On a single street in Chang'an's western quarter: overhead, the sky, splashed with the gold and crimson of dusk, is framed by the ornate eaves of a

Turkic prince's mansion, that is glimpsed between the wooden beams of a brothel, that is glimpsed between the stone vaults of a tax office, that is glimpsed between the sanctimonious shrines of a noble family; underfoot, pigs dragged by fraying ropes looped twice round the neck, gangs of skinny barefoot children grasping rusted blades and running along grey paths, the grey of dirt, of dust, of people making a life for themselves within a city's walls; on the horizon, Buddhist monasteries and Taoist pagodas looming over taverns, the blossom from the imperial gardens' peony and magnolia trees raining down in spring showers; inside, rice wine sloshed from clutched cups, men's soles stuck to worn floors, and the melodies of instruments carved from gourd and bamboo reverberating from room to room.

At dawn, camels, donkeys, and cattle pull the caravans from the city. At checkpoints, paperwork is confirmed, taxes are paid, and the journey begins again. On the western road from Chang'an, the merchants will pass mercenaries and monks, bands of travellers and mandarins, all heading for the safety of the Great Wall. Emperor Wudi of the earlier Han dynasty extended the wall to protect his borders from raiding parties of northern nomads, and the recent feat of engineering maps safe passage between the Gobi Desert and Tibetan Plateau. At the end of the wall waits the Gate of Jade in Yunnan. Garrisons of soldiers greet the caravans and trade their wages, paid in silk, for Chang'an's delights.[42] Passports are issued to those wishing to pass the borders of the Tang dynasty and depart the safety of the wall. The journey ends here for some, but for others it is only beginning.

When I was a child and first heard about the Silk Road, I imagined it as the flight path I took every few years from Ireland to visit my family in Malaysia. On a globe, I traced a line through mountains, deserts, seas, and forests. My fingertip began on the western coast of Portugal, crossed Europe, hopped over the Black Sea, entered the broad plains of Central Asia, ran the ridge of the Himalayas into China, and then dipped through Myanmar and Thailand to finish at the tip of the Malay Peninsula. Once I reached Singapore, I returned to Western Europe as the bird—or the aeroplane—flies. Anytime I came across a black borderline, my finger jumped over it without hesitation. In my mind, the Silk Road was a path, like Oz's yellow brick road, where a flow of purple silks, orange spices, and green stones moved from east to west and back again.

The ancient trade routes that run from Chang'an across the Eurasian continent to Constantinople, and onwards to sub-Saharan Africa and Western Europe, exist and expire without a collective name for centuries. Then, in 1877, Ferdinand von Richthofen, the German baron and geographer, popularises the name die Seidenstrasse, or the Silk Road, for the ancient passages of trade that led to the Far East. An orientalist's romance of the past is conjured for nineteenth-century Europeans, who, like my younger self, imagine that the Silk Road is a single path, beginning in Italy and ending in China. But reducing the network that covered the Afro-Eurasian landmass to one single road shrinks its histories. The Silk Roads are better understood as countless exchanges that took place along routes that linked Asia, Europe, and Africa across land and sea, crossing and countervailing, stopping and restarting. The historian David Christian offers a conversative but concise definition of the Silk Roads as "the long- and middle-distance land routes by which goods, ideas, and people were exchanged between major regions of Afro-Eurasia."[43] These are roads that are both literal and metaphorical and that conveyed materials and ideas, carried in merchants' hands and minds.

Caravans deliver silks, ceramics, livestock, glass, metal, precious gemstones, tea, herbs, medicines, spices, wine, apples, citrons, peaches, jasmine, sugar, and grain to different cities, communities, and societies along the Silk Roads. Over hundreds of years, the arrival of foreign products creates hybrid cultural cuisines: millet grain goes west to feed the Roman Empire, while wheat goes east to become noodles in China.[44] People move along the Silk Roads too; travellers marry into new families and communities, so that genes can be called one of the roads' most important exchanges.

Merchants also carry their cultures, religions, languages, politics, and technologies with them as they travel along the roads, leaving the remnants of ideas that began in faraway lands behind them. During the Tang dynasty, the city of Chang'an embodies the diversity of the Silk Roads' travellers. Its two million inhabitants include people from the northwest—Turks, Uighurs, Tocharians, Sogdians—as well as those from farther afield—Arabs, Persians, and Hindus.[45] They gather ideas on their journeys, pick up objects and ascribe to them new meanings. From 200 BCE until the Ottoman Empire ceases trading with the west in the thirteenth century, religions journey along the Silk Roads with its travellers. Buddhism, Judaism, Zoroastrianism, Islam, and eventually Christianity spread into the farthest corners of Afro-Eurasia and turn minor faiths into major religions.[46]

By the end of the Silk Roads' golden age, communities in Asia, Europe, and Africa have become multicultural hubs. In a Syrian cookbook first published in the thirteenth century, the anonymous author lists plant life originating in East and Southeast Asia such as citron, cinnamon, and agarwood as ingredients found in Ayyubid spice racks.[47] The majority of food that we eat today has migrated to our kitchens: either as a product grown elsewhere and shipped to us, like oranges to the UK, or as a foreign plant that has, over generations, naturalised to a new land after crossing continents. Diet staples, like apples, potatoes, garlic, and cabbage, were all once exotic new foods introduced to the British Isles. As food, people, and ideas travel the Silk Roads, they are adopted into new lands. The borders between what is native and what is foreign become hazier as we step into the past.

IN 2019, I FLEW over the ancient Silk Roads. Leaving from Dublin, my plane crossed over Turkey, Iraq, Iran, and India before descending over the Straits of Malacca, where ships journey along the maritime Silk Roads, to land in what was firmly modern Kuala Lumpur.

It was September, and West Malaysia was engulfed by haze. Palm oil plantations had been razed by slash-and-burn clearance fires in Indonesia; forest fires were raging in Borneo, Thailand, and Vietnam; and Southeast Asia had been plunged into a polluted cloud.

I was in Malaysia to be with my ah ma. She had been diagnosed with breast cancer at the end of the previous year. I had already planned to stay with my Auntie Sian for three months—the longest I could stay in the country without a visa—but Ah Ma's illness gave the trip a sudden urgency. Each year since I was a child, I had spent weeks with my Irish grandmother. We had no language barrier and spoke with ease. I knew her intimately. But my Malaysian grandmother existed mostly in my childhood memories. We could not converse freely; she had emigrated from China as a girl and learned English as a young bride in Malaysia. I could not speak Longyan or Mandarin. We conversed in fragmented English and spoke about each other to my father or aunt, and they translated for us. And now she had cancer. Her death, once unimaginable to me, now loomed as a foregone conclusion. I was consumed by pangs of fear that I would run out of time and she would disappear from me before I could ask her about the things I had always wanted to know: about her childhood in Longyan, her memories of Japanese-occupied China, her experience of immigrating to British-occupied Malaya, the joys and sorrows that had marked her life. This trip to Malaysia took on a new meaning for me. I wanted to help care for Ah Ma as she underwent her treatment, but I also wanted to make sense of her past. It might be my last chance.

When I arrived at my aunt's apartment in the city, my grandparents greeted me. Their own home was in the city of Ipoh, but they had been staying with their daughter while Ah Ma underwent chemotherapy in KL. I hadn't been sure how I would fit into my grandparents' new routine. I soon learned they rose early in the mornings. They had breakfast with my aunt before she drove into the city for work. After she left, I would drag myself from the sofa-bed in the study—my makeshift bedroom for those three months—to join them. On some days the haze from the fires lingered outside my aunt's building and clung to its pale concrete walls. Other days it was gone when I woke up, leaving nothing but a smear on the window that I opened each morning.

Ah Kong spent his mornings running through qi gong moves and walking a lap or two around the building. He returned with copies of local Chinese and English newspapers that were delivered to the lobby each morning. While I yawned and drank oily black coffee and bit into toast slathered with kaya and peanut butter, he read. Before he had retired, Ah Kong was a teacher and wrote geography textbooks for students. He did not peruse the papers like Ah Ma, who sat back on the sofa to flick through the news. Instead, he hunched over the inky pages. In a shallow dish by his elbow waited a wet sponge, which he dabbed his finger into to turn the broadsheets. Occasionally he sucked his front teeth, jabbed at a flimsy page with his finger, and scolded a corrupt politician or foreign president. In the afternoons, Ah Kong napped under a slow-spinning fan, while Ah Ma called her sisters, my Auntie Anna and Auntie Chui Lee, who often stopped by the apartment to bring us lunch from the market.

When I arrived in KL, I had expected to find my grandmother a shadow of her former self, a fragile cancer patient who needed constant care. But besides the loss of her hair and diminished energy levels, Ah Ma appeared to be the same grandmother I had always known: quiet, except when scolding my grandfather, and content to dedicate most of her time to cooking for her family. She watched Chinese shows with Ah Kong in the evenings and gambled against my great-aunts on weekends. I loved the sound of the clinking ceramic as the women shuffled the mahjong rummy tiles over the green velvet table, spreading them around with hands that were marked by freckles and wrinkles and adorned with simple bands of gold. I lost twenty or thirty ringgit to my grandmother every time I dared to join their game. She always returned the money to me when I left the apartment to visit the mall.

It was easy to slip into the rhythm of my grandparents' lives in KL. In the afternoons, I worked, mostly writing articles. When Auntie Sian returned from her office, we ate simple meals of rice, tofu, fish, and root vegetables. Every dinner finished with my aunt carrying battered plastic boxes of cut fruit from the fridge to the table: cubes of melon, slices of dragon fruit, and peeled rambutans. Ah Kong sneaked away with his daily bowl of vanilla ice cream back to the television, while Auntie Sian and Ah Ma gossiped in Chinese and folded me into the conversation with English.

On the wall by the dining table was a small gallery of black-and-white photographs. I was often distracted by them at mealtimes and asked my aunt about the pictures. They were of our family, most of them taken years ago and featuring my aunt, uncle, and father as kids. In one, which must have been taken in the early 1970s, the tallest child, my father, looked about ten years old. My aunt wore a white dress and my uncle a striped shirt. Behind them stood Ah Kong, thin and serious, his round glasses reflecting the sun. In the foreground was Ah Ma, sitting beside her children, who were gathered around her. Her hair was short and thick, and the black curls bunched beneath her jawline. She looked into the camera's lens, and she did not smile.

"No one smiled for photos then," my aunt told me. "Everyone stood in a straight line and wore their best clothes."

Ah Ma would have been in her early thirties in the photograph. She had a few more years with her children before, one by one, they were sent away for school: my father to the north of Ireland, my uncle to England, my aunt to Australia. My grandfather wanted his children to excel through academia and to be educated in foreign schools, which he saw as superior to any in Southeast Asia. They would be trained by white men to become doctors, professors, or lawyers, and then they would return to Malaysia. My uncle and aunt followed this destined narrative and came back. My father dawdled after medical school, enjoying his independence in Europe too much, and then he met an Irish woman and began his own story with her.

I knew this origin tale well; it was mine after all. I had heard it time and time again as a child. What was hazier were the roots of our grandparents. I remembered my father telling me that Ah Ma grew up in China during the war. She had to practice drills in case the Japanese army marched on Longyan, and, with her siblings, she would run and hide in cupboards. The image of my wartime grandmother thrilled me as a child, until I learned about the atrocities committed during that occupation. Ah Ma was born in 1937, the same year the city of Nanjing was seized by Japanese soldiers and a six-week hell began: twenty thousand people raped and two hundred thousand murdered in acts of violence so evil I couldn't finish reading the accounts of British and American war correspondents who witnessed the massacre. What happened in Nanjing was a possibility for any Chinese city during the war. My great-grandparents in Fujian, only a few provinces south of Nanjing, would have heard the news as the Japanese army spread across China.

I asked my aunt if the Japanese invasion was the reason Ah Ma's family had migrated to Malaysia. She said that was unlikely to be the only reason; when Ah Ma left China in the late 1940s, the war was over but the country was poor. "It was a time when people left China in junks for greener pastures," she told me.

They immigrated to North America, Europe, Australia, and, closer to home, Malaysia, which was then British Malaya.

Aged twelve, Ah Ma arrived on the Malay Archipelago. She carried no birth certificate with her, and we still don't know her exact birthday. She sailed from Fujian with her mother on a junk ship and was greeted at a port in Malaya by her father, who had travelled ahead of his family. On a map, I traced the country's west coast, wondering where her ship would have arrived. Penang perhaps, or Port Klang (which was then called Port Swettenham, after a British colonial officer), just outside KL. Stepping onto the dock would have been the first time my twelve-year-old grandmother saw a white person.

Ah Ma married my grandfather in 1959, two years after Malaysia gained independence. My father was born a year later. By the time Ah Ma was twenty-five, the same age I was standing in my aunt's apartment looking at old black-and-white photographs, she had three children. I realised how ignorant I was of my own family history and asked my aunties for the memories, hearsay, and gossip they had collected over their lifetimes.

"Ah Ma doesn't talk about her past," my Auntie Suan said when I badgered her for more information about my grandmother's childhood in China. "She didn't go to school when she arrived in Malaya, I think because your ah ma came from China," my aunt told me. "But she's not sure."

Ah Kong's story was easier for me to trace. He was born in Teluk Intan, then called Teluk Anson, a small town on the coast of West Malaya. His father had left our ancestral village near Longyan at the turn of the century and started a peanut factory in British Malaya. Despite his father's dismissal of academic studies, Ah Kong aspired for an education that would pull him into the middle class. He convinced his parents to send him to an English medium school rather than a Chinese one, so that he could learn English, the language of the colonial government and the education system, which would help him rise among their ranks. He devoted himself to his books until he earned a place to train to be a teacher near Wolverhampton in England. When he returned, Malaysia was independent, and he was a geography teacher with a British qualification. He had met my grandmother at a wedding before he left for England, and on his return, they married.

"Wait, let me draw a family tree," Auntie Suan said. She started with my great-great-grandfather in the village in Fujian and then began splitting the trunk into branches.

"One of his sons stayed in China, and the other one—Ah Kong's father, your great-grandfather—left China to migrate to Malaya. Do you remember that old lady from our trip to the village near Longyan?" she asked as she added names to the branches. "The son who stayed in China had a son who married her, which makes her your ah kong's . . . uncle's . . . wife. Aiyo, so confusing." She continued drawing and the tree grew, its branches thickened with names and relations.

I inspected my grandmother's branch, which was grafted onto my grandfather's tree. "Where's Auntie Anna and Auntie Chui Lee? Aren't they Ah Ma's sisters?"

"Not blood sisters," replied Auntie Suan. "Your ah ma's family adopted Auntie Anna. It was very common in China and for Chinese immigrants in those days."

"I had no idea."

Auntie Suan shrugged. "Of course, you wouldn't lah. If not for the adoption, Auntie Anna would be Ah Ma's cousin. Anna's father was your ah ma's mother's brother. It was common in those days for siblings to adopt each other's children for one reason or another. So Auntie Anna, Auntie Chui Lee and your ah ma are sisters and cousins all rolled up!"

She finished the tree. I traced the roots where my great-great-grandfather's name was inked and followed the unbroken line with my finger until it forked into two paths. I picked my grand-father's branch and moved my finger along it. Great-uncles, great-aunts, my father, my aunt, my uncle, cousins, second cousins.

I saw them all as fruit, each name hanging from the tree. I came to the final branch of the tree, where Auntie Suan had written my name beside my brothers'. On the page it was more a sprig than a branch, waiting to grow future fruit. I took the pen to where my grandmother's name was, and beside it, I extended the branch and added in the names "Anna" and "Chui Lee." My handwriting was messier than my aunt's and my lines fitted awkwardly on the page but there they were, aunts to me, grafted onto the tree. I wondered how many other names were absent from the lines that followed the male bloodline.

BEFORE LEAVING MY AUNT'S APARTMENT, Ah Ma swapped her colourful headscarves for a short black wig. It sat snug on her head, cut with care so that the artificial strands fell around her ears and temples in a near-perfect replica of her pre-chemo hair. When she appeared from the bathroom wearing it, I complimented its likeness to her natural hair. She looked at herself in the hallway mirror and smiled.

While Auntie Sian drove the three of us to the market, Ah Ma patted at her wig as if to check it was still there. There was no haze that Saturday morning and, above KL's concrete, the sky was a sure blue. Ah Ma and my aunt spoke to each other in Chinese, about friends' sons and lunch plans and what we would bring to a potluck dinner in my aunt's building later that week. In the back seat I was content to watch flocks of sparrows shoot above the treetops which lined suburban streets.

The Saturday market was held in a multi-storey concrete block in Petaling Jaya, a satellite city on the outskirts of KL. Cars were parked at the base of the complex and shoppers walked up wide concrete ramps to enter the sheltered marketplace. We were there to buy next week's groceries and a bulk of fresh ginger roots—my aunt had read that raw ginger was the secret to successfully regrowing hair after chemotherapy.

In the heart of the market Ah Ma and Auntie Sian disappeared to haggle with the ginger seller while I wandered away to discover tofu that emerged glossy from buckets of water to be sold by the brick. Tables buckled under the weight of kuih seri muka cut into lime squares and crates of haphazardly piled fruit glowed in the dull hollows of concrete walls. Alone, without my aunt and grandmother, I stood out as a foreigner, pale and beguiled by the food on display. The women behind the stalls followed me with curious eyes. Tourists did not come to this market. I wondered if I was another orang putih—a white person—to them, or if some part of my body gave away a different heritage.

I stopped in front of a stall to pick out some fruit, one of the few food purchases Auntie Sian entrusted to me when we went shopping. The proprietor was a middle-aged Chinese man, charismatic and loud as he squabbled with a group of young women over his prices. He exclaimed each time a number was offered and gestured to his wares. I didn't understand what he was saying to them in Cantonese, but I understood the essence. Did they not know this was the freshest fruit at the market? Green apples imported from Australia! Papayas plucked fresh this morning! I dodged around them as a bartering battle began and moved closer to the piles of fruit: spiky rambutans, shelled mangosteens, and scaly dragon fruit. I fought the urge to reach out and touch the rind with my fingers. If I picked up a fruit, the stall owner might consider it sold and my aunt would never forgive such bad market tactics.

"Ah!" The stall's owner was finished with his customers, who were dropping papayas into their plastic bags, and had noticed me. He held out a fist. With the indulgent showmanship of a salesman, he turned his hand over and unfurled his fingers from around a fruit. Its skin shone under the market's fluorescent lights.

"Oh." I stared, cross-eyed, at it, unsure if I should take it.

"Organic, fresh . . . no chemicals," the man said, serious now. I recognised the fruit resting in his hand as a Java apple. I understood the seller's pride. It was a perfect fruit; the shape like an inverted bell or an oily womb. Its skin transitioned from flushed rose to unripe green so gradually that I couldn't see the exact spot where nature had decided to switch colour palettes. An artist might spend a lifetime trying to replicate that ombré in watercolour paint.

The seller broke his own spell first, pulled his hand back, and the fruit disappeared. He was merry again and chuckled at the stunned expression on my face.

"Kate?" My aunt appeared beside me, rustling with plastic bags. Ah Ma and the stall owner began to haggle over prices in rapid Chinese.

We brought a small bag of Java apples home and I ate one that evening, after dinner, the flesh snapping off in a crisp crunch with each bite. As I ate the fruit, Ah Ma left the table and returned with a small red jewellery pouch.

"What's this?" I tipped it over the palm of my hand and gold cascaded out in a single chain. On the end was a beautiful, strange pendant. It was two globes, one slightly bigger than the other, connected by a narrow belt. I couldn't recognise the shape of it.

"Is it an hourglass?" I asked my grandmother, holding it up to the light.

She replied in Chinese and then translated herself: "Gourd."

My aunt came to look. "You know the gourd vegetable, Kate? The calabash? In China, they used to hollow them out and use them as bottles." She nudged the gold pendant with a fingernail. "I think it means luck?" She turned and conferred with Ah Ma in Longyan. "Luck and healing, maybe? This was Ah Ma's necklace. That sort of charm is passed to girls."

I fastened it around my neck. Ah Ma beamed a satisfied smile back and patted my arm. I thanked her.

"Only granddaughter lah," she said as she shuffled in her plastic slippers from the room.

A fruit is a seed-bearing vessel. It is, quite literally, a fertilised ovary. Its one job is to disseminate the genes of its plant as far as it can, so that an offspring plant may grow and continue the lineage of the parent plant. Fruit tastes so deliciously sweet because it has evolved to appeal to our taste buds, as well as to the taste buds of all kinds of mammals and birds. We are the fruit-carrying vehicle through which plants have spread their seeds throughout the world. A citrus fruit is a hesperidium, a type of berry that develops a tough rind which covers the ovary wall—the white sponge which gets trapped under our finger-nails as we peel an orange.

A gourd is also a kind of fruit. After Ah Ma gave me the necklace, I searched online for the traditional meaning of the calabash. It is, like many symbols revered in Chinese culture, connected to auspiciousness: the first character of its Chinese name, 葫芦 (húlu), has a similar pronunciation to 福 (fu), meaning "fortune," and its shape resembles the figure eight, considered a lucky number. Many cultures in Asia and Africa hollow out gourds and turn them into bottles, bowls, decorations, and musical instruments. In ancient China, doctors carried medicine inside the bottle gourd, and the vegetable became associated with longevity, health, and strength. Femininity, too, was connected to the calabash, its bloated belly implying an impregnated womb.

I wondered why Ah Ma had decided to pass it to me now. Around the time that she had been diagnosed with cancer, my maternal grandmother had been too, with lymphoma. Inheritance was something I was considering more now than before their diagnoses. Perhaps Ah Ma was thinking about it too, as she began to sort through her jewellery boxes to decide what to pass on to her daughter, her granddaughter, and her sisters.

There is material inheritance, but there is also what gets passed down through our genetics. In KL, I had reread Susan Sontag's book *Illness as Metaphor*, written while Sontag was living with breast cancer in 1978. I was struck by how she imagined illness as a place. "Everyone who is born holds dual citizenship, in the kingdom of the well and in the kingdom of the sick," Sontag writes. "Sooner or later each of us is obliged, at least for a spell, to identify ourselves as citizens of that other place."[48] Having two grandmothers undergoing chemotherapy at the same time felt like I had walked right up to the borders of that other place. My grandmothers had migrated, and I was still on the other side, trying to see what lay ahead of me.

When my mother was going through menopause, she suffered terrible pain and discomfort. "You have this to look forward to," she said to me, her words partially a joke and partially a promise. "My mother was exactly the same."

Growing up I had been told that I had inherited my paternal grandmother's hands and my maternal grandmother's chin. If I had inherited these features from my grandmothers, then surely their cancers would be waiting somewhere inside me too? Ever since I was a teenager, I had been concerned with origins but I hadn't given much thought to endings. Here was a future unfurling before me, a blank page already outlined.

The narrative of every living creature—plant or animal—begins and ends the same, with a birth and a death. The French philosophers Gilles Deleuze and Félix Guattari describe this middle—this journey between destinations—as a plateau, and for them it is a place of excitement where divergence and possibility occur.[49] In geology, the plateau is a high flat land, typically surrounded by mountains. The Tibetan Plateau, where the first wild orange is thought to have been cultivated, is often called the roof of the world because it is this planet's vastest plateau. Its grasslands and lakes pass through eight national borders without hindrance. The plateau is liberated from a singular origin point and exists without the burden of a beginning or ending. It is where new connections can be formed, and old ones left behind.

In Malaysia, I felt bordered by beginnings and endings. Every moment in my family's history had led me to this moment, to be sitting here in Kuala Lumpur with my grandmother's necklace around my throat, with inherited illness on my mind. Life seemed like a road that I had been plodding along before I had sense enough to look up and take in my surroundings. I was no longer at the beginning now, nor was I at the end. I was in the middle of a plateau and any borders were of my own making. Perhaps there was still enough time to bypass them. Perhaps there was still enough time for the road leading from the past into the future to diverge and graft and multiply.

BEFORE SPRAYED PRESERVATIVES and artificial climates which will arrive in a millennium, fresh food does not last on the Silk Roads. Leaving China, merchants sell what they can in the remote towns and caravan cities in the western lands. The remaining fruit which has made it this far without spoiling now begins to gather a layer of blue-and-white fuzz on its skin. The travellers excavate the seeds from stale flesh. Pips and strips of peels are dried on flat stones in the sun, or dunked in jars of honey and wine. Heat, sugar, and alcohol do their work to slow death, preserving and dehydrating the fruit so that it is caught between ripe and rotten. The seeds are gathered in cloth, ready to be disseminated along the Silk Roads, migrating one by one from hand to hand, each to be planted in foreign soil.

The first citrus type to go west is the citron, one of the parent fruits of the genus's hybrids. The citron looks like a larger lemon; its yellow peel is wrinkled and rough. There is little juice in a citron, and instead its thick rind is used to fragrance cooking. The myth goes that it is Alexander the Great who first brings citrons west to Greece, but more probable is that the fruit arrives by merchants from China and India, reaching Persia in the fourth century BCE, and Spain in the seventh century CE.[50] Citron is used for both medicinal and ornamental purposes, as an antidote to poison and as a fragrance; but it also becomes a holy fruit, used in Jewish rituals and decorating the sides of Jewish coins issued between 66 and 70 CE.[51] Its trees are the first citrus to be planted in Italy during the Roman Empire.

Following citron, bitter oranges are the next citrus to arrive in Europe. They, too, are carried from China and India, first by Arab traders and then by Arab armies of the Umayyad dynasty, which march through North Africa to conquer Spain and Portugal. This first great Muslim dynasty brings irrigation and agriculture to the Iberian Peninsula, and by the eleventh century groves of bitter oranges and lemons thrive in the hot Mediterranean climate.[52] For its fragrant blossom and bright fruit, the bitter orange is beloved in Islamic cultures,[53] as are gardens and groves, which are noted in the Qur'an as gifts bestowed by Allah to the faithful: "From the date palm come clusters of low-hanging dates, and there are gardens of vines, olives, and pomegranates, alike yet different. Watch their fruits as they grow and ripen! In all this there are signs for those who would believe."[54]

Trees line mosque gardens, planted with perfect symmetry to conjure the garden of paradise, or Jannah, that awaits Muslims in the afterlife. By the eleventh century, immigrant Asian orange trees trail across the Silk Roads. Now on both sides of the Eurasian landmass, in its native land of China and in its new home in Portugal, the orange is a symbol for prosperity and abundance.

With fruit, language migrates west. The word "orange" evolves from the Sanskrit naranga, and as the orange fruit travels from China and India, its name is adopted into each new language it encounters. The Persian naranj is carried by Muslim traders and armies along the Mediterranean Sea, where it becomes the Spanish naranja, the Portuguese laranga, and the French orange.[55]

The first oranges to arrive in Europe are the bitter variety and are rarely eaten without modification. Arab traders arriving in Western Europe bring candied peel, which is eaten either dry or syruped with little forks.[56] Sweet oranges, at first called China oranges, will take longer to migrate west, arriving in Europe in the sixteenth century when Portuguese sailors return home from East Asia.[57]

When they arrive in Europe, citrons, bitter oranges, and lemons are grown in pleasure gardens for the rich and the holy to enjoy. Then, slowly, they leave the garden walls, to be disseminated farther afield and amongst the common people. Trees will be planted with the intention of selling their fruit as produce, and it will be discovered that grafting, not planting from seed, overcomes citrus's inherent instability. Severed from their parent tree, offspring buds will adapt to their new rootstock, and soon they will thrive across the continent. A single tree grows to be a grove until, one day, the gardener pauses under the green boughs and realises he can no longer tell which is the original parent tree that came from a place far away in the east. The assimilation is complete.

WHERE LIFE MOVES, so too does death. For as long as the Silk Roads have existed as an international network of commerce, they have been paths for illnesses too. The first recorded plague pandemic comes during the reign of the Byzantine Emperor Justinian I in 541 when diseased rats arrive in Constantinople on grain ships from Egypt.[58] Nearly half the city's population succumbs to the plague. Outbreaks return in waves of death for two generations until Justinian's once-grand empire, buoyed by international trade and commerce, suffers a demographic collapse of over half its people. But life endures. Tribes from the Arabian Peninsula migrate and gain control of the weakened Byzantine Empire.[59] Cultures and ideologies hybridise as the Eastern Mediterranean recovers. It is surprisingly easy to forget about something like the end of days. Historians, holy men, and city administrators preserve records of the pandemics, but the children and then the grandchildren of the dead are clumsier with the stories of past devastation which they inherit.

Babies are born, grandparents pass away. Memory slips into mythology.

Five hundred years after the end of Justinian's plague, a second pandemic and a new apocalypse is delivered along the Silk Roads. It comes from the west. Merchants arrive in China's southern cities with stories of a disease that is sweeping down from Tian Shan, the steppes just west of China and north of the Tibetan Plateau.[60] When the illness arrives in a town, it spills from body to body, showing itself in buboes that swell to the size of almonds, oranges, and cucumbers,[61] black welts that bloom like roses, and blood that drowns the lungs. The fourteenth century has arrived in Ming-dynasty China with disaster. The earth suffers quakes, floodings, and famines. Off the coast of Fujian, dragons are sighted by the superstitious, roaring through tornadoes and storm clouds.[62] Nature is volatile, and the fantastical is collapsing into reality. Something terrible looms. While the people of China look to the skies for guidance, it is from beneath their feet that catastrophe comes. Disturbed by flooded rivers and violent earthquakes, rodents are shaken from their shelters and severed from their food chains.[63] They migrate into human settlements to find new homes and carry with them fleas infected with a bacterium called *Yersinia pestis*. In city centres, infection leaps from rat to human, and disease spreads throughout China, following the trade routes of merchants. In 1334, thirteen million people die from the same illness.[64]

Pandemics do not acknowledge borders. Illness sweeps from east to west, carried in the hollow bellies of ships filled with grains, spices, and silks, where hungry rodents race through the sacks, crates, and baskets. They mix with the food that will be delivered to market stalls, picked up, paid for, taken home, and devoured by other bodies. Fleas are shaken from their animal carriers, and they find new hosts in fabric and food. After months at sea, the merchants arrive in the Mediterranean's seaports with crates of foreign luxuries and news of a pestilence sweeping across China and Central Asia. They are greeted with exuberance by European shoppers, who are gathered, greedy for whatever commerce they can afford. The ships are emptied out and the rodents, finally free, disappear into these new lands.

The sick soon stretch along the lands of Asia, North Africa, and Europe. Christians call this new plague the Great Pestilence, while Muslims call it the Year of the Annihilation, but regardless of religion, it migrates along the Silk Roads.[65] Health passports and quarantines are imposed on travelling merchants. Warriors returning to western Europe from their Crusades adopt the hygienic use of bitter citrus customary in the Holy Land. In Italy, oranges are carried and held to noses with the hope that the fresh scent of their peel will keep the plague at bay.[66] But citrus is not enough to curb the pandemic that kills a third of Western Europe's population, a third of the Eastern Mediterranean and North Africa's population, and over half of China's population.[67] Along the Silk Roads, mass graves overspill. Villages are abandoned. Supply chains collapse. Marketplaces sit in ruin. Gods are forsaken.

Death and grief linger on the street, in the air, along the rivers, amongst the trees. In the *Muqaddimah*, the fourteenth-century historian Ibn Khaldûn observes that "[the pandemic] was as if the voice of existence in the world had called out for oblivion and restriction, and the world had responded to its call. God inherits the earth and all who dwell upon it."[68]

A meaning for all this suffering is necessary. In Europe, those who are seen as social polluters are condemned: foreign migrants, sex workers, and Jewish people are targeted as the sinners responsible for bringing about unclean conditions for the plague. Christians in western Europe, desperate for their god's mercy, begin to cleanse their lands of anyone perceived as contaminated. In an intensification of pre-pandemic anti-Semitism, Jews are persecuted as plague-bearers, run out of cities, tormented, and killed. Other places find different scapegoats.

When the pestilence arrives on the shores of Cyprus in trading ships, the people of the island round up their Muslim prisoners and kill them all in a single bloody afternoon.[69]

The Silk Roads are woven from different cultures, religions, and societies to create braids of hybridity running from Chang'an in Central China to Rome in Italy. These networks of exchange make the world what it is today, both for the better and for the worse. Perhaps it is human nature to band together with the majority to blame and ostracise a minority. History repeats our cruelties; the cycle turns over and over again, across different times and different lands. The Silk Roads deliver exotic fruit, new gods, and hybrid societies, but they also carry with them sorrow and suffering and violence—all of which we still inherit today.

DECEMBER WASHED INTO KUALA LUMPUR with teatime storms and sweet Taiwanese mandarins. Most days it rained and we ate dinner late, waiting an extra hour, or sometimes two, for my aunt to ease her car along the city's flooded roads. When I first arrived in KL, I had been transfixed by the tropical storms which seemed to ripen all afternoon, charcoal cumulonimbus clouds choking the blue sky until they burst and an hour of rainfall flushed out the city. When the deluge passed and the sun returned, steel and glass glistened anew in rainbows. I never got used to the violence of monsoon season's thunder and lightning, but I craved the cool mists that arrived with the sudden downpours. While we waited for my aunt, I sat in the threshold of the balcony's open doors, listening to Ah Ma's gentle snores coming from the sofa. In one hand I took oranges apart, and in the other I crushed a novel's spine flat against the storm's gusts. In another room, Ah Kong watched the television, always on the same channel broadcasting from a studio in Beijing. He refused to wear his hearing aid indoors and instead blasted the news in surround sound so that the entire apartment floor vibrated with the newscaster's steady voice. If I had understood Mandarin at the time, perhaps I would have heard of an illness that was spreading through the city of Wuhan. Perhaps if I had known that I would not be able to return to Malaysia for the next three years, I would have been more careful with the time I had left in KL with my grandparents. Or perhaps I would have just carried on chewing fruit and reading my aunt's old paperbacks, content to wait out the storm.

As Christmas came closer, Auntie Sian and I strung red and white decorations around her bamboo plants. On a visit to one of the city's many malls, I saw that an automated Lapland fairy tale had been installed, complete with flying reindeer and robotic elves hard at work. Caught in an air-conditioned current, the artificial snow blew across the mall's marble floor. White petals stuck to the bottoms of my sandals as I browsed the shops for Christmas presents to take back to Ireland.

My time in Malaysia was nearly up, but before I left, my grandparents would be celebrating their sixtieth wedding anniversary. My father and oldest brother were coming to KL for the dinner, as were my Singaporean cousins, and an extensive web of relations from across Malaysia. When I asked if some of us would be staying in a hotel, Auntie Sian laughed. "Ah Kong would never allow it. The family must stay together." Her apartment filled with ten more people, and I was demoted from sofa-bed to floor to crash with my brother and cousins on the soft, thin mattresses we had slept on as children.

For my grandparents' anniversary dinner, I wore the necklace with its little gold gourd and greeted aunties, uncles, and cousins whom I hadn't seen in years. When the meal started, I looked around at the faces of our extended family. I wanted to keep track of how each person was related to me, and in my mind, I began to put faces to the names on the family tree Auntie Suan had drawn for me.

The tree in western culture has come to order patriarchal lineage. It dominates how we envision genealogy: each branch a new family with buds for offspring to grow. The tree is also the model for other genetic relationships: animal and plant species as well as language families. It's a structure that is useful for visualising connections, but one that is also limited to direct inheritance. Hybrids like spontaneous mutations and pidgin languages, as well as communities which operate like families but are not blood relatives, are not so easily grafted onto this tree model.

At the family dinner, I tried to keep track of our family as a tree, each old branch splitting away as new families were created and new grafts added as marriages connected families. The tree grew more and more expansive as I drew it in my mind, with more and more branches, until the weight of the boughs became unbearable for the roots and it collapsed to the ground. Its arborescent linearity lost, our family no longer resembled a tree in my mind, but instead a tangled web of branches that sprawled outwards and roots that bulged through the earth. New connections were made possible as the top and the bottom of the tree became lost in the mess. I could no longer see where it began or ended. The singular path of inheritance disappeared. Instead, the plant could grow in any direction. Now each of us was in the middle of its entanglement.

Deleuze and Guattari reject the tree, "which has dominated Western reality and all of Western thought." Instead, they propose the rhizome, the subterranean stem of ginger, turmeric, and lotus, as a truly radical structure which allows for multiplicities and new connections and which they see as characteristic of "eastern" horticulture and thought: "The East presents a different figure: a relation to the steppe and the garden (and in some cases, the desert and the oasis), rather than forest and field; cultivation of tuber by fragmentation of the individual; a casting aside or bracketing of animal raising, which is confined to closed spaces or pushed out into the steppes of the nomads."[70]

For Deleuze and Guattari, the rhizome is a much less rigid model. "Any point of a rhizome can be connected to anything other, and must be," they argue. "A rhizome may be broken, shattered at a given spot, but it will start up again on one of its old lines, or on new lines."[71] A rhizome is thus a kind of plateau.

The philosophers concede that a tree branch has the potential to burgeon into a rhizome.[72] I wonder if they ever saw a citrus tree with lemons, tangerines, and mandarins all growing from the same branch. The spontaneity of citrus, its instability and unreliability when grown from seed, strikes me as an anti-genealogical image full of queer potential. A citrus tree may still be a tree, but the way in which it can carry on its lineage is rhizomic to me. If a seed produces a hybrid mutation of its parent tree, then it cannot be relied upon to carry on the family lineage.

As citrus moves from east to west, it shakes off its old meanings to instead be assimilated into new cultures, religions, and lands. The orange has liberated itself from one singular point of origin, but new challenges come from being foreign in a strange land.

I had travelled to Malaysia, in part because I had wanted to better understand my heritage. But what I discovered was much more complicated than the single, clean narrative that I had desired since childhood. There were roots moving in every direction, old grafting scars and severed branches that I was still learning about. As I left KL to return to Europe, I said goodbye to my grandparents and aunt and promised to return soon. I had a renewed curiosity about the past now and not solely for my own family history. I wanted to better understand how we connected to other communities and lands, not just in East Asia but across the world. Flying back home, my plane followed the trail of the Silk Roads, the ancient networks of connection that first delivered the orange from east to west. But arriving in Europe would not be the end of our journey.

THREE

· · · · · · · · · · ·

HOLLAND

IN THE SPRING OF 2020, LIFE STILLED. AS A VIRUS ACCELERATED into a global pandemic, illness spread with little regard for borders on maps. Governments mandated lockdowns. We were to remain at home; there would be no travelling, no leaving, no moving, no mingling. No other bodies beyond the domestic immediate. The initial action to curb the spread of infection was expected to last three weeks. Stuttering and restarting, it lasted over a year.

When the north of Ireland mandated a lockdown, I was at my parents' house, close to Belfast. In the first weeks of the pandemic, I was made redundant from my job, and on the first day of every month, I scraped around a pot of savings to pay rent on my now empty flat in Edinburgh. Nervous editors hesitated to commission new work, so I stopped writing, and, for the first time in my adult life, I had the anxiety-inducing privilege of nothing to do. My world shrank to my childhood neighbourhood. It was as if the last decade of my life had been a fever dream, and each morning I awoke a child again. The only windows into life beyond our street were dispatches from my father, who continued working in a now deserted accident and emergency department, and, of course, the internet.

Nine-to-five routine gone, I slept late and woke late. At night I got lost down the infinite scroll of the internet. I watched an Italian priest wearing a hazmat suit deliver last rites in a hospital ward. I watched white people shouting "kung flu" at East Asian people in the streets. I watched prisoners dig the final resting places of their fellow inmates beneath the Manhattan skyline. I watched a group of British boys beat a Chinese boy for being Chinese on a British street. I watched undertakers hammer plastic crucifixes to mark mass graves. I watched a man throw a woman the same age as my grandmother to the ground and tell her to get out of his country. I watched dolphins swim through the green canals of Venice, and then I watched a man debunk the videos of dolphins swimming through the green canals of Venice as fake news. As the sun began to bleed through the curtains, I finally switched off my phone to see my reflection staring back at me on the blank screen.

As my routine and my future slipped away together, my concept of time became unwieldy. Beyond waiting for the six o'clock news to start each evening, there was little else to occupy my time other than worrying and scrolling and then worrying some more. Things became desperate enough for me to spend an afternoon clearing out my old bedroom, which had remained mostly unchanged since I had moved to Scotland at eighteen. I reached a hand under my bed and pulled dusty boxes and papers into the sunlight. Most of what I unearthed were old art projects from school: sticky canvases, yellowing sketchbooks, and stacks of paper wrinkled with age. The spines of old sketchbooks groaned as I cracked them open. In a plastic folder, I found the project I had based on my trip to Longyan: the drawings of temple dragons and watercolour cityscapes I had created in my last year of school. I was sure the city of Longyan would be locked down, but I wondered if the pandemic had reached our village yet. I sorted through the pages to decide what I would keep and what I would throw away.

As the discard pile grew, so too did a strange sensation. It was thrilling to hold a sketch that had taken me hours of focus, skill, and dedication to complete, and rip it up, toss it aside, ruin it as meaningless. If the world were fair, destruction and creation would take the same effort. It is far too easy to destroy something. A red strike through a sentence. A flame through a forest. A fist through a flower's roots. What took life a hundred years to create could be felled in mere minutes.

Time came loose during the early months of the pandemic, or perhaps more accurately my ability to pin time in place with meaning came loose. Things that I had cared about in the past—writing, reading, drawing—left me. The act of creation could not compete with the conveyor belt of violence that algorithms served up to me inside my tiny screen. I felt untethered from reality. I had floated away and was now watching a person who looked like me and sounded like me move through the mundanity of lockdown. I had stepped over the frame and out of my life. Now I was watching from the gallery floor, as curious as a stranger, to see what would happen next.

BEHIND US IS THE LIGHT; ahead, a pool of darkness. But let our eyes adjust. There are shades to this void: a true darkness that moves away to leave a corridor of depth. There is an end beyond us, a point that we cannot see. But we should focus on what is closer, what lies between the light and dark. Look carefully now.

We are in a room, although it is a room without borders. In the centre is the sharp edge of a table. Atop the marbled surface is the tasselled skirt of a tapestry folded with nonchalance, and atop *it* is a silver plate shining like a mirror, and atop *it* is fruit: two pieces; an orange, two leaves of its branch still attached, and a lemon, half peeled, its rind coiling through air. On the far side of the table, a blue-and-white jar catches the light. Its porcelain surface winks at us. Beside it are two ornate amber goblets, each half empty with half-drunk wine. An array of trinkets—a watch, a pen, a crescent of cheese—litter the rest of the table. No space is empty; no surface is unfulfilled. The arrangement hangs, glistening and still, between light and dark, an offer of temptation.

The artist Willem Kalf paints this small moment in 1669, at the height of the Dutch Golden Age. Kalf has spent most of his career in Amsterdam, and although this scene seems set in Holland, the objects on the table are not Dutch in origin. The provenance of the Wanli-period porcelain jar is in China; the peeled lemon and whole orange grown along the Mediterranean; the glassware arriving maybe from Venice; the decorative crimson tapestry perhaps from Turkey. The imported goods evoke wealth; the imagined owner of this laden table is a rich, refined citizen of Holland. A moment of pleasure, of good taste and luxury, has been caught by oil paint—that is, until the eye moves down the curves of the golden goblet to rest upon the open watch. Time, even in a painting, is ticking away. The serenity of the scene is interrupted by its precarity, suddenly obvious. The plate's careful balancing act seems now reckless and the lemon's dangling spiral about to tear and drop at any moment. Time has entered the scene, which means that corrosion, rot, and dust are inevitable. The background plunges back into the void. The domestic tilts into the unfamiliar. Look again. Where exactly are we, anyway?

When Kalf sits down to paint his still life of foreign goods, Amsterdam's reputation as the finest commercial hub for global trading is a recent acquisition. In the sixteenth century, war-torn Western Europe is at the margins of the world's network of trade, still reliant on the middlemen merchants of the Arab nations. Across the Eurasian landmass, the port of Malacca, on the west coast of present-day Malaysia, is the nexus of trade in

Southeast Asia, where ships full of spices set sail to reach the ports of India, China, Syria, East Africa, and eventually the Mediterranean.[73] Of all the foreign produce that has reached Europe since medieval times, spice has become the most desired. An appetite for clove, pepper, and nutmeg—all of which derive from trees grown on the islands of Indonesia—has developed, their use for food, medicine, and holy rites becoming essential in everyday life. As Europeans begin to map the world and navigate their ships across oceans, these western nations are on a mission to find a direct trade route to the spice islands of Southeast Asia.

Portugal arrives first. In Malacca, the fleet is received with hostility and suspicion. The naval admiral Afonso de Albuquerque decides that conquest is the only way to gain dominion over the port, and his small army captures Malacca in 1511, disrupting the Southeast Asian trading markets.

Portugal expands its control into the Indonesian islands, but it struggles to retain conquered land. When the Dutch arrive with their superior ships and naval tactics, they fight off their European rivals. Competing Dutch companies set up shop on the spice islands of what they call the East Indies, each eager to establish a monopoly on exported pepper, nutmeg, and clove. The rivalry among traders tanks their own industry as the European market is flooded with an abundance of spice. The States General of the Netherlands proposes a merger of the twelve competing businesses into a single chartered company, and so the Vereenigde Oostindische Compagnie (VOC) is born.

The creation of the VOC in 1602 begins two centuries of colonial expansion, unprecedented in its rapid, global growth. The Dutch company controls Southeast Asia's spice trade, operating as both a multinational corporation and a sovereign force. Its merchants have the power to wage war, invade land, establish colonies, and replace Indonesian rulers with their own company administrators. The VOC is brutal in how it obtains total domination over the spice trade. The tropical tree species from which nutmeg and mace derive are native to a small cluster of volcanic islands in the Banda Sea. When the Bandanese people break their contract for exclusive trading with the VOC, the Dutch Governor-General Jan Pieterszoon Coen lands on the islands with over a thousand soldiers and eradicates the native population. In the largest massacre in the VOC's history, the army kills, enslaves, and forcibly deports fifteen thousand of the islands' inhabitants.[74] A small fruit's seed has become one of the most lucrative products in global trade, and the island society which has cultivated its trees for centuries is obliterated in the race to own the means of production.

"The Dutch are human ants," writes the French philosopher Denis Diderot a century after the VOC is established. "They spread over all the regions of the earth, gather up everything they find that is scarce, useful, or precious, and carry it back to their storehouses. It is to Holland that the rest of Europe goes for everything it lacks. Holland is Europe's commercial hub. The Dutch have worked to such good purpose that, through their ingenuity, they have obtained all of life's necessities, in defiance of the elements."[75] In the nineteenth century, Karl Marx notes a chain reaction from the mission of the VOC to the birth of modern capitalism. "The colonial system ripened trade and navigation as in a hot-house," he writes in *Capital*. "The treasures captured outside Europe by undisguised looting, enslavement and murder flowed back to the mother-country and were turned into capital there. Holland, which first brought the colonial system to its full development, already stood at the zenith of its commercial greatness in 1648."[76]

Any resident of the United Provinces of the Netherlands can buy shares in the VOC, a lucrative investment for a new Dutch mercantile class that emerges in the seventeenth century. Wealth from the spice trade brings a pleasant lifestyle: honey and milk, lemons and oranges, fowl and fish, all served on porcelain and silverware. Art, too, becomes a commodity for the new market.

Before the seventeenth century, Western Europeans who owned art were wealthy, religious, or usually both, and artists were tasked with painting family portraiture or biblical scenes. But as the VOC imports new money and new commodities into Dutch ports, a cultural obsession with material possession sees a boom in still life artworks. These small oil paintings hang in cosseted parlours and living rooms, and they reflect the household's wealth, not only through their chosen subjects—flowers and fruit, spices and wines, seafood and fine china—but also through the exquisite new techniques still life painters employ. In Dutch still life, objects gleam and they glisten. The surface is emphasised; in Kalf's paintings, the plates, jars, and even a lemon's cut flesh shimmer with the light of a hundred small mirrors. "What can be the justification of such an assemblage if not to lubricate man's gaze amid his domain, to facilitate his daily business among objects whose riddle is dissolved and which are no longer anything but easy surfaces?" asks Roland Barthes about the sheen of Dutch still life.[77] Gazing upon these displays of colonial wealth is pure pleasure.

The extravagant aesthetics of Dutch still life, particularly glossy arrangements like Kalf's, have been interpreted as a celebration of what they are representing. These *things*, flung recklessly upon a table, are the spoils of violent, expansive warfare and greed. The popularity of still life in Holland points to a country that wants to relish, even gloat about, its recent accumulation of national wealth, hanging it for all the world to see. This reading of still life implies that the objects within the frame are a kind of catalogue of empire: a miscellany of exotic produce that has arrived into Dutch ports to be auctioned off to a new class of citizens with fresh money to spend.

But look again. Kalf's glassware is so intricate, his lemon peel so perfect, his silverware so blinding. There is nothing natural about his still life paintings. We have become so familiar with the still life genre that we take for granted the assumption that what we are looking at is a perfect representation of life four hundred years ago. But glass, fruit, and metal do not shine with their own luminescence; the artist bestows light on his subjects. The gleam is seductive, but its artifice becomes more obvious the longer you stare at it.

The German poet Johann Wolfgang von Goethe argues that Kalf's still life paintings prove the power of art over reality, writing in 1797 that "one must see this picture in order to understand in what sense art is superior to nature and what the spirit of man imparts to objects. For me, at least, there is no question that should I have the choice of golden vessels or the picture, I would choose the picture."[78]

If given a choice between the orange that sits half crushed at the bottom of my fruit bowl or the orange of a Kalf painting that shimmers like a mirage, I, too, would choose the picture.

When I studied art in school, I took inspiration for my still lifes from the impressionists and post-impressionists, not the masters of the Dutch Golden Age. There is a playful warmth to the apples, oranges, and pears of Paul Cézanne, Claude Monet, and Vincent van Gogh; the edges are hazy, and the nineteenth-century artists propose rather than order their subjects. I appreciated the technical expertise of the Dutch masters, but I had become more interested in art that knew that it was art. Trompe l'oeil paintings seemed too safe, too traditional, and, despite their brilliant gleam, too dull.

The year after I returned from Longyan, my grandparents visited our family in Ireland. They decided that before they left Europe to fly back to Malaysia, they would transit through the Netherlands. My father and I travelled with my grandparents to Amsterdam for a few days of sightseeing before the four of us split up to go our separate ways, returning west and east. Walking through the crowded corridors of the Rijksmuseum, I passed still life after still life. It is thought that a million still lifes were painted during the Dutch Golden Age, and two hundred of them hang in the Rijksmuseum.[79] As I strode past scenes of fruit and flowers and food, the mass of oil paint blurred together into a single lustre of colonial riches.

I am a child of the 1990s, born during booming globalisation, and so I didn't stop to consider how few of the objects featured in Dutch still lifes were native to the Netherlands. Inside the frames were tulips from Turkey, oranges from Sicily, rugs from Damascus, bowls from Jingdezhen. Nowadays, we hang a still life in our kitchen because it reflects a cosy domesticity. But I wonder how it would have felt to be a seventeenth-century Dutch person admiring her newly purchased still life of exotic ephemera. Perhaps placing the painted objects in her home turns them into her possession. Or perhaps they stay foreign, so that every time she passes them in their frame, she thinks of where they came from—the faraway lands that are only half real to her. The world is so big and so unfamiliar, and she is so small and so innate, and perhaps she loves the painted oranges and lemons because their foreignness roots her in the only land she has ever known.

DURING LOCKDOWN, THE FRUIT on supermarket shelves had a discombobulating effect on my sense of place. Under bright lights, I held apples and oranges in my blue-gloved hands and read the names of the countries of origin that had been stuck to their skin. Spain, South Africa, New Zealand. In 2020, these places seemed unreal. The world seemed unreal. Or maybe I was the unreal one. My mind, bombarded by violence, guilt-ridden by anxiety, and unmoored by loneliness, could not imagine life beyond the borders of my own skin. I sank into a void that I now recognise as depression. My own brain became a foreign place to me.

My mother gave me packets of seeds and told me to take a small barren patch of the garden. In April the soil was still too cold, too tough to nurture life, so I sowed the seeds in little pots and placed them in a window where they would get the midday sun. I poked holes into the dirt, sprinkled in the seeds—sugar snap peas, raspberries, tomatoes, curly-leafed parsley—and crumbled some soil over them.

In days, the green heads of seedlings pushed through the darkness like tiny miracles. They grew, straight and strong, towards sunlight until it was finally warm enough to acclimate their roots to the outside garden. The rhythm of my days changed to move with the weather. I sank my fists into the earth and felt the sun on the nape of my neck. I watched green stems grow and branch and multiply. I watched new leaves unfurl and small flowers bloom. Fruit arrived and I watched the clusters ripen, their pale skin flooding with colour. When the first raspberry was ready, I plucked it from its stem and popped it into my mouth. It burst, sharp and jammy, and I savoured every bite. *I grew that*, I thought. *I watched a seed become a fruit. I watched something be made.* It was the most real I had felt in months. Raspberry pips still caught between my teeth, I continued my work in the garden, trimming, watering, feeding, fastening, growing. Clouds roamed over my little patch of earth, ferrying water from a distant place on to somewhere new. The world was still moving. The sun was still rising and setting. The wind was still carrying seeds from one place to another. As I knelt in the garden on the cusp between spring and summer, dedicating my time to ripening fruit, the borders between myself and the life that I was nurturing became indistinguishable. For the first time in a long time, I felt rooted to the land that had raised me.

BY THE SEVENTEENTH CENTURY, most Europeans are familiar with citrus. The northern nations import oranges and lemons from the Mediterranean coasts, where Italian and Spanish farmers cultivate new varieties. Although the orange evokes the sun of Southern Europe, its Chinese roots are not forgotten. The

Dutch word for the orange is *sinaasappel*, meaning "China's apple." At the height of the Dutch Golden Age, the fruit is an exotic reminder of the VOC's grasp on the world, more emblem than food for the burgeoning middle class.

And so, in the hollow of a blue-and-white china bowl sits an orange. It has been freshly plucked from its tree. Two leaves and a white blossom remain connected to the fruit, and its stem holds them high in the air, with none of the droop that comes with the passing of time. The orange's citrus cousin, the lemon, sits beside it. Unlike the intact orange, the lemon has been sliced so that its oval flesh gleams, a flat mirror. A spiral of peel escapes over the bowl's borders.

A Willem Kalf still life is a familiar scene now: fruit, porcelain, glass, table, all set against a dark void. But in this painting—which hangs in the National Gallery of Art in Washington, DC, where it is labelled "*Still Life*, c. 1660"—it is the shallow porcelain fruit bowl that is the centrepiece. Kalf has tipped it towards us, showing off the patterned, glazed ridges which decorate its yawning mouth. It is an unnatural angle for a ceramic of that width, and it rests a little too close to the table's edge. Two pieces of fruit are not heavy enough to keep the bowl weighted down for long. I imagine the moment after the painting is finished and the scene has been captured: the bowl crashes back to its centre of gravity and the orange and lemon are catapulted into space.

Nowadays, this style of blue-and-white patterned ceramic is so ubiquitous it is unremarkable when spotted on a kitchen counter. My parents had their own blue-and-white patterned fruit bowl modelled after a Dutch ceramic. As I left for school, I pulled satsumas from its mouth. The same style of blue-and-white ceramic sat on my parents' living room shelf, in the form of small Chinese porcelain vases. These objects were so familiar to me as a child that I never asked how the same decorative style could be found on the rim of a European fruit bowl and on the curve of an East Asian flower vase.

Porcelain first arrives in the new Dutch republic as stolen goods. In 1602, the VOC captures the *San Jago*, a Portuguese carrack, off the coast of Saint Helena, an island in the South Atlantic. On board, the sailors discover a cargo of fine Chinese porcelain, which they cart back to the Netherlands.

Creating porcelain from the clay mineral kaolin began in the city of Jingdezhen over a thousand years ago, but the art was mastered during the Song dynasty, between the tenth and thirteenth centuries.[80] The glossy ceramics were exported to other Asian countries for centuries before the first European encountered porcelain. Then, in the fourteenth century, the Venetian merchant and writer Marco Polo returned from his travels in China with a small jar made from a material he called *porcellana*, because of its resemblance to the shiny, hard cowry shell.[81] No one in Italy had ever seen anything quite like this before, and as with citrus and flowers and spice, Europe was soon mesmerised by it.

Porcelain trickles into Europe as kings and emperors covet the rare exotic ceramics. Merchants in Jingdezhen export their ceramics into this new market, shipping the "white gold" west as trade routes become more secure. As the VOC grows in power and Holland becomes rich from its overseas trade, Chinese porcelain fills Dutch cities. As with spices, the Dutch would rather cut out the middleman, and European ceramists attempt to make their own versions of porcelain, but no one can master the secret recipe. (Western accounts of the time suggest eggshells, special eastern "juice," and "umbilical fish" are the raw ingredients that are then shaped and cocooned in the earth to be reborn as porcelain.)[82]

Jingdezhen porcelain makers begin catering for the newly wealthy European market. They make shaving mugs and mustard pots and sell them to VOC merchants. But while the Dutch want functional ceramics, they also want their porcelain to look Chinese. One account sent from Batavia, the VOC's capital in Indonesia, to Taiwan in 1635 lists Europe's favoured motifs:

"Chinese persons on foot and on horseback, water, landscapes, pleasure-houses, their boats, birds and animals, all this is well liked in Europe."[83] The market for Chinese-looking porcelain is captured in many of Kalf's paintings, such as his *Still Life with a Chinese Bowl, Nautilus Cup and Other Objects* (1662), which features a relief of Chinese figures in traditional dress affixed to a blue-and-white sugar bowl beside peeled citrus.

Europe does eventually master its own porcelain. Augustus II the Strong, elector of Saxony and king of Poland, desires porcelain with such a burning greed that by his death in 1733, he owns a thirty-five-thousand-piece collection, the largest in Europe. The ruler is a rampant spender on the luxurious, the exotic, and the desirable, so much so that he diagnoses himself with "porcelain sickness," that is not unlike a hunger for citrus. In a letter, he writes: "Are you not aware that the same is true for oranges as for porcelain, that once one has the sickness of one or the other, one can never get enough of the things and wishes to have more and more."[84] In 1701, Augustus imprisons the German alchemist Johann Friedrich Böttger, who boasted that he had discovered how to spin gold. Unable to make good on his lie, Böttger instead works on a recipe for the porcelain-sick ruler with the scientist Ehrenfried Walther von Tschirnhaus. After four years they finally succeed, and in 1710 they establish a porcelain manufactory in Meissen, which continues to produce porcelain today.

Vienna in Austria, Plymouth in England, and Delft in Holland all begin producing their own porcelain. This is not authentic Jingdezhen porcelain but a cheaper, thinner earthenware that resembles the imported items. European ceramists interpret Chinese visual culture for themselves, reproducing popular motifs such as dragons, plants, birds, and people, but severed from their original cultural significance.

In the eighteenth century, reinterpretation of East Asian designs by Europeans becomes its own decorative style, called chinoiserie, which expands to encompass furniture, wallpaper, paintings, and architecture. Like the painted sinaasappels in a still life, silks, lacquered furniture, and porcelain in European households are fashionable for what they signify—the exotic. Chinoiserie is a European interpretation—an appropriation of Chinese aesthetics made palatable for western tastes. It is a hybrid aesthetic, a crude creation of China through a European gaze. This reinterpretation of other cultures is not one-way. In Beijing, the Emperor Qianlong commissions Jesuit artists to design eighteenth-century baroque-style European pavilions in Yuanming Yuan, the city's Summer Palace.[85]

Authenticity is prized high in culture. We want "authentic" food, "authentic" travel, and "authentic" experiences. "Authentic" may as well be synonymous with "real." But authenticity is a nebulous quality. As the Silk Roads taught us, societies have been exchanging food, ideas, religions, and genetics for thousands of years. I wonder when an inauthentic creation becomes a style in its own right. When does Dutch porcelain with its Chinese motifs assimilate into the history of art, not as a cheap version of East Asian ceramics but as its own hybrid visual identity?

Immigration is the hybridising of multiple cultures, as is the mixing of families of different races, nations, and religions. My father using the leftover trimmings of a roast dinner in his Malaysian curries is perfectly inauthentic and perfectly delicious. Immigrants who open restaurants of their national cuisines often transform their cooking to cater to western palates. Chinese, Indian, and Thai takeout restaurants may not be authentic, but in their inauthenticity, something new and hybrid and delightful is created.

Being mixed race is, of course, being a hybrid of two cultures. The language of mixed identity, from the more innocuous—half of this and half of that—to the more insidious—the one-drop rule—is loaded with accusations of inauthenticity. I could fill the rest of this book with the offhand comments that have been levelled at my racial identity, but all of them had the same effect: of segmenting me into halves and quarters until my sense of self was almost entirely cut away. During the pandemic's surge of anti-Asian violence, these voices from the past returned as a whisper in my mind that questioned if I was even Asian enough to have the right to feel this much sorrow.

Looking back now, I see that my childhood obsession with authenticity—and my frustration when I failed to capture what I thought was authenticity in art—was about trying to feel real. Growing up, I felt out of step in a world that was rigidly organised into categories of difference. I was not Asian or White but Other; not Straight or Gay but Other; not British or Irish but Other; not Protestant or Catholic but Other. This third, hybrid identity had no borders and no models to guide me. Now I know and love so many people who live along the spectrum of Other, between what our society considers fixed identities. But I felt alone as a child, and I thought that if I couldn't pin myself to one identity, then I did not exist. I felt half finished, half authentic, and half of something else—which really meant that I totalled nothing.

But the world is made of hybrids. Purity is an illusion. We are born of two parents. Even the orange is the offspring of different parents: the mandarin and the pomelo. Art has always taken its inspiration from numerous wells of ideas. A still life is a construction half of imagination, half of reality. A contemporary ceramist shapes their porcelain after both Chinese and Dutch models. History is too various to offer a single narrative. Life is composed of shards of glass, all slotted together to make a mosaic. No one is born complete.

Some Dutch painters use Delftware in their still lifes as a cheap stand-in for Jingdezhen porcelain. When we look at a painting, like Kalf's *Still Life* with its fruit bowl, we can't be sure if we are looking at "real" porcelain, fired in southern China, or an inauthentic imitation, crafted in Holland. But does the provenance of an object matter, when what we are looking at is neither Jingdezhen nor Delft ceramic but rather the idea of porcelain painted inside a frame?

And it's not just porcelain that calls into question the authenticity of still life's subjects. "Seventeenth-century Dutch still-life painters seldom made their compositions from nature," writes the art historian Seymour Slive. "Close examination of the works by the flower painters shows that their colorful bouquets are based on carefully executed preliminary studies which served as patterns, and that they were not painted from freshly cut flowers."[86]

It had never crossed my mind that the Dutch masters did not work from life, but it is so obvious. Of course they couldn't; it would have been an expensive set-up for the artist—an arrangement of half-eaten food, flowers, and fruit that needed to be in a perfect state between ripeness and decay for all the weeks it took to complete a single oil painting. Separate sketches of different objects were brought together with careful skill by the artist. In some cases, oranges never met porcelain bowls and lemons never touched silverware. These painters were less concerned with capturing what was in front of them in a frame and far more interested in drafting fantasy arrangements. They sought to find new meanings by placing a half-peeled citrus fruit beside a watch. By doing so, what new allegories would be conjured in the viewer's gaze?

AS LOCKDOWN CONTINUED and the summer stretched on, I found a set of crumbled oil pastels and tubes of half-congealed acrylic paint, and I began to create on paper again. For weeks I sat in the garden and made bad art. Any skills I had developed in school were gone, and I struggled to represent life around me. So, instead, I let abstraction seep onto the page. Colour became my focus. When I sought to capture what a tree meant to me and what I brought to it, a page of sage and pine and fern blotches seemed more true to me than trying to force a shaky imitation of reality.

I also began to write again. I turned away from personal writing about the rise of anti-Asian hate crimes. Attempting to articulate myself—my own history, as well as the UK's far longer history of migration, colonialism, and racism—in a few hundred words felt like a futile task. I had once been willing to package parts of myself into neat boxes for quick money, but now I sought an alternate means of expression. So instead, I wrote for myself and not for a marketplace.

Across history, art and economics have been inseparable: from the funding of the Renaissance by Medici patrons to the billions that creative industries contribute to countries' economies each year.[87] The history of porcelain in the Dutch Golden Age is the history of art moulding itself to a new market. Chinese artists adapted their designs to appeal to the west's new mercantile class, while European ceramists took inspiration from the influx of East Asian earthenware to create their own version of porcelain that diluted its Chinese origins.

Still life paintings—both in subject and in market—tell the story of how modern Europe becomes a global nexus of power, beginning with the expansion of overseas territories and the ever-tightening control of foreign resources. This story becomes mythology as European nations justify invasion with religion, ideology, and manifest destiny. The myth that Europe is destined to own the earth gathers momentum as nations continue to lay claim to conquered land and draw borderlines on their new maps. Roland Barthes writes that myth is so powerful a force because "it abolishes the complexity of human acts, it gives them the simplicity of essences . . . it organizes a world which is without contradictions because it is without depth, a world wide open and wallowing in the evident, it establishes a blissful clarity: things appear to mean something by themselves."[88] For centuries, the myth of European colonialism is one of "blissful clarity," as history becomes stories set firmly in the past. But myths haunt and they linger. As recently as the early 2000s, when I was a child in the British education system, I was not taught why the UK, a tiny island, remained connected to a commonwealth that stretched to Fiji, or why English was the official language of sixty countries, or why a Union Jack haunted the corners of so many flags. I was not taught about the cost of empire: the resources taken, the blood spilled, the cities built. The complexity of Britain's history had been polished into a tale of empire, royalty, and greatness that was taken as truth. It was a myth so shiny, it blinded.

But during the lockdown of 2020, the myth began to dull. The rise of pandemic-related anti-Asian violence galvanised many young people of East and Southeast Asian heritage to seek solidarity within their communities for the first time, and to push back against the myth of the model minority Asian, the myth of the docile Asian, the myth of belonging through assimilation into whiteness.

Then in May, the Black Lives Matter movement garnered renewed energy when police officers murdered George Floyd in Minnesota. I watched from my bedroom as the public outcry rippled, not just through the US but across the globe. In Europe, countries like France, the Netherlands, and the UK had public reckonings with their colonial pasts. The myth of empire cracked when protestors took to the streets. It cracked when people toppled statues of slave traders. It cracked when street signs that bore the names of slave owners and tobacco lords were renamed to honour Black civil rights activists. In the summer of 2020, it seemed like the myth might truly shatter.

But national myths have deep roots. They are entrenched in our collective consciousness, and they bloom as truism. History seems so distant from where we are now, that the events of the immediate past become narratives. If we are taught about

European colonialism and the Atlantic slave trade in school, it is as stories with beginnings, middles, and endings. The threads that run from there to here, and from then to now, are not made visible; the fruit, the jewels, the people, all that was taken from the continents of Africa, Asia, and America and used as the raw resources from which rose the great cities of Western Europe that we still live in today. The corporate infrastructures of the VOC, the British East India Company, the Royal African Company, and the Virginia Company laid the foundations for modern-day capitalism that still thrives on the exploitation of people and land. I learn about the colonialisation of Indonesia and Malaysia, and the nutmeg and pepper that built European empires, and I condemn the Dutch mercantile class who profited from that system—and then I remember the spices in my own cupboard, the clothes in my wardrobe, the objects that decorate my home, all sourced, created, and bolstered on supply chains of exploitation. I ask how artists like Willem Kalf could paint their still lifes of shiny colonial luxuries—and then I remember that I am using technology that runs on cobalt mined by children in the Congo to write my own stories.

The myths that structure our world seem unshakeable. They are our inheritance, forming how we think, feel, and live today. It seems impossible to dream of alternative ways of being when history seems to have doomed our future.

But at their core, myths are stories, and like all stories, they are flawed. When I was a child, my parents brought me to the Giant's Causeway, the basalt columns which interlock like hex-agonal tiles and jut out from the north coast of Ireland. The myth goes that the giant Fionn mac Cumhaill built the Giant's Causeway as a bridge to cross the sea and reach the Scottish giant Benandonner, who had foolishly challenged Fionn to battle. As I scrambled over the columns as a child, the causeway existed, not just as a natural geological formation but also as the epic arena of ancient warring Celtic giants. I didn't have to try and imagine this mythology; it was, like all national myths are, so lodged in our collective consciousness that it was real even though we knew it was fiction. But the myth of the Giant's Causeway varies depending on whether its teller grew up in a republican or loyalist neighbourhood and therefore knows the causeway to be the myth of Fionn mac Cumhaill or his anglicised name, Finn MacCool. I wonder then, if by having two names, Fionn and Finn are two giants with two stories and two causeways which exist simultaneously. When a myth branches, a single story is free to grow towards various meanings.

In seventeenth-century Holland, oranges and lemons are a luxury, imported from the sunny groves of Italy and Spain. In still lifes, where they are nestled amongst silver and porcelain, they evoke the wealth of their owners. But artists like Kalf do not simply paint the fruit so that it sits, pretty and still, with its skin intact. Instead, lemons and oranges are caught mid-motion. Their peel is half removed, dangling in spirals over blue-and-white bowls and rolling towards tabletop edges as if they are about to plummet out of frame. Their segmented insides lie exposed to the air, respiring while rot burrows into their flesh. Decay is inevitable. Arranged beside clocks and watches, rancid fruit is a reminder that we are all at the mercy of time. To its owner, the orange might be a trinket of newfound wealth from overseas, but Kalf is also offering a warning: nothing lasts forever.

The art historian Stephen Bann offers a distinction between representation and presentation in art.[89] Representation is a depiction of what is already known in the world; it is both familiar and expected, seemingly originating in mundane reality and placed within a frame by the artist. Presentation, on the other hand, makes the canvas the originating place of the subject. When we look at Kalf's still life, we know that citrus, cloth, glass, and porcelain all exist outside the frame, yet those specific objects appear only in the world of the painting. You cannot bite into an orange that looks like Kalf's in the real world. It is too lavish, too shiny, too artful. This is Kalf's own version of the objects of empire. It is within that artful presentation of artifice that myths can be challenged and fractures can appear.

A painted orange can be an allegory for morality. It can be a commodity of brutal empire. It can be a symbol of modern capitalism. It can be a piece of fruit that an artist passes by, picks up, and puts down amongst porcelain bowls and fish heads and ticking timepieces to re-create on canvas. It can also be a figment of an artist's imagination, plucked from thin air to exist only in paint.

It is impossible to know when an object will take on new meaning. It can happen when you least expect it. One morning, in the second lockdown of the pandemic, I ate five oranges, and the fruit changed for me. The past associations I had with the orange emptied out: childhood easy peelers, Christmas, breakfast orange juice, sunshine—all gone. As I ate orange after orange, the fruit gained a new meaning, becoming imbued with uncertainty and contempt and frustration for the myths that haunt our present—the myth that leads to a white man murdering six Asian women.

There are the myths we inherit, and then there are myths we make for ourselves. During lockdown, when I began to lose the things that I had accumulated over my lifetime—a sense of linear time, of the importance of creation, of the future I was moving towards—one narrative fractured. It was like I had been staring at a painting all my life and was only now beginning to notice the details: the decay spreading from the fruit, the droop of the severed flower heads, the buzzing of flies landing on warm meat. What I had thought I knew as familiar was in fact foreign. The gleam of Europe had once blinded me, but now I could step back and see the whole picture. I had taken for granted the land I had rooted myself to—a land where we live amongst the unevenly distributed spoils of empire. But then something startles you out of complacency. Five oranges, sitting in a blue-and-white imitation of porcelain, did that for me.

Dutch Delftware reimagined Chinese porcelain. Dutch still life represented foreign objects as displays of colonial wealth. The meanings of those objects transform depending on who is looking at them, which means that they can change again. On a recent visit to the Los Angeles County Museum of Art, I visited an exhibition on seventeenth-century Dutch collector's cabinets. I wandered through the halls, peeking at porcelain and globes and cabinets of curiosities. On a wall, two paintings had been placed side by side. In a golden frame was a still life, painted by Abraham van Beyeren in 1667. Its subject was a feast of wealth: melons and peaches beside shining goblets and a coral lobster atop silver dishes and pale silks. To the painting's left, a curator had placed another still life. This one was by Sithabile Mlotshwa, an artist born in Zimbabwe in 1975, who now works in the Netherlands. In Mlotshwa's painting, white people dressed as Roman leaders and gods sit and stand atop a mountain of coins. In the centre of the painting and this excess of wealth is van Beyeren's still life. Surrounding the Dutch painting and amidst the money are the forms of Black and Brown people, bent and broken before the spectacle of white wealth. Skulls and crows and death lurk in the gold. The artist has chosen to make visible the suffering that was rendered invisible and silent in van Beyeren's painting. See the cost of this pleasure, the painting says. See the cost of this world founded on the bodies of others. What was once forsaken can be made real again. Myths can still be fractured.

FOUR

· · · · · · · · · · ·

VIENNA

IN THE BEGINNING, THERE IS FRUIT. "SEE, I HAVE GIVEN YOU every plant yielding seed that is upon the face of all the earth, and every tree with seed in its fruit; you shall have them for food," says God on the fifth day of creation. After the fruit comes the garden, "in Eden, in the east," planted for the first man and his wife.[90] Adam and Eve's exile from the Garden of Eden is the first biblical story I can remember learning as a child. In a damp church hall I used maroon and green crayons to colour in apples and snakes. The image was seared into my memory, as was what the drawing represented: that woman's first sin was pursuing knowledge and that man's first sin was being led astray. I pitied Adam and Eve when they were forced from Eden. Their grief at losing paradise, their place of origin, resonated with me even then. How would they orient themselves through a world that was cold and barren and hostile to them? I imagined the pair roaming the earth for the rest of their lives, searching for a home where they could truly belong.

The story of original sin is the story of biting into forbidden fruit and the story of losing your place in the world. As a child, I understood nature to be God's creation, with trees, flowers, and fruit taking on a literal holy significance. I even saw God once. I was staying at my grandparents' farmhouse, near the river Foyle in the northwest of Ireland, and a bright light woke me up. It was too early to be morning, and I stumbled across the floor to pull away the curtain from the window. A crimson blaze bolted through the clouds to illuminate the fields just beyond the house. Nothing was able to escape its glare: every blade of grass shone orange and was made pure. I pressed my palms against the pane of glass, and I looked up at the light that was pouring down from heaven. It was the first time I realised just how small I was, a child in crumpled Hello Kitty pyjamas, and how everything I took for granted—the sun, the sky, the earth, the trees—existed beyond my consciousness. It was a moment of intense humility. I understood that this thing we called nature served a higher purpose. It could even be the manifestation of God on earth.

As I aged, I lost my faith in Christianity. It became impossible to ignore the cruelties and hypocrisies of organised religion, which seemed everywhere. Abortion was a sin and queerness was a sin, and choosing to live with joy seemed to be a sin, too. Morality governed the laws of the north of Ireland, and it was difficult to see where the politician ended and the preacher began. Religion was more about classification and order than the spiritual. God left me, but I never lost my sense that nature was a sublime force beyond my control. The rush of self-abnegation I felt standing in that window was something that I continued to seek: on top of a Scottish Munro, beside a Canadian lake, inside a Malaysian rainforest. To surrender to the sensation, to let it pass through you, to feel connected to something bigger than yourself is a glorious annihilation. It's why I suspect I would have made an excellent pious peasant in the Middle Ages.

Genesis is the story of God creating nature in his image, and throughout Abrahamic religions and cultures, paradise is a garden. Even the word itself derives from the Old Persian *pairi-daêza*, which means "a walled space." Adopted by the Greeks as *parádeisos*, it describes the gardens of the Persian Empire, and Greek translations of the Bible use the word for both the Garden of Eden and heaven.[91] Eden was not only the perfect pleasure garden, but it was also the perfect agricultural farm, and Adam, the first man, was its gentle farmer. After Adam and Eve commit the first sin of eating from the tree of knowledge, "cursed [becomes] the ground." Their punishment is not solely exile but also toil. They will eat, God tells Adam, only "by the sweat of [his] face."[92] After the fall, we lost our right to the free harvest of the garden, forced instead to work the land and to take from it our daily bread.

The garden of Eden—once our home, now lost—has long been held up as a metaphor for redemption. We labour to one day regain access to the garden, to pass through its gates and reach paradise. In medieval times, Eden is thought to be a real garden, one full of flowers and fruit, that lies beyond the edges of half-finished maps. Spices, like pepper and nutmeg, arrive in Europe and are thought to derive from Eden itself. "The Garden of Eden, the terrestrial paradise, was thought to lie at the eastern extreme of Asia," writes the historian Paul Freedman. "The odor of paradise and the image of purity and eternity were not just abstract metaphors but vivid concepts that permeated the geographical lore."[93] The source of spice is paradise, and when the Portuguese, and then the Dutch, arrive to the Indonesian islands, they find a different kind of paradise: one that will make them economically and politically, if not spiritually, rich.

The discovery of foreign plant life—and particularly the discovery that foreign plant life can be exploited to accumulate capital—creates new interest in botanical science in Europe. In the Italian city of Padua, one of the first botanic gardens, the Orto botanico di Padova, is founded in 1545 by the Senate of the Republic of Venice, who are incentivised to invest in botanical research as the spice trade booms in their ports. Medicinal herbs are grown in these physic gardens, as well as imported plants so valuable that thieves risk exile by scaling the walls to swipe them for the black market.[94]

The first botanic gardens are academic sites, constructed to maintain a collection of living plants to be studied. In Padua, the garden is planted as a perfect circle. Four segments each contain the plants of a different, newly discovered continent. This design becomes common in botanic gardens that are built across Europe in the sixteenth and seventeenth centuries. The first English botanic garden is a physic garden founded in Oxford in 1621, and its function is laid out in a 1658 catalogue: "As all creatures were gathered into the Ark, comprehended as an epitome, so you have the plants of this world in microcosm in our garden."[95] As well as serving a medicinal purpose, these early botanic gardens are hubs for the trading of "raw" plants that can be processed into colonial wares, such as spices, tobacco, and rubber.

Orange trees have been cultivated in Italy since the thirteenth century, protected by hefty wooden shelters in the winter months, but in the sixteenth century, the Orto botanico di Padova builds the first identifiable orangery in Europe: a purpose-built structure designed specifically for housing citrus.[96] Botanists can now observe the life cycle of these exotic plants as they would in the tropics, and artichokes, pineapples, and tomatoes soon appear alongside oranges and lemons in Italian gardens.[97]

In 1648 the Eighty Years' War ends and an era of relative peace comes to Western Europe. As trade routes and overseas corporations like the VOC garner unpreceded wealth for European nations, more money, time, and effort are invested into elaborate gardens, and orangeries are erected. The cost of building, upkeep, and heating—as well as the hundreds of plants imported to fill the space—means that only the wealthiest can afford to enjoy orangeries. They are pleasure houses, as well as places of scientific study, and they are flaunted as status symbols for European royalty and nobility. At first they are heated by open fires, but more elaborate steam-powered heating systems are soon engineered. As the only consistently heated room in many palaces, orangeries become the settings for festivities, dinner parties, and concerts in the winter months. Hail, wind, and snow may batter the gardens outside, but inside, the richest sliver of society sweat through their finery in a theatre of the tropics with its artificial humidity, evergreen foliage, and colourful fruit. Paradise is a garden, and it has relocated to Europe.

AT THE EASTERNMOST TIP of the Alps, where the mountain range's rocky basin reaches far and low to meet the Carpathians, and where the river Danube sweeps south with sudden intent, sits the Austrian capital city of Vienna. I arrived in June when the city was hot, humid, and awake after years marked by lockdowns and uncertainty. During the day, residents took their small dogs and dozed in parks, or took the U-Bahn to lay their bodies down by the river that runs into the city from the Austrian hills. When the sun set, people stirred themselves and met on balconies and beside restaurants, smoking and drinking and talking. Being alive felt precarious and precious that summer. When people gathered, there was a giddiness in the air; here, as in the other cities across the continent, was amazement: that we were together, that we were outside, that we were the ones who had made it.

At first with caution and then with caution be damned, people began moving through the world again, leaving and returning and leaving once more. In the shadows of Schönbrunn Palace, tourists crowded by its pale yellow walls to avoid the afternoon sun. Umbrellas acted as parasols, and hats flopped over sweaty foreheads. Water sloshed out of crushed plastic bottles, hit the concrete, and evaporated in seconds. When it was time to move across the palace courtyard, people raked their feet through the gravel, so that clouds of dust greyed their white shoes.

I sat on a wall between two squat concrete pillars as crowds streamed around me. I drank from a can of lukewarm juice and looked down to study the map again. It unfolded on a leaflet about the history of Schönbrunn Palace. Beside a paragraph about the palace's origins as a royal hunting lodge, I traced my finger along the glossy paper until I found what I was looking for: Schönbrunn's orangery, nestled in the northeastern gardens a short walk from the palace. I swung my legs over the wall, crushed the can, and turned to face the sun once more.

In front of Schönbrunn Palace, two rainbow flags began to lift themselves in the breeze before abandoning their effort and collapsing against their masts. As I passed under them, I wondered what the House of Habsburg would think about their summer residence identifying as an LGBTQ+ ally during Pride Month. Moving through historical sites turned tourist hotspots requires some suspension of disbelief. The past is offered up to the present through re-enactments, museum labels, and audio guides. Horse-drawn carriages trotting through the gates of Schönbrunn Palace are supposed to carry you into the past, as you—the tired tourist—see the city from the same motion-sickness-inducing perspective as Empress Maria Theresa. I passed a group of women in corsets and wigs, holding electric fans up to their crimson faces. Do people really want to climb inside history, to live in it, or is this all play? I remembered my own daydreaming about Longyan's tulous and the yearning I had felt to connect with my own family's past. Perhaps a similar pull was what drew tourists here to play dress-up. Or perhaps they had watched too much *Bridgerton* during lockdown.

But I do understand the desire to get closer to history and why we visit places like Schönbrunn Palace to do just that. Physically moving through historical sites lets us embody the past; standing inside them closes the distance of time, and chronology gets a little hazy. As I passed through the gate that read

"Orangery," I began to feel that haziness. The present was slipping away and the past was encroaching.

Before I could reach the long building that housed oranges centuries ago, there was the garden to contend with. On browning grass, scores of bushes, shrubs, and trees were planted in wooden buckets, each coated in the same sage-green paint. They had been arranged in perfect lines, and this neat formation allowed for paths between each row, so that curious visitors could stop to admire the specimens. Each pot came with a white label that named the plant's genus and species in Latin; then its common name and place of origin, first in German and then in English. I stopped to read some. A stocky, tough-leafed shrub was identified as a sweet box from eastern China. A small palm tree was a Spanish dagger from the USA, although its name suggested a longer history of migration, as did that of a spindly Chilean myrtle from Argentina guarding the end of its line. A tall grey mountain apple from Southeast Asia had split into two branches, and then another two and then another two, and the branches had begun to weave with one another. I searched the rows for citrus trees and to my surprise found none.

Thick steel wires ran parallel to the rows, and each plant's thin trunk was tied to them, to keep their spines straight as the leaves grew heavier—and perhaps to deter thieves. There was no obvious logical order to the placement of the plants; it seemed they had been put down wherever there was space in a row. Their genera differed, their names differed, their origins differed. What seemed to unite them was their foreignness. I didn't see a single plant from Europe amongst the rows I traversed.

I left behind the assortment of green leaves and grey bark and came at last to face the orangery. The building was one storey, and longer than it was tall or deep. Brown tiles sloped down to meet walls that were painted the same creamy yellow as the palace. Enormous windows, each nearly the full height of the wall, ran along the length of the building. Several panes made up a single window, and the smallest sheet of glass was pulled open on a hinge to allow fresh air to flow in from the garden. I stepped through a door which, like the windows, was built from glass and green iron. Inside, the orangery was hollow. I stared down more than six hundred feet of empty space. I couldn't imagine the festivities it had held nearly three centuries ago: the dances, the feasts, the parties amongst the citrus trees. Perhaps if it had been filled with greenery, it would have been enchanting, but after the hot sun, the bare stone floor and whitewashed walls left me cold.

As I walked through the building, white walls gave way to a series of vaulted ceilings which caught the sound of my footfall and returned it to me. On the far side of the room, I found some information, printed on placards beside several old black-and-white photographs. Around the year 1754, the Schönbrunn Orangery was built where it still stands today. It is thought to have been designed by the court architect Nikolaus Pacassi, who supervised the rebuilding of the imperial summer residence during Maria Theresa's forty-year reign. When completed, it was almost the largest in Europe, second only to the orangery at Versailles. The Schönbrunn Orangery is warmed by a Roman hypocaust system: beneath my feet were ten chambers heated by fires in the winter, the hot air then pumped through ducts trapped in the bricks which line the orangery. This ancient heating system allows the temperature to remain at a constant fifty degrees Fahrenheit, even in the winter months.

The pots that I had walked amongst in the garden would stay outside until winter arrived, and then they would be carried back inside, safe from the Austrian frost. It is this seasonal relocation which allows the orangery's tropical plants to thrive year-round, in consistent heat that is intermittently sun-made and man-made.

Being so climate dependent means that the plants stand in their own individual pots of soil, so that they can be transported at a moment's notice; they will never be rooted to the land they find themselves in. Instead, their pale tendrils wrap around themselves again and again, until they are tangled beyond separation. There is nowhere for them to go.

I have read about the language of the forest: how in the earth, a rhizosphere microbiome allows trees to communicate with one another.[98] The plants at Schönbrunn's orangery stood in silence. I wondered if they had been brought here from their countries of origin and therefore were conscious of what they were missing, or if they were bred in a European greenhouse, and so, like tigers born into captivity, they lived in quiet ignorance but with an ache within them; an inherited grief for something that had been lost which they did not have the language to articulate, even to themselves.

"CITRUSMANIA" GRIPS EUROPE at the end of the seventeenth century when orangeries peak in popularity. The historians James Wearn and David Mabberley describe this era of oranges: "Citrus-inspired designs became commonplace additions to embroidery, sculptures and paintings, while the plants and fruit featured more and more in poems and song lyrics."[99] In earlier centuries it was the fruit that was imported into northern Europe, but now orange and lemon trees arrive to be contained behind glass in European royalty's orangeries. And no orangery is more grand and no garden more elaborate than the orangery and garden of Versailles during the reign of the French Sun King, Louis XIV. Cultivating a garden takes on symbolic significance in this period, which is marked by warfare as France is expanding its borders and establishing colonies in North America, Africa, and Asia. Across Europe, expensive imported flowers like tulips and carnations become fashionable tokens for the rich, and plants discovered in the New World are carried back to Paris by French explorers. They are assimilated into royal gardens and cultivated by botanists, who are eager to understand exotic plant life and if further riches can be extracted from their seeds, petals, and fruit. These gardens are sites of knowledge and power, paid for by royalty, operated by botanists, and bolstered by Europe's expansion of colonies.

The early modern era is a time of discovery and cataloguing. "The natural history room and the garden, as created in the Classical period, replace the circular procession of the 'show' with the arrangement of things in a 'table,'" writes the philosopher Michel Foucault about the transition from the Renaissance to the Enlightenment's "Classical period." "What came surreptitiously into being between the age of the theatre and that of the catalogue was not the desire for knowledge, but a new way of connecting things both to the eye and to discourse. A new way of making history." This new way of making history, he writes, is organised through "the classification of words, languages, roots, documents, records."[100] Scientists are discovering evolution, which complicates the story of life's origin told in Genesis. A new relationship to God, and to humanity's purpose on earth, is required. Better understanding the natural world—dissecting a plant, studying its flower, stigma, stamen, fruit, and stem, and documenting each part—is one way a man of the Enlightenment can dedicate himself to God's creations.

"The world is a garden, or the nursery of the great God," proposes an anonymous gardening manual published in 1692. "It is there that he opens every day that flowers to be placed on the altars of his glory, and in making the ornaments of Paradise."[101] And so, little Edens spring up all over Europe. Nature is pruned, compelled, and perfected in these paradises which are altars to God's glory. In his treatise on horticulture, the French author Olivier de Serres notes in 1600: "Here are plants and fruits which are very helpful towards embellishing the garden, and which intelligent people will make use of if they wish to make their homes really beautiful and pleasant. Nor will they find it difficult to do so, since oranges, citrons, lemons and such-like valuable fruit-trees flourish in any climate, provided one is ready to incur the necessary expenditure. . . . All these trees are very delicate, being extremely fearful of cold. That is why, to keep them alive, more artifice is required the further one gets away from the regions where time has naturalized them."[102]

Forests are levelled and walls are erected to privatise huge swathes of land for the pleasure of the rich, closing them off from disappearing public commons. Hedges are trimmed into ridiculous cones and flower beds planted in geometrical patterns. But the centre of the garden's power is the orangery, where spring blooms eternal. "No monarch but Louis XIV had the power and resources to produce the physical attributes of the perpetual springtime—to maintain sumptuous gardens like those at the Trianon able to resist the inevitable succession of the seasons and inevitable decay," writes the botanical historian Elizabeth Hyde.[103] Imported flowers are replaced as soon as their petals show signs of rot. Versailles is less a garden, and more an artwork. Flora makes its way inside the palace, too; in 1673, 171 bouquets of "diverse kinds of flowers from China," crafted from a single roll of silk, appear in the royal inventory.[104]

The labour that transforms wild land into gardens goes unseen at Versailles, and at royal residencies throughout Europe. Workers disappear when the gardens are to be enjoyed, as though nature is simply magicked into perfection. Cultivation is supposed to bring men closer to God, but really it brings them closer to *being* God. The shocking poverty of Europe's cities, the distant rumblings of industrialisation, the moral dilemma of relying on colonialism and slavery for resources; all this reality is kept unseen, hidden by the high walls of the garden. Outside, the moral landscape is turbulent and wild, but inside a man can remain in control of his kingdom. Cultivating the natural world is a way to cultivate certainty in faith: faith in self, faith in national agenda, faith in a higher purpose.

In my own tiny Eden during lockdown, I had a taste of this faith. I soon learned that gardening is at the mercy of luck and climate. Seeds did not germinate and fruit did not ripen. Slugs moved silent and slick under the cover of night and left behind carnage: half-munched zucchini flowers, demolished lettuce heads, shredded pea shoots. Too much rain came and then not enough and I hurried outside at dusk with a watering can. But I kept going because I had faith that something would grow from my labour and the earth. It was a different sort of religious reckoning from what I had experienced before; not the sublime thrill of the smallness of the self when faced with mountains and oceans and ancient rainforests but a hope that something— anything; a seed, a fruit, an idea—would take root and ripen, to find its place in the world.

At Schönbrunn, I exited the empty orangery and retraced my steps: past the potted plants, past a stone fountain spluttering brown water, past young trees that lined a broad stone path. Tiny rosy apples poked out from behind their deckle-edged leaves. Their strange design stopped me. A gardener had tied the thin trunks of the saplings to wooden posts, and then bound the even thinner branches to steel wire. Rather than growing upwards, each apple tree had been manipulated to grow horizontally; a gardening technique which creates a flattened tree called an espalier. Rather than offering shade, espalier trees are decorative, growing only a few feet off the ground. The effect should have been pretty, but the trees looked strained, their grey branches twisted at sharp forty-five-degree angles. We force nature to do our bidding all the time—I trick my small houseplants to follow the sun by moving them around my living room—but forcing an apple tree to grow at such an unnatural angle struck me as a strange desire. Who was this manipulation for?

The answer to that question was immediately obvious: it was for me. It was for tourists like myself who visit historical sites to imagine what life was like in the past, as if we would have been allowed to enter the garden paradises of royalty. Apple trees are bent into place, exotic plants are potted, and hedges are trimmed into perfection. Wild variation is cultivated out of nature to serve our whims and pleasures.

I reached my hand out and ran a finger along the pink skin of a ripe apple. On the ground below the trees, fruit had fallen and lay broken. Split open, the apples rotted in the heat, and lines of ants marched over the sweet flesh that had smashed through broken skin. I wondered what would happen to the rest of the ripe apples. Perhaps they would be taken home by the gardeners. Or perhaps the trees would lose their apples, one by one, until their coerced branches were bare and their fruit lay ruined in the shadow of the orangery.

CARL LINNAEUS IS INTENDED for God before botany. Born in Sweden in 1707, Linnaeus is the son of a curate, responsible for the cultivation of souls in a small village clergy. As a boy, Linnaeus is expected to follow his father's path to God, but instead he inherits his father's other passion, for flowers and gardening. In the eighteenth century, Sweden is a colonising nation: the resource-rich, northern parts of the Swedish Empire, now called Lapland, are home to the Sámi peoples. The drive to utilise the Sámi land is spearheaded by Scandinavian governments, naturalists, and priests, who set up learning centres to "Christianise" the indigenous population. As a young botanist, Linnaeus ventures north himself and is impressed by the Nordic landscapes. Later, in 1754, he encourages the Royal Swedish Academy of Sciences to establish plantations on the Lapland mountains.[105]

Linnaeus leaves Sweden as a young man to travel to the Dutch Republic, where flora and fauna are arriving from foreign lands. On his way to Harderwijk, Linnaeus stops first in Hamburg, where he encounters a creature from the Bible: the Beast of Revelation, a famous taxidermised seven-headed hydra kept in the city. The eighteenth century is a time when the borders of myth and science are still hazy, and the hydra had been created from snake and weasel skin to represent the many-headed dragon of the Apocalypse. Linnaeus claims that he was "the first who discovered from the teeth that this monster was not by nature but an artis miraculum" and he exposes the taxidermy as a falsehood.[106] The time of spectacle is coming to an end. Empirical revelation gains dominion over the natural world.

In his book *Systema Naturae*, published in 1735, Linnaeus begins organising the visible world. In it, he proposes three "kingdoms": the animal, the plant, and the mineral; which are then broken down further into phyla, classes, orders, families, genera, and species. A human, for example, falls under Linnaeus's classification as *Animalia* (kingdom), *Chordata* (phylum), *Mammalia* (class), *Primates* (order), *Hominidae* (family), *Homo* (genus), and *Sapiens* (species). It is these two final classifications that give a living thing its scientific name. Linnaeus's system of nomenclature makes him the most famous botanist of the eighteenth century and the "father of modern botany" to future generations—his classification remains the universal naming system used today. At the orangery at Schönbrunn, each potted plant I saw was labelled with Linnaeus's taxonomy of a general genus and a specific species.

Science and faith are inseparable for Linnaeus. During his lifetime he is known for a much-repeated motto: "Deus creavit, Linnaeus disposuit"—"God created, Linnaeus organised." The frontispiece for *Systema Naturae* is a drawing of Linnaeus in the Garden of Eden. The naturalist positions himself as a second Adam, tasked with cataloguing God's creations, including all that are arriving into the European ports from foreign lands. Linnaeus believes that plant species are consistent in their reproduction: the fruit of parent plants bear the next generation, never departing from a predetermined destiny of immaculate reproduction. Later in life, when Linnaeus is confronted with hybrid plants like citrus, he is forced to alter his thesis: he still believes that God has created life, but, he admits, perhaps the constancy of species can be interrupted by nature. Perhaps God's creations can be "mingled," he proposes in his lectures, to make a new life form in a hybrid.[107] Linnaeus's suggestion, which gives nature even slender autonomy, is still enough for him to be accused of atheism.[108]

Naturalists like Linnaeus play a pivotal role in Europe's colonising mission. "In Sweden and Holland especially, the East India Companies acted as patrons of science, encouraging scientists to avail themselves of their ships and urging their personnel to help collect specimens and make observations," notes the Swedish historian Sverker Sörlin. "Science and commerce formed synergetic powers in the process leading towards Western world hegemony."[109] There is also a thread that runs from Linnaeus's hierarchical taxonomy to the science of genetics and the rise of eugenics. In *Systema Naturae*, Linnaeus catalogues humans into four "types": people from Europe, Asia, the Americas, and Africa, who are distinguished by their skin colour and facial features as well as geography. For Linnaeus, behaviour also differentiates these four varieties of humans: Native Americans are "unyielding, cheerful, and free" and Asians are "stern, haughty, greedy," while Europeans are "light, wise, inventor," and Africans are "sly, sluggish, neglectful." While Linnaeus continually changes his preferred ranking of humans, people from Africa—a continent in which Sweden holds colonies that participate in the Atlantic slave trade—always comes in last place.[110]

In the eighteenth century, religion justifies science, which justifies commerce, which justifies colonialism, which justifies violence. It is this cycle of ideology that establishes European dominance in the modern world. Botanic gardens are laboratories for Linnaeus, his naturalist contemporaries, and European governments. They are the heart of a supply chain along which faith, science, business, discovery, and expansion come together, both at home in Europe and overseas in the colonies. Dutch botanic gardens in Java, Ceylon, and Malabar exchange plants with Amsterdam, while the French acclimatise coffee plants in the hothouses of Versailles before sailors take them to plantation colonies in the Caribbean.[111] In the 1780s, the botanist and naturalist Sir Joseph Banks begins to turn Kew Gardens in London into "a great botanical exchange house for the [British] empire"; from the gardens, plants are sent to colonies in India, Africa, and the West Indies.[112] Acclimatising and transplanting plants is how European colonies accumulate wealth, while enslaved people work the stolen land upon which these new crops are grown.

"God gave the World to Men in Common; but since he gave it them for their benefit, and the greatest Conveniences of Life they were capable to draw from it, it cannot be supposed he meant it should always remain common and uncultivated. . . . Subduing or cultivating the Earth, and having Dominion, we see are joyned together," writes John Locke in his *Two Treatises of Government*, a foundational text for European liberalism, in 1689.[113] In the centuries that follow Locke, naturalists, like Linnaeus, take to heart the belief that God has bestowed nature upon men for their use. Every aspect of the natural world could, and should, be utilised, and eighteenth-century Europe gets to work: tilling, sowing, and reaping every inch of God's green earth.

In the seventeenth and eighteenth centuries, the world grows bigger and becomes more known, and people begin to bend nature to their will. To name something becomes a way to gain power over it. Labels, stories, and maps catalogue new species, new lands, and new people. In orangeries and gardens, plants and their fruit reflect how European empires perceive themselves: as ordered, as powerful, as commanding. Nature is both real and metaphor; yes, its fruit contains pulp and juice, but it also holds identity and meaning.

IN THE BEGINNING there is fruit, which means in the beginning there is a sin and a betrayal, a fall and a poisoned chalice. In the beginning it is human nature to want more, to never be satiated with having enough. In the beginning there is fruit, which means, really, we are always going to lose paradise. It is a story told to classrooms of children to teach them about their origins and that to lose paradise is their God-given inheritance.

The temptation of the dangling apple in the Garden of Eden was probably the first metaphor I learned. There is another metaphor bestowed upon Christian children. Place an orange into a child's open hand and tell her that it represents the world. Tie a strip of red ribbon around the fruit's circumference. Red for the blood of Christ, dripping from his broken body on the cross. Four cocktail sticks pierce the peel; stuck into the flesh they represent the four corners of the world. Soft sweets are pushed through the spikes of each stick because each corner of this world has been blessed with God's gracious bounty. Finally, a knife pierces the skin and a candle is pushed inside until it is held steady by the fruit. Lit up, the little flame is Jesus, whose very existence illuminated the world's darkness.

The first Christingle ceremony takes place in Germany in 1747, when each child in a Moravian Church congregation is presented with a candle and ribbon as a metaphor for Jesus's light.[114] The tradition of creating a Christingle with a decorated orange is more modern. In a church at Christmastime, a few objects endowed with a story transform into the physical embodiment of faith. You give a child an orange, you give her the world. You give a child a candle, you give her the genesis for her existence.

Metaphor exists because we need stories to make the terror of being alive tolerable; because sometimes we don't have the heart to stare at it straight on, to pull it from the shadows and expose all its facets to the light.

The morning after a white man murdered six Asian women, I ate five oranges. I saw two stories branch out from that moment:

the story of a fruit and the story of why a white man might want to murder Asian women. I find the latter story unbearable to approach directly. It blinds my senses and my narratorial sensibilities. In the past I have tried to write different variations of that story, and I have failed because this language cannot encompass the shame and the suffering, the sorrow and the rage that come with reckoning with centuries of mythology. This language *created* the myth of race. I think it is too much to expect it to unravel its own work. An alternative form of expression is required. But the two branches—one of fruit and one of terror—that I thought would grow in different directions keep intertwining together.

Five oranges sitting in a fruit bowl became more than fruit to me the morning after an act of violence unravelled the terror that I had been struggling to articulate since I was a child—the terror of exile, of exposure, and of rejection; the terror of being a hybrid creation. I have been following the orange as it makes its way from east to west, as literal fruit and as metaphor. It is a hybrid creation. It is foreign. It is inauthentic. Yet it has managed to carve out its purpose across history. I follow the orange because it offers a model for a hybrid existence and I, too, seek my own meaning in the world. But I also follow the orange because it offers refuge; it can cradle the terror for a little while, until I am ready to reckon with it once more.

I RETURNED TO SCHÖNBRUNN in the winter. This time, I entered through the park. The tourists had deserted the grounds, and instead Vienna's locals were jogging between the hedges, pushing prams by the fountains, hiking up to the Gloriette—an arched colonnade—to gain vantage over the city. The evening's frost was already settling into the tree branches. I huddled into my coat and stomped towards the palace. In the northeast gardens, I found the gate to the orangery already swung open. In the summer, I had bought a ticket to enter the orangery's grounds, but perhaps in the winter it was decided that there was nothing to sell to tourists. A maintenance worker was kneeling by the fountain. Perhaps he had left the gate open behind him, thinking no one would follow.

In the orangery's garden, the potted plants were gone. Only the rows of stony paths that I had walked down in the summer remained. I passed down one and remembered the plants from Asia, Africa, America, and Australia that had brushed their leaves against my bare arms and legs. As the sun set behind the rooftop of the orangery, summer felt impossible.

I had recently read Rebecca Solnit's *Orwell's Roses*, about the English author George Orwell's relationship to his garden. In it, Solnit describes how the dictator Joseph Stalin tried to grow lemons year-round in Russia, Ukraine, and Georgia. "Let them get used to the cold," he reportedly told his gardeners.[115] They never did, and their roots froze and withered in the winter months instead. The self-delusion of forcing citrus to grow where it simply cannot seemed even more stark to me as I stood shivering by the orangery. You cannot force acclimatisation. Even Carl Linnaeus knew this in the eighteenth century, when he tried—and failed—to grow opium, tea, and pineapples en plein air in his native Sweden.[116] He could represent nature through language, he could catalogue it, but he could not command it to do his bidding.

I walked to the orangery itself. In the summer, the building had been emptied out and turned into a function room for concerts and events. But now, in the winter, I saw the orangery's true purpose. Over a hundred plants were enclosed in glass and concrete, their leaves fanned out against the windowpanes. From the outside, I could see no order to their arrangement; the plants disappeared into a jungle of their own making. It could have been anywhere and therefore it was nowhere. It was a green paradise held captive by European imagination. In the bitter chill, a house of glass was the only thing that stood between the plants and expiration. It struck me as a precarious existence for these creatures: to rely on your appeal as foreign, exotic, *different*, to be worthy of care and not neglect. But was that not what I had done, when I turned myself, my heritage, and my identity into neat little packages of writing to be sold?

The sun was setting in earnest now, and it was becoming difficult to see beyond the glass. Against the blotched pink sky, the plants were fading into darkness, and my reflected silhouette and the gates behind me were coming into focus. It was going to be a cold night. I turned back and left the plants in their orangery.

On the way out of Schönbrunn, I passed by the front of the palace, where a Christmas market was being set up. Hollow wooden huts were being hammered into shape, and from white vans came boxes of glass baubles, wooden ornaments, and crocheted mittens to fill each stall. A vat of glühwein was mulling behind a bar, and a fragrance of citrus, cinnamon, and star anise was rising to spike the air. My stomach rumbled as I walked through the skeleton of the market. A woman was piling up pyramids of whole oranges studded with sharp cloves. Above them, slices of dehydrated orange were strung up on a glossy red ribbon with cinnamon sticks and shiny green holly leaves. Citrus and spices have become a common part of European Christmas traditions. The bloodstained history of violence that brought them here has been forgotten and replaced with festive nostalgia.

Globalisation is considered a modern phenomenon, but unjust supply chains that criss-cross the world are centuries old. In 1711, the essayist Joseph Addison writes a column for *The Spectator*, considering "what a barren uncomfortable Spot of Earth falls to [England's] Share" and describing the influx of commerce that is arriving into Britain from other nations. He continues: "We repair our Bodies by the Drugs of America, and repose ourselves under Indian Canopies. My Friend Sir Andrew calls the Vineyards of France our Gardens; the Spice-Islands our Hot-beds; the Persians our Silk-Weavers, and the Chinese our Potters. . . . Nor is it the least Part of this our Happiness, . . . That our Eyes are refreshed with the green Fields of Britain, at the same time that our Palates are feasted with Fruits that rise between the Tropicks."[117]

The brazen entitlement to possession stuns me. Everything is ours and everything is unseen. The atrocities committed by the British Empire are not imported with the drugs, the wine, the spices, the silks, the porcelain that arrive into British ports. Slavery and colonialism are kept offshore from Britain, yet the fruits of that terrible effort arrive in abundance, and they make life good for its rich citizens. "No Fruit grows Originally among us," writes Addison in his column. "[Our] Melons, our Peaches, our Figs, our Apricots, and Cherries, are Strangers among us, imported in different Ages, and naturalized in our English Gardens." The cities of Europe are born from the resources, the bodies, and the lands of other peoples. They are glasshouses decorated with plundered treasures.

There is a common saying about immigrant families: that the first generation survives so the second can be the artists and the storytellers. As I walked through Vienna that winter, that refrain haunted me. What story was there to tell here in Europe? A story of acclimatising to an inhospitable land? Or a story of foreignness, of remaining on the outside, of always looking through the window into paradise? Neither appeals to me and neither is correct, yet they have become the expected narratives for immigrants and for people of colour in Europe: You can be a good immigrant or a bad immigrant. You can become one of us or you can remain foreign. But the truth is somewhere in the middle of that binary: you can never truly assimilate, yet you can never fully remain a stranger.

I was tired of trying to hold two ideas stable simultaneously. I was tired of the two identities and the two narratives that bisected me yet never fully expressed my experience of being a person in the world. I was tired of being both native and foreign.

I was tired of being both impressed and disgusted by palaces and botanic gardens and orangeries built with the profits of empire. I was tired. I stopped walking. It was dark now and I found a bench to sit on along the river Wien. Perhaps the first generation survives so the second can choose: choose to remain or choose to leave. The worst of the pandemic was over, and the world was opening up again. Perhaps it was time to step across the borders of the garden to see what life was like beyond the fantasy of Eden and beyond the common narratives that I kept coming up against.

During the eighteenth century, the citrus that arrives in Europe finds itself retracing its journey, back along the old networks of the Silk Roads. European colonists take oranges and lemons back east, as their ships of settlers, workers, and prisoners rely on the fruits' vitamins to combat scurvy. The East India Companies leave a wake of orange and lemon trees behind them—along the coasts of Madeira, South Africa, Saint Helena, South Africa—so that sailors with bloody gums can pick the fruit on their voyages to India, Malaya, Indonesia.[118] The routes of empires are lined with citrus groves, and the story of the orange is turning back on itself. It is time to leave the theatre of paradise behind in Europe and instead follow the orange back east, back to lands where citrus trees can grow wild and free beyond the confines of glass.

FIVE

IPOH

THE WET TARMAC AND PETROL FUMES, THE CHUGGING
air-conditioning units and the rumble of a distant tropical storm
that would arrive soon to wash away what remained of the day;
I smelled, I heard, I tasted the humidity before I felt the heat.
The doors of the Kuala Lumpur International Airport slid open,
and I was back in the climate I was never quite prepared for. It
rushed forward to meet my body, and I had no choice but to
surrender to it.

The Malaysian border had closed to foreigners in March 2020.
Two years later it reopened. My family had made it through the
pandemic physically unscathed. After global lockdowns and
grounded flights and death tolls, it felt like a miracle to be back
in Malaysia and to reach my arms out to hug my grandmother.
Ah Ma had finished her chemotherapy, and her hair had grown
back as a soft white comb-over. I beamed at her and Ah Kong
and my Auntie Sian through my face mask.

After a week of acclimatising in Kuala Lumpur, we travelled
to my grandparents' house and my father's hometown. The city
of Ipoh sits in the state of Perak region, a two-hour journey

moving northwest away from KL. As a child, I sat in the back seat of my grandparents' car as Ah Kong raced along the highway between the two cities. However, the last time my grandfather had been behind the wheel of his car, it had ended up in a ditch, so now we were taking the train to Ipoh.

I boarded the train with Auntie Sian. My grandparents had gone ahead a few days before us, wanting to settle back into their home after several weeks in KL. I sat by the window and watched as we pulled out of the station and left behind skyscraping condominiums for Selangor's fields and groves. The sky cleared as we travelled farther away from KL's city haze. Between stops, we passed by Malaysia's kampongs, small traditional villages that are being swallowed up by land acquisition and housing developments. The train leaned so close to some houses that I could look panting dogs in the eye. Then, they disappeared and the morning sun shone down on the palm oil plantations we snaked past. New saplings had been planted, each lined up in regimented formation for future farming. The train's rhythm put me into a doze, and next thing I knew, my aunt was tapping my shoulder to wake me up. We were arriving into Ipoh.

I hadn't seen Ipoh's railway station in years. Tourist guidebooks feature the building as the pinnacle of the city's colonial architecture. Opened in 1917, the station, with its white walls, high ceilings, and columns, is a hybrid of English Edwardian design and the nineteenth-century Indo-Saracenic architecture that the British built in India. Its architect, Arthur Benison Hubback, employed the same style in his other famous designs built during the colonial period, like Kuala Lumpur's railway station and Kuala Kangsar's Ubudiah Mosque.

Ipoh's railway station is impressive from the outside. But although its exterior has been maintained as a site of heritage, its insides haven't been updated in years. It is crowded, with too few barriers and seats for the number of passengers who arrive on electric trains. We joined the long queue to enter the station from the platform. I saw my Auntie Suan waiting beyond the barrier. When she spotted us, she waved and held her phone up to take photos that would inevitably be circulated in multiple family group chats. When our tickets were scanned and we finally passed the barriers, I hugged my aunt. She herded us through the station and into the car park. The heat was formidable after the train's air-conditioning.

"Aiyo!" she exclaimed as we walked through the midday sun to find her car, which was baking in the heat. "I couldn't find any shade to park in lah."

We settled into her car, its leather seat covers burning into the backs of our thighs. I made sure not to touch any metal while Auntie Sian fiddled with the dials of the AC. Soon, cold stale air was blasting, and we were on the way to lunch.

After KL, Ipoh seemed rural. Surrounding the city are tree-topped limestone mountains and caverns. Ipoh's food is famous for its freshness because of the limestone-filtered water which feeds the region's crops. Most famous are Ipoh's bean sprouts, which people come from far away to buy. Auntie Suan had already gone to buy bags of the vegetable for Ah Ma before the market sold out by midday.

After a lunch of Ipoh's specialties—plates of salty bean sprouts, bowls of slippery hor fun, spoonfuls of wobbly caramel custard—the three of us drove on to my grandparents' house. We slipped out of our sandals and let our feet cool on the grey marbled tiles of the porch as we waited for Ah Ma to unlock the front door. She turned the key in the ornamental metal grate that had been secured to the doorway for as long as I could remember; my grandparents prefer the grate's open airflow to the heavy wooden doors, which are kept open all day. I followed my aunts into the house, which had remained the same since my childhood.

My grandparents moved to Ipoh when their children were young, and into an open-plan mid-century designed house. In the middle of the main room an archway slopes down to separate the living spaces, while the floor sinks down near the front door to create a reading nook. As children, my brothers and I would leap down there, landing on the soft, secluded sofa, before charging back up the tiled steps to make the jump again, while our mother shouted at us that we were going to break our necks.

My favourite room in the house has always been Ah Kong's study. After saying hello to my grandparents, I went to find it, tucked away, far enough from the living room to give my grandfather peace. I dropped the two steps into the room. Marcel Proust had his madeleines; I have this room and its fusty smell of old paper, dust, and lacquered furniture which launches a childhood's worth of memories. It's where I escaped from loud aunties and uncles to take refuge under the desk with my Famous Five paperbacks and where I crowded on the sofa with my brothers and cousins, sticky thigh glued to sticky thigh, to watch pirated episodes of *House*. When I promised I would be careful, Ah Kong would let me use his electric typewriter, and I spent afternoons hammering out long letters to friends that I never sent.

Ah Kong's study was my first cabinet of curiosities. A lifetime of travel is laid out in display cases and on wooden shelves. Ever the geographer, my grandfather arranges his artefacts by location, marking each shelf with a printed label that states its contents' place of origin. On the "ASIA (CHINA, KOREA, ETC.)" shelf, tiny porcelain cups sit beside a Hello Kitty key chain and a hair clip shaped like a bird of paradise. In faded photographs, a much younger Ah Kong and Ah Ma pose with their friends in cities across East Asia. As a child, I travelled the world by roaming the shelves. Vietnam, Tasmania, America, Spain. A few years ago, I visited the Pitt Rivers Museum in Oxford for the first time. Its mezzanines of overflowing paraphernalia and handwritten labels brought me straight back here, to Ah Kong's study.

The room's walls are just as cluttered as the shelves. The covers of Ah Kong's textbooks have been carefully pinned to the wallpaper alongside family photographs, travel posters, and Chinese prints. Above the desk is a map of the world, curling at the edges with age. I sat in my grandfather's chair and looked up at it. At some point in the past, he had pushed pins into the countries where his three children live: Malaysia, Singapore, Ireland.

I left the study and crossed the living room, the soles of my feet slapping the tiles, to join Ah Kong, who was sitting on a collapsible chair on the porch. Through his thick glasses, he was watching the commotion on the other side of his garden wall, where a team of construction workers was laying the foundations for a new build. When he noticed my presence, he began complaining that the house would eventually block the view of the limestone hills in the distance.

"Go see the view while you can," he said, waving me into the garden.

With reluctance, I left the house's shade and wandered into the afternoon blaze. Yellow grass and fallen leaves from the rambutan tree tickled my ankles. Standing in the middle of the grass, I could see, through the scaffolding, the cragged hills that outlined Ipoh. On the drive through town, I had noticed that amongst the deep wild green, bald patches had appeared on the sides of the mountains. Some hills had turned a dusty brown as developers cut into the slopes to quarry for concrete. The range close to my grandparents' house remained green for now. Something in the air had shifted since the morning. There was a fullness that felt as if it would overflow soon, which, coupled with a dull pain behind my eyes, usually meant a storm was on its way. An hour later, when the rain began to fall, I looked out the kitchen window to see that the limestone hills had disappeared behind a veil of grey.

IPOH SITS INSIDE the Kinta Valley, the largest tin field in Malaysia. Mining the land for small quantities of tin has been common practice for centuries. Malay workers used a panning method called lampan to pull down earth in tin-rich valleys and then wash away the loose soil to reach tin ore. Chinese immigrants brought open-cast mining methods and they soon became the major workforce operating Malaya's mines.[119] This changed when English traders realised the depth and richness of Perak's tin fields.

In 1786, England leases the island of Penang as a base for trade with China. Silks, tea, and porcelain are coveted by the English, but China has no interest in British-made produce. Instead, the East India Company becomes the middleman of trade in Southeast Asia.[120] In Penang, pepper, nutmeg, and clove plantations are established, but cultivating these foreign plants is time and labour intensive. The British instead decide to import rubber plants from Brazil, which thrive in the hot, humid climate. Chinese workers who once relied on crops they knew from their homeland—oranges, pineapples, coconuts—soon neglect growing fruit for working the expanding rubber plantations.

As Britain's control expands on the mainland, rubber and tin become Malaya's greatest exports. Chinese immigrants' grip on tin mining is loosened by European technology during the Industrial Revolution at the end of the nineteenth century. Although Chinese miners have superior skills, Britain has the capital required to generate a boom in the tin industry, so that British Malaya produces half the world's tin by 1904.[121] The Malay Archipelago becomes the British Empire's resource reserve. Its tin builds cities, ships, and railroads. Its rubber steers automobiles. Its rainforests supply timber. In 1952, a British lord describes Malaya as "the greatest material prize in South-East Asia."[122]

Colonial control over Malaya's natural resources devastates the landscape. Mass deforestation razes entire ecosystems. The indigenous population, the Orang Asli, are forced from their homes to lowlands, and hundreds of people die.[123] Chinese and Tamil immigrants toil in the rubber, timber, and tin industries for little pay. British Malaya, the colonial project, described by one historian as "the creature of Chinese labor together with European capital and supervision,"[124] is an extraordinary achievement: a foreign land is mined, harvested, and felled so that Britain, half a world away, can become a global superpower.

Malaysia gained its independence in 1957, three years before my father was born. Over sixty years later, I walked through modern Ipoh. On every block, I was reminded of the city's colonial history. It was not only Arthur Benison Hubback's railway station that was built before the empire retreated but also Ipoh's high court, its city hall, and old town buildings. British Malaya's colonial administrators made Ipoh in the image of their old country. Other cities in Malaysia were treated to a similar fate, like George Town in Penang, which was transformed into a fantastical reimagining of Edwardian Britain, complete with quaint tearooms, hat shops, and publishing houses. Now these colonial-era buildings are occupied by modern banks and businesses, hawker stalls and bakeries.

The legacy of empire is seared into nations. In Britain, tin and rubber, extracted from faraway lands, built the country's infrastructure, its rail tracks and banks, its universities and museums. In Malaysia and other previously colonised countries, European empires left behind depleted natural resources and beautiful empty buildings. In the 1930s, Ipoh's tin industry went bust because the economic recession in the western world placed tin restrictions on Malaya. Chinese immigrants who had come to Perak to work the tin mines were repatriated back to China by the colonial British government. Others were left behind in poverty.

Now, rather than tin, tourism is major business in Ipoh. The city's past has been reconstructed for curious westerners. In an Old Town restaurant, I bought a bowl of hor fun and slurped the white noodles under an arched veranda held up by white columns. I walked down Concubine Lane, which dresses up its derelict colonial buildings to transport tourists back to British

Malaya with old-fashioned painted signs, red paper lanterns, and wooden shutters.

One day, my Auntie Suan suggested we eat at Ipoh's oldest bar and restaurant, opened in the early twentieth century by Hainanese immigrants from China. Inside, we were greeted by an enormous portrait of a young Queen Elizabeth II hanging on the wall. In it, she was maybe in her late twenties, when Malaysia was still under British colonial rule. I laughed in astonishment at finding the portrait hanging, not in an English country club or village pub but here, in a Muslim country, in a multicultural country, in a country that had fought for independence from this very woman's crown.

While my aunt spoke to a well-dressed waiter, I studied the portrait. There was something nostalgic about the painting and the restaurant, which had been decorated to resemble colonial-era British Malaya. The scholar Sharmani Patricia Gabriel describes this performance of the past as "not history but rather the selective appropriation of history. . . . Like tradition, heritage is an invention—but it also invents its own past."[125]

Heritage also sells its own past. The restaurant wore Malaysia's history like a costume that was decorative and apolitical; a painting on a wall rather than colonial governance. In the restaurant, colonial Britain—and its young queen—could not impose on present-day Ipoh. For my aunt, the restaurant's decor made it a fun, quirky place to grab lunch, the same way that for her the British royal family—which she followed fastidiously through issues of Hello! magazine—was an entertainment.

I could not so easily enjoy Ipoh's funhouse mirror of empire or separate it from the Britain I had left behind a few weeks earlier, a nation that also lives in its own fantasy—one that refuses to acknowledge how its ugly history still causes harm today. The painted queen gazed towards the front door. I wanted to follow her line of sight, turn, and bolt from this claustrophobic playhouse of history.

HALF A WORLD AWAY from the Malay Archipelago, the sun rises over an island. Pink and orange light spills, first upon the waves, water turning to glass, then upon the beaches, each grain of sand a glistening ember, then upon the brown earth, the long grass, the treetops, and the creatures who awake to a new day. Soon, the light sharpens into a blue horizon. Life on the island is noisy. The sea throws itself against rocks, leaves ripple in the breeze, insects shrill in the grass.

For ages, nature's cacophony is the island's only sound, until sail masts flying strange colours break the horizon. Men descend from boats to map the island. Over the years, its land is reshaped, broken, segmented into plantations to grow a foreign crop. People are abducted from their homelands, taken to the island, and forced to work the land, so that the foreign men can steal more people and take more land and build more cities on the other side of the ocean. Britain has found its paradise and decided to wreak hell upon it.

During the age of sail—the age of conquest, of terror, of warfare over water—ships become vessels for seed dissemination. Sailors who discover new plants take specimens home or bring them to their next port of call. Carried along the maritime trade routes of empire, a plant leaves one land, native, and arrives in another land, foreign. In the trading ports of Malacca and Java, British and Dutch sailors eat pink-and-gold-fleshed pomelos, the largest of the citrus fruits and indigenous to the Malay Archipelago. The fruit will not survive the sea journey, but the dried seeds might, so the sailors fill their sacks. By this time, European trading companies have bisected the world into the East Indies and the West Indies.

In 1627, the English settle on the island of Barbados in the Caribbean. Over sixty years later, a first generation of pomelo trees have grown from seeds brought here from the Malay Archipelago. Hans Sloane, a physician and naturalist who will use his wife's wealth—money that comes from sugar plantations in Jamaica—to gather the founding collection of the British Museum, visits Barbados and notes the pomelos, which he calls shaddocks, and sweet "China oranges" growing on the island.[126] Years later, Sloane pens their origin tale: "The seed of [pomelo] was first brought to Barbados by one Captain Shaddock, Commander of an East India ship, who touched at that island in his passage to England and left its seed there."[127] This legendary Captain Shaddock eludes future historians for decades, until they discover a Captain Philip Chaddock who seems a likely match for the Barbados folktale.[128] But myth takes on a life of its own, and the pomelo has a new name in a new land.

Unlike the Spanish and the Italians with their groves of oranges and lemons, English colonisers are inexperienced with citrus cultivation. They have grown pomelo trees from seeds rather than by grafting, and scattered them across the island with reckless abandon. In 1814, the planter John Lunan remarks on the unruliness of Barbados's pomelos when grown from seed: "About the shaddock, they say if you plant the seed, there is but one in a whole fruit that will bring forth good and pleasant fruit," he writes. "I have seen many of them planted and come to bear but never saw a good one produced from the seed. The best way is to take a stem or a twig, and ingraft or inoculate it on a good China Orange stock."[129]

But before the English colonialists discover grafting, citrus's inherent nature—its promiscuity, its spontaneity, its instability—takes root. On the island, hybrid fruit is born from the pomelo and sweet orange.

It is Lunan who makes the first recorded use of the word "grapefruit," in that same piece of writing dated to 1814. The grapefruit is the most famous of the Barbados-born hybrids. It is also known as the "forbidden fruit" in the eighteenth and nineteenth centuries, as well as, confusingly, the shaddock and the golden orange. Later, it is categorised by the botanical name *Citrus paradisi*.

The history of the grapefruit, and the other hybrids of the pomelo and sweet orange in Jamaica, is, like so many histories of citrus, guesswork. Some modern pomologists propose that the forbidden fruit was not a grapefruit but instead its own hybrid variety of citrus, a delicious popular fruit that went extinct before the nineteenth century.[130] In 1990, two scientists come across a citrus known locally as "forbidden fruit" growing and widely eaten on Saint Lucia. Three trees of forbidden fruit are aged between seventy and one hundred years old by the scientists, and local Saint Lucians tell them that the trees have never successfully propagated by either seed or grafting. When the scientists ask the origin of the forbidden fruit's name, the only explanation offered is the story of Genesis. "Despite this, they exhibited no hesitation in eating [the fruit]," note the scientists.[131] The fruit of Eden is found, lost, and found again.

ANOTHER TALE OF KNOWLEDGE LOST, then found, changes the course of history forever. In the fifteenth and sixteenth centuries, the world becomes boundless. Setting sail from the corner edge of their continent, Europeans seeking new trade land on far-flung shores. South Africa in 1488. America and India in 1492. Malaysia in 1511. Australia in 1606. There is a new world to discover, then encounter, and then conquer.

In the age of sail, knowledge of trade routes is worth more than silver, and warring European kingdoms seek to hold the monopoly on access to spice, silk, and sugar. Kings and peasants share visions of fortunes across the water. Men and boys from all walks of life venture from their plague-ridden hamlets and cities to discover their destiny in foreign lands. If they can just survive the months on the open seas—the hard toil, the murderous storms, the maddening infinite horizon—if they can just survive long enough to get to the land on the other side of the blue expanse, they will be rewarded with paradise. And so they board ships stocked with beer, biscuits, weapons, and fantasies of future fortunes.

Half of these men will perish on the open sea.[132] This is not unexpected to the men on board; a voyage of discovery is an adventure full of risks. But these sailors will not die in the blaze of battle, fighting natives or foreign adversaries, nor will their deaths be delivered by drowning or dashing against rock—these are endings fit for an odyssey. Instead, half the men setting sail will succumb to an invisible enemy.

After a few months at sea, the symptoms appear on the body. Gums blacken, bones collapse, scars ooze, and teeth fall from skulls. The body will forget linear chronology as once-healed wounds weep and the stench of decay emanates from still-living souls. Some of the afflicted will fight the inevitable, turning their knives on themselves to release foul pus and blood from sores. But soon the body is too weak to try and save itself and hundreds of men will wait to die, swinging on hammocks in the belly of a ship which now resembles a morgue.

The sixteenth-century Portuguese poet Luís Vaz de Camões, who journeyed to and lived in Asia, included a description of what had become known as the plague of the sea in his epic poem The Lusiads:

> A dread disease its rankling horrors shed,
> And death's dire ravage through mine army spread.
> Never mine eyes such dreary sight beheld,
> Ghastly the mouth and gums enormous swell'd;
> And instant, putrid like a dead man's wound,
> Poisoned with foetid steams the air around.
> No sage physician's ever-watchful zeal,
> No skilful surgeon's gentle hand to heal,
> Were found: each dreary mournful hour we gave
> Some brave companion to a foreign grave.[133]

The "dread disease" that ravaged European voyages was named scurvy in the 1560s. It is estimated that over two million sailors died from scurvy between Columbus's first voyage to the American continent in 1492 and the invention of steam-powered ships in the nineteenth century.[134] In his 1757 *Treatise of the Scurvy*, the physician James Lind notes that "armies have been supposed to lose more of their men by sickness, than by the sword. . . . Scurvy alone, during the last war, proved a more destructive enemy, and cut off more valuable lives, than the united efforts of the French and Spanish arms."[135] Lind will be remembered for discovering the cure for scurvy; his *Treatise* concludes that oranges and lemons relieved his patients. At the University of Edinburgh, where I studied and where Lind earned his medical degree, a plaque commissioned in 1953 by the California citrus cooperative Sunkist memorialises Lind's work. To be read by students and staff walking by the medical building, the plaque declares that Lind's *Treatise* "led to the conquest of scurvy, the development of modern naval hygiene and the growth of tropical medicine." Although hindsight will prove the veracity of Lind's findings, in the eighteenth century, his work goes mostly ignored by the British navy.

In the age of sail, scurvy is the single greatest hindrance to a nation achieving domination over foreign waters. Between the fifteenth and nineteenth centuries, it kills more than two million sailors, making it deadlier than storms, battles, and all other disease combined.[136] Vitamins are a modern revelation; vitamin C will not be discovered until 1912, and it will not be recognised as the cure for scurvy until 1932. In the sixteenth and seventeenth centuries, sailors levy a range of accusations as to what brings on scurvy: rats, damp ships, putrid air, laziness, salty food, the sensibilities of northern people, and God's wrath are all proposed as potential causes of the affliction.[137]

Now we know that it is a lack of ascorbic acid, found in fresh fruit and vegetables, that causes the body's metabolism to fail.

Without ascorbic acid—or vitamin C—we cannot produce collagen, the glue which holds our bones, teeth, muscles, and skin together. Scurvy is an agonising disease, and it is also a very human disease. Nearly every animal species has the enzyme gulonolactone oxidase, which can convert glucose to ascorbic acid when it is deficient in the diet. Only some primates, guinea pigs, and Indian fruit bats lack this enzyme.[138]

Although ascorbic acid will remain a mystery for centuries, sailors discover that when they eat fresh fruit, it relieves them of the symptoms of scurvy. Long before British, Portuguese, and Dutch fleets set sail, Norse, Arab, and Chinese sailors knew that fresh fruit abated scurvy, and they carried cranberries and ginger on their voyages.[139] Arriving in new lands after long stretches at sea, European sailors gorge themselves on fruit. On a voyage to Asia in the 1500s, a Portuguese sailor notes that fresh oranges bought en route in Kenya—"the best in the world"—cured his fellow sailors of "amalati de la boccha," or "the curse of the mouth."[140]

Access to fresh produce at colonial ports of call becomes essential for successful maritime missions. To solve the issue of food spoilage, sailors carry citrus seeds and saplings with them on their voyages. By the sixteenth century, Spanish vessels are required to carry one hundred citrus seeds for planting whenever they arrive on a new island.[141] For the British and the Dutch, who do not have access to ripe citrus, unlike their Mediterranean competitors, groves along their East India Companies' trade routes become vital. A Dutch citrus plantation is established in South Africa, and soon the west coast of the African continent is besieged by lemon and orange groves.[142]

A ring of citrus soon circumnavigates the world. The historian S. R. Dickman proposes that "one might say the British Empire blossomed from the seeds of citrus fruits," so crucial a role do the fruits' antiscorbutic qualities play in colonial expansion.[143]

In the seventeenth century, Dutch and British fleets make regular stops at the island of Saint Helena in the South Atlantic.

Early Portuguese seafarers planted citrus saplings on the island to form "citrus clinics," so future vessels can stock up on fresh fruit before heading east. A Dutch sailor who visits Saint Helena in 1608 notes the island's "valley of Oranges," where "one finds . . . good oranges, pomegranates, and lemons, enough to serve for the refreshment of the crew of five to six vessels."[144]

The British East India Company takes possession of Saint Helena in 1659. Settlers from the empire's metropole arrive on the island to cultivate the land, although immigrating to a remote island is a hard sell for the British people. Instead, enslaved people from East Africa and Madagascar are brought to work on Saint Helena, so that two years after the arrival of the first colonists, its inhabitants number fifty-three white Britons and twenty-one enslaved Black people.[145]

As the British East India Company expands its colonial outposts in South and Southeast Asia, its vessels increasingly traffic enslaved African and Asian people. By the late seventeenth century, it is made a requirement for all ships trading with Madagascar to deliver a slave to Saint Helena.[146] In 1792, when the enslaved population threatens to outnumber the white British, Saint Helena ceases to import enslaved people for fear of uprisings. Instead, hundreds of indentured labourers are imported from China.[147]

As a stop between the African and American continents, the island comes to play a crucial role when the slave trade is finally abolished in the nineteenth century. British navy vessels patrol West Africa's coastline to intercept illegal Portuguese slave ships and deliver an estimated twenty-seven thousand "liberated Africans" to Saint Helena.[148] On the island, however, these people are not free. Over ten thousand of the rescued will die and be buried in unmarked burial grounds, in sites which have been described as "the most significant physical trace of the transatlantic slave trade."[149] The majority of those who survive are claimed as indentured labourers by the British Crown and are shipped onwards to its colonies in South America and the Caribbean.[150] A minority are allowed to remain on Saint Helena, but first they are quarantined at the Liberated African depot in what was once known by passing seafarers as the valley of oranges.

On a Saint Helena tourism website, the island's contemporary population of 4,550 is described as "mainly descended from people from Europe (mostly planters, government employees and ex-soldiers serving in the local St. Helena Regiment), Chinese (itinerant workers from about 1810) and slaves (mostly from Madagascar and Asia, only a few coming from Africa from 1840 onward)."[151] Saint Helena's society could be called multicultural, or diverse, or a melting pot, or any of the words we use to describe the legacy of British colonies and stations of empire, as well as modern Britain itself. There is a long unspoken history that comes before a society can describe itself as multicultural or diverse or a melting pot. For Britain, this is a history of violence; of people abducted, displaced, and dispersed. Many centuries ago, on new islands and in foreign ports, it grew from a few citrus saplings and the desire to make empire.

THE LOCATION OF the pomelo farm was a secret. At 9:00 a.m. on the dot, Auntie Suan arrived at my grandparents' house to drive me to the fruit trees. When Auntie Anna and Auntie Chui Lee berated her from the kitchen for not sharing where cheap pomelos could be bought, Auntie Suan replied with a long "Aiyo!" and told them that the point of a secret pomelo source was that it was a secret. "I know this guy," she added. "That's why it's so cheap lah. Tell one of you and you all will swarm him!"

Auntie Suan was taking me because she knew I loved the taste of the bright green fruit that ripens to be as big as a human head. But more crucially, I was a visitor and therefore not a threat to her pomelo source. I promised Auntie Anna and Auntie Chui Lee that I would bring them back some fruit.

Close to my grandparents' house in eastern Ipoh is the small town of Tambun, which is pressed between the city to its west and the limestone mountains to its east. Tambun is famous for its pomelo trees, which were planted by Chinese immigrants and are now tended to by second-generation Chinese Malaysians. The Perak earth contains the perfect chemistry for fruit cultivation—mostly pomelo, but also guava and rambutan—and farmers pride themselves on the freshness of their produce. There are two common varieties of Tambun pomelos: one is called sweet-sour and the other only sweet. Auntie Suan's farmer grew the sweet-sour type.

We drove away from Ipoh and turned onto a highway, then onto a road, and then onto a long dusty lane. The car bumped up and down potholes as tangled vegetation grew dense. We passed through a narrow tunnel underneath the highway, and then, finally, we arrived in a clearing in front of a small house. I clambered out of Auntie Suan's car and into the morning humidity. The smell of insecticide and baked earth filled my nose. Almost immediately, my T-shirt clung to the small of my back. I squinted in the sunlight. In front of the single-storey house, three chimneys which looked like giant incense sticks were belching smoke. Red lanterns with yellow Chinese characters hung from the porch rafters. On the wall, a mural depicted eight lines emanating from a golden sauvastika like rays from the sun's core.

My aunt, a devout Christian, waved her hand towards the smoking incense. "I don't like all that stuff." The farmer, a Chinese immigrant, had held on to his family's religion, unlike my second-generation relatives, who had converted to born-again Christianity. I have a fading memory of visiting a temple with Ah Ma when I was a child: a pile of sandals, incense tickling my nose, an offering of food left by the altar. Her family observed some Chinese folk traditions when she was a child in Longyan, but she hasn't returned to a temple for years.

"Let's go find the farmer," my aunt said. We left the house and walked towards the farm buildings. As well as fruit, the farmer also bred fish. In the shade of a roof made from metal sheets, hundreds of tiny goldfish swam in long troughs under black netting. The fighting fish—beautiful with black-scaled bodies and vibrant blue fins—were kept separate to prevent loss of stock. On shelves, each fish was held in a plastic pint-sized cup of algae-tinged water.

My aunt nudged me. "Hey, don't tell your ah kong, but this is where I came to replace his fish," she said. A few months ago, a mystery had lit up various family WhatsApp chats. Auntie Suan, who had been tasked with sprinkling food in my grandparents' small tank, had arrived at the house to find fish littered across the hard tiled floor. The scene of the crime suggested a mass suicide pact, but the motive of the dead fish had yet to be uncovered. My aunt chose to keep quiet and replace them before my grandparents returned. Ah Kong still had no idea that the fish he fed each morning were changelings.

We spotted the farmer near one of the troughs. He was squatting in yellow rubber boots and sorting through a tangle of netting, while his dogs dozed in the shade. My aunt shouted hello, and the farmer and his dogs stood to greet us. While he and my aunt conversed in Cantonese, my gaze wandered away towards the green mountain beyond the farm. Only a few patches of pale limestone were exposed amongst the treetops.

"Come on, Kate." My aunt was calling for me to follow the farmer, who had set off in front of us with his dogs.

"So, this is the farmer's brother," she explained in hushed English as we snaked between the troughs and followed the man back towards the driveway. "The farmer I knew died during Covid, so his brother has inherited the farm. But he says he has pomelos!"

By the driveway was a grove of fruit trees. From the ground, I could see no logic to their arrangement; this was no commercial plantation. Instead, the trees were planted close to the house for easy picking. The farmer had picked up a long metal rod on our way to the trees. He stopped at one and asked my aunt a question in Cantonese. She nodded and replied with enthusiasm. She pointed upwards. "See up there? Rambutans." In the canopy of leaves, the round crimson fruit with its green urchin spikes dangled in bunches. The farmer extended one side of the rod until the arm could reach where human arms could never. At the end were shears for cutting stems, which could be controlled by the rod's handle. The farmer began to cut at the tree, and fruit tumbled down with broken branches to the earth.

The farmer motioned towards my aunt. She laughed. "Aiyo, he wants us to have a go!"

She went first. Gripping the rod like a weapon, she aimed it towards the tree and began to slash at the branches. When it was my turn, my aim was even clumsier. Rather than snipping neatly as the farmer had done, I crashed the rod into the leaves and tried to tear rambutans from the branches with sheer force. The farmer, who had been watching us with an amused expression, suddenly looked concerned and stepped in before I could do any real damage to his tree. He shook a plastic bag from his pocket and handed it to me so my aunt and I could gather the prickly fruit as he finished plucking the tree.

We left the heavy bag by my aunt's car and headed for the pomelo trees. The farmer led us through a thicket of hanging branches. Dead brown leaves and yellow long grass crunched under our sandals. Afraid of lurking snakes, I scanned each patch of earth before committing to a step. I was so focused I didn't realise we had reached the pomelo trees until my aunt and the farmer stopped.

I looked up and my heart recoiled. What looked like ten or twelve white ghosts floated amongst the dense branches of a tree. I blinked and my brain caught up. Newspaper. It was newspaper wrapped around fruit. Still, it was an eerie sight to behold. Each pomelo had the circumference of a classroom globe and was wrapped in a sheet of Chinese newspaper. The trailing white paper gave an illusion of little Halloween spectres.

The farmer walked over to the lower branches and lifted a sheet of paper to inspect what it hid. He was dwarfed by the pomelo tree, which was as wide as it was tall. The morning light pooled on glossy green leaves. My aunt and I watched the farmer as he took a pair of secateurs from his trouser pocket and cut a branch with three pomelos from the tree. He carried it over to a rusted wheelbarrow and untied the sheets from the fruit.

I asked my aunt why the fruit on the tree was covered in newspaper.

"It protects them from insects. See the string?" She pointed to the plastic knots which tied the newspaper to the fruit stems. "He uses different colours of string to keep track of when each pomelo began to grow."

The farmer and my aunt walked back over to the tree as they spoke together. The fruit sat naked in the wheelbarrow now, its paper removed. The botanical name for the pomelo is *Citrus maxima*. It is the largest citrus fruit and the ancestor to many of the family's hybrids, including the grapefruit. Tambun pomelos differ from the honey pomelos, which are more commonly exported from China and Taiwan to the west. They grow to be much larger—I have struggled to carry some Tambun pomelos— and their skin is almost as green as a lime.

I reached my hand out and cupped my palm to the curve of one of the fruits. Its skin was smooth and rough, and marked with pores of dark pigment like a teenager's skin. I knew that when it came time to pull apart the fruit, my fingernails would break the skin to reveal a thick layer of soft white pith. Buried beneath would be the segmented pink flesh. Peeled pomelos look dry; their vesicles tear apart easily and don't leak juice like a messy orange or grapefruit. But a bite explodes the fruit into juicy pulp.

My aunt returned with the farmer. He laid four more pomelos down in the wheelbarrow.

"Can you ask him how long he's been here?" I asked my aunt.

She had a short conversation with the farmer and then said in English: "They've been here for around sixty years."

The farmer wandered back through the trees and disappeared into the shade with his dogs.

"He's going to get another two for us," my aunt said with glee. "Much cheaper than the supermarket lah and it'll keep your aunties happy."

I asked her why there were so many pomelo farms in Ipoh. We had driven past signs for a few on the way to this farm, as well as stalls where green pomelos harnessed in red string dangled from hooks.

"The ground around Ipoh is rich in minerals," my aunt said, pushing loose soil with the toe of her sandal.

"From the limestone?"

"Exactly," she said. We both looked beyond the treetops at the mountains which watched over the city. The water is so rich in nutrients, the farmers claim they don't use artificial fertilisers on the fruit trees, she explained. And for some reason pomelos grow especially well in the soil.

"And they're all Chinese farmers?"

She thought for a moment. "Yes, all from China or their parents were from China," she said. They might have been part of the generation who immigrated for Ipoh's tin and were forced to pivot to pomelos. "But this land is very valuable lah," my aunt said. "The government is coming to claim it. All around Ipoh, farmers have been losing land." She tutted. "So many of them have been here for fifty, sixty, seventy years."

I asked what the government wanted with the land.

My aunt shrugged. "Development, housing, roads lah."

In the lull of the conversation came the sound of the rushing highway in the distance. I have always appreciated trees for their beauty, but I was struck by how their existence is a living testimony of history. The pomelo groves of Tambun were a reminder that sixty years earlier, some Chinese immigrants had planted roots in their new home. To grow a tree is to express loyalty to a future: that you will still be here in five, ten, twenty years to pick its fruit. But to plant a grove, that is a declaration that you don't simply want to survive off the fruit; you want to prosper from it. Now, a second generation of growers in Tambun were reaping the harvest of their parents' labour. They continued the work of tending to the trees, which still fed their families. When groves were felled to make way for highways, it was not only livelihoods that were lost but also the stories of these Chinese communities in Perak. What a shame it would be to uproot this history, I thought as I stood amongst the pomelo trees.

The farmer returned with pomelos under his arms. He added them to the pile of green fruit. He looked at me and smiled and then spoke to my aunt.

"Go look over there, Kate," she said. Close by the wheelbarrow was a low wooden structure. Half-empty sacks and coils of metal fencing and blue canisters were stored there, held on floorboards raised off the ground by columns of bricks. Old newspapers and brown leaves lined the gaps between the brick stacks. This was what the farmer and my aunt were looking at. I stepped forward. I was about to ask what I was meant to be seeing when a sudden rustling disturbed the nest. My first thought was *Snake!* and I took a step back. Then a puppy stumbled from under the wooden boards, its tiny tail whipping the air. Another puppy followed and then another, all white with brown splotches on their bodies. I peeked through the dark and saw a litter waking from their mid-morning nap. The sun's heat kept the puppies in the shade, but we watched them wrestle with one another, small body tumbling over small body.

"They're lovely," I said to the farmer. He patted one of the adult dogs sitting by his feet—the litter's mother, I presumed. Her happy tail tilled the soil.

The farmer took a reel of red string from his pocket and began to make harnesses for the pomelos, so that three of the fruits could be carried with a single handle. When he was finished, he slipped an arm under the red string and carted the pomelos over to my aunt's car. She opened the trunk and in went the green fruit beside the bag of rambutans.

Then my aunt began her favourite pastime: bartering for the best price. I left her to haggle with the farmer and walked over to the closest pomelo tree. It was still to be harvested; wrapped in newspaper, the fruit hadn't yet ripened to the size of a globe.

Pomelos are native to Malaysia, but they have migrated across the world now. These trees could have returned here from China sixty years ago, with the farmer's family. Or they could be the offspring of saplings that were taken by British and Dutch colonists to the Caribbean. Over the centuries, they might have ambled over to America before returning west to China and Southeast Asia in the hands of homesick migrants. Perhaps they were the offspring of seeds that were once carried—by creatures, by wind, by water—up the Malay Archipelago, moving through tropical lands and onto the plateaus of China, Tibet, and Nepal, where they rested long enough to parent the first wild orange. Or they might have never gone beyond the limestone hills of Ipoh.

But no matter their provenance or the journey they had undertaken, these trees still bore pomelo fruit. Each year they blossomed, and from their flowers, green fruit ripened in the winter. Did it matter if their trees were native or foreign to this land when, no matter their origins, their pomelos bestowed the same meaning—one of auspiciousness and good luck—at Chinese New Year?

After one last playful cry of "Aiyo!" my aunt had finished her deal with the farmer.

"Kate," she called to me with a wide smile on her face. "He is throwing in some soursop as well. Ah Ma will be happy, soursop is very healthy."

The farmer returned with two of the green, prickly fruits, their grey stems still attached. I recognised the fruit from when I had stayed with my grandparents while Ah Ma was receiving chemotherapy. My aunt Sian had bought the fruit at the weekend market to make juice drinks with its white flesh.

I insisted on paying the farmer; I wanted to fulfil my promise to my aunties that I would return from the secret grove of pomelos with a fruit for each of them.

BEFORE I LEFT IPOH, Auntie Suan wanted to take me on one last road trip. The night before she picked me up, she warned me to bring something warm. The next morning, we would head southeast from Ipoh towards distant hills.

A mountain range runs down West Malaysia like a scar, separating Perak from the peninsula's eastern coastal regions. As the British settle in Malaya, starting with Penang in 1786, the colonial administrators build hill stations, where they can escape the tropics for cool altitude. In 1885, William Cameron, a government surveyor, finds a highland plateau between Perak and Pahang, and in 1925, British administrators begin development plans. British Malaya's hill stations are designed as sanatoriums, places of relaxation. The developers decide on an English Tudor revival style for the architecture, and by the 1930s, a golf course, botanical gardens, inns, and clubhouses are all constructed in the Cameron Highlands—named for the land's first British surveyor.[152]

On the drive to Tanah Rata, the largest town in the Cameron Highlands, my aunt and I passed women selling fruit and vegetables in small stalls by the roadside. Some children played with toys by their feet.

"They're the Orang Asli," Auntie Suan said, pointing a finger without releasing her grip on the steering wheel. "Our native people."

Comprising eighteen different ethnic groups, the Orang Asli live in villages throughout the rainforests of Malaysia. There, they build their homes, forage, hunt, and grow crops for a few years, before leaving the land to regenerate.[153] During the British colonial period, and since independence, as industry has boomed in Malaysia, the Orang Asli have been displaced from their ancestral forests to make way for new infrastructure. Mass deforestation—for palm oil and rubber plantations, as well as roads and housing—has wreaked havoc on the country's natural ecosystems, and the Orang Asli have felt the brunt of the loss of animal habitat, the rise of water pollution, the risk of zoonotic diseases. Some villages now welcome tourists to visit their homes, to make a living. Others sell produce at the sides of roads.

In the town of Tanah Rata, the mock Tudor buildings still stand. My aunt drove me to one of the hotels, the Smokehouse, which was built in 1939, complete with black timbers lining its white, pebble-dashed walls. Looking up at the hotel, and the other Tudor buildings we passed, I was reminded of the hyperrealism of Disneyland's mock storefronts. Had the homesick British who arrived in the Cameron Highlands really found solace in this facade of Englishness? Maybe if they ignored the borders where the cultivated world of hotels, golf courses, and racetracks rubbed up against the Malay wilderness, they could pretend as though this little Britain was the only reality that existed.

After Malaysian independence, the Cameron Highlands became a major tourist destination, and further land was cleared for tea, strawberry, and flower plantations. My aunt and I visited the BOH Tea Garden after a deluge of rainfall. BOH, one of Malaysia's most popular tea companies, was founded by a British man, John Archibald Russell, who arrived in Kuala Lumpur as a child, and who became an entrepreneur in tin, rubber, and later tea production. He named the company after the Wuyi Mountains in Fujian, known in English as Bohea, where the mythical second emperor of China, Shennong, is said to have discovered tea.[154]

With the rest of the tourists, my aunt and I slipped along the sodden path that overlooked the sloping tea plantation, each row of green disappearing over the hills and into the clouds. In the centre's café, we sipped our cups of hot tea, grateful for a moment to warm our hands before we headed back to the car. I said to my aunt that it felt strange to enjoy the remnants of colonial Britain in modern Malaysia. She frowned over her cup and asked what I meant.

I was unsure how to articulate the queasy feeling inside me. "You know, like how the Cameron Highlands were built as a place for the British to enjoy themselves when they occupied Malaysia," I began. "It feels strange to try and separate the fake Tudor buildings and the tea and the strawberries from the things they did to the native people."

I asked how she felt about it, as a Malaysian.

She set down her cup with a steady hand. "The British did some good things and they did some bad things," she said. "But what they did is in the past lah." She shrugged and picked her cup back up. "In Malaysia we need to think about the future."

I admired my aunt's practical outlook, but I still felt trapped by the past, incapable of moving into the future because I was overwhelmed by the history I saw everywhere I went. Ipoh was a palimpsest: of my own childhood memories and of Britain, the country I had hoped to leave behind. A Tudor inn, a painting of a British queen, a white-walled railway station were reminders of a past that Malaysia preserved, reimagined, rejected, and memorialised. Auntie Suan was educated in the colonial British system, as were my father and his siblings, and that education got them into commonwealth universities, where they graduated as doctors, professors and lawyers. I once asked my aunt about her colonial education, and she called it a gift.

Colonial legacy is seared into the world in terrible and wondrous ways. In Ipoh, I found a city that occasionally played in a fantasy of the past, one which was safely contained within a nostalgic sheen, like exotic flowers inside a glasshouse. The rose-tinted look at history had made me uncomfortable, coming from Britain, a country which excels at both ignoring and glorifying the repugnant chapters of its past. But our relationship to history is complex and it is ever-changing. How we interpret the past through our present moment speaks to the state of a nation now as much as it does about its previous actions. Malaysia is moving forward from centuries-long occupations, while Britain is still basking in the glow of an empire that dimmed years ago. I could not find comfort in either form of mythmaking.

Recently, my mother told me that she and my father had planned to move to Malaysia before my brothers and I were born. "I had all my nursing paperwork ready and everything," she said. I hadn't known this had ever been a possibility. Ultimately, they decided to stay in the north of Ireland, in their hospital jobs and close to my Irish grandparents, but I wonder if I would have been a different person if I had been born in Malaysia. There are an infinite number of paths a life can take, but I can't help but fantasise about a childhood rooted in Ipoh. Everything would have been reversed. I would have learned English and Malay, maybe Mandarin and Cantonese, and Longyan as well. I would be able to converse without a barrier with my grandmother. Words that I wrestle with, and stumble over, would fall from my tongue. I would know the heat and the sun and I would mark the year by its monsoon seasons. I would have grown up in a country that had shaken off its British occupiers long before I was born. Would I have been less self-conscious of my skin, my heritage, my name?

Perhaps. But I suspect I would have yearned for Ireland and felt the loss of growing up away from it, the same way I feel an absence when I am away from Malaysia. I think that is just the nature of loving two places. No, I think, when this fantasy childhood fades away. If I had the choice, I would not change my past or the troubled land that made me. As a child I thought loving two places—embodying two places in one body—meant dividing yourself. Now, I know that the act of loving multiplies the heart; it does not segment it.

That old refrain about immigrants: the first generation survives so the second can tell the stories. This generational distinction has never rung quite true to me; in my experience, first-generation immigrants are the far superior storytellers and the second generation has its own struggle for survival. While shame and violence seep into my narratives, my father's stories are full of character and colour and light. I grew up hearing about the snakes that swam to the top of the staircase when my grandparents' house flooded. There was the story about the neighbourhood boys who gathered outside the window when Ah Kong bought the street's first television. The tales of food and mischief and coming of age at the end of empire in a childhood that my father once described as glorious. His stories were probably why I yearned for a childhood in Malaysia myself.

But the stories stop around the time when my father moved to the north of Ireland, aged seventeen, during the Troubles. I don't know much about this time in his life, but I can imagine the homesickness of a teenager, the uncertainty of assimilating into a new culture, and the hostility that met a boy with a foreign face.

Each generation thinks they are the first: the first to break away from the past, the first to envision a new way of living, the first to experience the strangeness of moving through this world.

When I told my father that I was writing a book that was, in part, about how I felt pulled between two places, I confessed to him that I wasn't sure if I could, or should, do it.

"It's a lot to write about," I said, holding my phone to my ear as I paced around my flat's small kitchen. "I don't want to make our family sad. I don't know if it's worth it."

"Hmm." He listened to my panic. I could picture him at his desk in our house, leaning back in his chair and looking up at the noticeboard of photographs, bills, and to-do lists. Or maybe he was in the kitchen, watching the time tick by on the two clocks that hang above the doorway—one set to Irish time, the other to Malaysian.

"I know it's not easy," he said finally. "I left home when I was young. Your aunt returned and your uncle returned after their studies, but I stayed here. I'm not the black sheep of the family, but I didn't go back."

I stopped pacing. He didn't often talk about his feelings.

"I feel like I have two homes, here and Malaysia," he continued. "It's a good thing and it's not a good thing to want to be in two places at once."

It was the first time I could remember him expressing the melancholy of being pulled in two directions, a sensation that was familiar to me. It shocked me and it comforted me, and it made me realise that whatever feelings of uncertainty I had, my father had experienced similar feelings while also trying to survive in a foreign country.

For years, an origin tale had mattered to me. I had thought that in Ipoh, I would feel more connected to my family and closer to Malaysia's past, but the more I chased a desire for belonging, the more it eluded my grasp. I couldn't find a satisfying ending here. Instead, I felt as unsure of where I fit in Malaysia as I felt in Britain and Ireland. Since I was a child, I have held on to two places, two homes, two possibilities for myself. But what would happen if I let them go? What if I slipped away and left these two poles for somewhere new? A ring of citrus circumnavigates the world. What if I kept following it?

SIX

· · · · · · · · · ·

SOUTHERN CALIFORNIA

BEFORE I LEFT FOR CALIFORNIA, THE TEST RESULTS ARRIVED.

"Welcome to you!" the email exclaimed. "A world of DNA discovery is waiting."

I clicked through the link. My heart began to beat a little harder as I tapped my desk, impatient for the web page to load. There was nothing, and then there was the earth. On the screen, a world map was all white except for two areas: blue in the west and red in the east, with continents of terra incognita between them.

A graph beside the map split my ancestry DNA into perfect semicircles. In blue: European 50 percent. In red: East Asian 50 percent. I clicked for the breakdown. Blue: British and Irish 50 percent. Red: southern Chinese and Taiwanese 50 percent.

Huh? I looked at the map beside the composition again. Blue British Isles. Red southern China. I hadn't expected many surprises to lurk in my DNA, but there was something about the clean cut down the graph that disturbed me. Not even a 0.5 percent French or a 2 percent northern Chinese. Just two halves, divided more perfectly than you could slice a cake. There were no hidden stories in the results, no secrets and no mysteries to discover. My ancestors had stood still in their parts of the world, generation after generation putting down roots.

I clicked on the link for southern China and Taiwan and scrolled through the information the company had compiled about the region's history and traditions. At the bottom of the page was a photograph of Fujian's ancient tulous at golden hour. I laughed then at the absurdity of my disappointment. What had I expected? Some great secret inheritance hiding in the saliva I had posted to a test lab a month ago?

I sent my parents a screenshot of my test results. My father replied a few minutes later. "I could have told you that for free."

Since at-home DNA ancestry tests began to be sold to the public in the 2010s, I had been half sceptical, half curious about them. The decade had seen the popularity of genetics testing accelerate into a billion-dollar industry. By 2019, more than twenty-nine million people had sent their saliva to private corporations which archive the data indefinitely unless biobanking consent is withdrawn.[155] The risk of lost, stolen, or sold DNA was enough to warrant my unease about ancestry tests (and it was not unfounded: a few weeks after I received my results, the company storing my DNA sample was hacked, exposing half its customers' data).

But what I found even more uncomfortable was the desire to find oneself through genetics. DNA testing simplifies the past. It untangles messy webs of histories, stories, and journeys into neat percentages and pie charts. Ancestry DNA testing is particularly popular in countries that are current or former European colonies, where the majority of the white population have recent local histories that begin with their ancestors arriving in ships from Europe. For people of colour in these nations, DNA testing can provide answers to uncertainties about where their ancestors came from or where they were taken from. And for mixed-race people, unsure of where parts of their families are located, it can be a lifeline back into the past. But a genuine desire to learn about your family's history is often exploited by companies that dress up biomedical data mining with marketing. My test's company encouraged me to take a "heritage trip" to a tulou because "journeying to your roots only extends that sense of belonging"[156]—in partnership with Airbnb, of course.

I knew that DNA cannot be conflated with cultural identity, and that race is socially defined, not biologically essentialist. And I knew that white supremacists had recently co-opted ancestral testing to prove their racial "purity" and to perpetuate eugenicist rhetoric. I knew the foolishness of seeking a sense of self by buying it from a corporate entity.

And yet.

You can be told all the reasons why something is bad for you, and you can still take the bite. Or, rather, you can spit in a tube, seal it in an envelope, and ship it to a laboratory in North Carolina. The temptation of self-knowledge was a lure impossible for me to ignore.

I WAS REPEATEDLY REMINDED of my results when I arrived in Los Angeles a few months later. Friendly locals, always white, were eager to tell me about their own ethnic ancestry once they learned I was from Europe. One woman was able to give me her family history in percentages as I browsed her store in Pasadena. Another man enthusiastically asked me for my surname after I told him I was Irish. When his face crumpled with disappointment, I explained that I had a Malaysian father. He cheered himself up by telling me he was from a long line of Dublin Murphys.

A desire to understand one's heritage is often played for laughs, as a mocking stereotype of white Americans, Canadians, and Australians—the descendants of immigrants, colonisers, and settlers who call themselves Irish or Scottish or German without ever having stepped foot in those countries. But I've always sympathised with the innocuous, if naive, faith required to self-mythologise, to romanticise, to shape the past into your own story. I have felt that deep desire within myself, the pull to be anchored to history. But for now, I was in Southern California because I wanted to leave my own roots behind. I was here seeking orange trees in a new land.

My search began in Los Angeles, a one-time swamp that was paved with concrete in the twentieth century and assembled into a sprawl of freeways. I loved being in LA. I loved that my brain flooded with serotonin every time I went outside and felt the heat of the sun on my skin, so sudden and strange in the middle of winter. I loved waking up to a blue sky and the sound of helicopters. I loved the taste of tomatoes and limes ripened in the California sun. I loved that I could face west to the sea, turn, face north to the mountains, turn, face east to the desert. I loved the smell of fuel and tar and weed because it smelled like a city and I loved being in a city, especially the anonymity of this contradictory one. I loved that I could still love a place despite itself and all the repugnant discrepancies it contained: between poverty and wealth, concrete and greenery, creativity and consumerism.

I had come to California for orange trees, but in LA, in January, it was quicker to find their fruit. On my first morning, I walked to a food store and bought more citrus than I could possibly eat in a week. Blood oranges, honey pomelos, daisy tangerines. I carried them back to my guesthouse in Larchmont and sat in a sun-dappled patch to eat. With a blunt knife, I hacked into a blood orange, its ruby juice splattering the patio. Its taste was bitter and sharp and flooded my mouth with saliva and pinched my cheeks. I ate the messy segments and took in the little green garden. I had expected LA to be inundated with citrus trees, that I would land into a paradise of lime-, lemon-, and orange-laden boughs, but they proved surprisingly elusive. That afternoon, I glimpsed a flash of gold amongst green leaves through the greasy window of the Metro. The next morning, I passed a house with a lemon tree in its backyard. I stopped on the sidewalk and turned to walk up the driveway to take a closer look. But there was still a metal fence between us, and, more importantly, I didn't know if California's gun laws covered trespassing. I decided the lemons weren't worth the risk of finding out.

What LA seemed to lack in citrus trees, it made up for in palm trees. They careened overhead in the breeze, hunched over by the weight of their own fanned leaves. In parallel pairs, the trees lined boulevards, each planted with immaculate symmetry. I had thought palm trees were native to Southern California, but my guidebook informed me that they were in fact imports, planted in the early twentieth century to ornament the streets. The year 1931 alone saw twenty-five thousand palm trees planted in LA in a beautifying spree to prepare the city for the 1932 Olympic Games.[157] Palm trees give LA its allure as a western oasis, but the planting of a desert tree that yields decorative pleasure but neither shade nor fruit conjures a mirage rather than delivers a bounty.

Palm trees, orange groves, and crashing waves. Picture California and that vision shimmers in the mind's eye. In the state's iconography, palms and citrus don't just symbolise Southern California: they have become Southern California. Since the country's founding, the US's great power has been its self-mythologising. The nation has been telling its own story— building its foundations upon it—ever since Europeans reached its eastern coast and convinced themselves that they had discovered an empty land, here for their taking. The Americas were, of course, not empty in the fifteenth century. Nor were they undiscovered. Complex ecosystems of people, animals, and plants had thrived on the continents for centuries, and they were severed when Christopher Columbus opened America up for European business.

ORANGES LAND IN THE AMERICAS with Columbus in 1493. On this second voyage to the New World, Columbus's fleet carries citrus seeds alongside Iberian plants, animals, and food to settle a Spanish colony on the island of Hispaniola, where Haiti is located today. Oranges arrive on mainland America with Spanish missionaries, who plant the trees in their wake as they spread across the continent. Eventually, citrus, in the hands of colonisers, reaches the west coast in the eighteenth century. Foreign crops are planted in California, and the Spanish missionaries use imported nature to subdue the Native population. California's first orange grove is planted by Native Californian children at the San Gabriel Mission in 1804, ordered by Franciscan fathers who see these four hundred trees as a gift from God.[158] California's landscape is forever altered with the planting of citrus groves, vineyards, and wheat fields—all imports from Iberia and all necessary to feed the increasing population of Spanish and Mexican settlers whose descendants called themselves Californios. California's Native population, who have lived on the land for ten thousand years, estimated to number three hundred thousand at the beginning of European colonisation in 1769, are halved by the mid-nineteenth century.[159]

California is soon to become the US's thirty-first state when flecks of gold are discovered in what is now called El Dorado County. The Gold Rush of 1848 brings eighty thousand Americans west, a population boom that enables California to apply for official statehood in the same year.[160] News reaches other shores and by the following year, a third of the miners seeking their fortune are foreign.

California as a land of abundance, the place where men can arrive with only the shirts on their backs and leave with treasure, is no longer pure myth. The lure of power and wealth comes with dire consequences for the indigenous population. In twenty years, the number of Native people murdered in the state, most often by vigilantes who are assisted—and rewarded—by state officials, is estimated to be between nine and sixteen thousand.[161] Blood and gold rush forth in California.

Manifest destiny is how Europeans-turned-Americans justify their claim on the continent, a story which is part nationalist agenda, part territorial expansion, and part religious mission. "We see that it is the manifest destiny of North-Americans to colonize and control the continental," announces an 1856 article in the *Democratic Review*.[162] An entire continent is mythologised as the "New World" and as a new Garden of Eden waiting for Anglo-Americans to civilise it. The land's Native peoples are considered just another part of the landscape: to be controlled, curtailed, and culled if necessary.

After the Gold Rush populates California and wealth floods the state, new settlers see the land as a wild frontier ripe for cultivation. Groves of citrus trees are planted throughout California, but it is the southern reach of the state, with its Mediterranean-like climate, where a citrus industry booms in the late nineteenth century. Oranges become an industry—the biggest industry in California's economy after oil[163]—and it is this industry that transforms nature's fruit into a manufactured product.

But first oranges need to ripen. New groves are the "handsome, symmetrical, electrifying Golden Glory of the Pacific slope," as the writer Thomas A. Garey calls them in 1882.[164] Even then, Garey knows an orange can be more than a piece of fruit. "Those who are fortunate as to tread the soil in the shade of the majestic trees, and breathe their fragrant exhalations, look upward," he writes. "They thank the Great Author of the grand, useful and beautiful in nature for so sublime a manifestation of His works, and His good gifts to mortals. There is inspiration, as well as beauty and princely profits, in an orange orchard." A Christian God and his missionaries have bestowed California with the orange, and manifest destiny will see it deliver America's promised paradise.

IN 1873, THREE SMALL CITRUS trees arrive in the city of Riverside.[165] They have travelled far. From a grove in São Salvador de Bahía, Brazil, twelve saplings were carried northwards at the request of William Saunders, head of the experimental gardens division of the US Department of Agriculture. In the US capital, the saplings were rechristened the Washington navel orange, and, now American, three of them journeyed west to the garden of Eliza Tibbets, a friend of Saunders, in Riverside, fifty miles east of LA. Planted in California soil, one is trampled by a cow, but two grow into fruit-bearing trees, nurtured by the sun and Eliza's dirty dishwater—the Tibbetses' house is not connected to Riverside's fresh water canal. When the oranges ripen, their sweet, seedless flesh is immensely popular. Naturally sterile, navel orange trees are cultivated through grafting, and Eliza's gardeners begin cutting budwood from the original trees to be grafted to other citrus rootstocks. By 1910, over a million Washington navel orange trees have sprung up in Riverside. Each tree, a perfect clone, can trace its lineage back to one of Eliza's parent trees.[166]

One of Eliza's Washington navel trees still grows in Riverside. In the armpit of Magnolia and Arlington Avenues, the 150-year-old tree stands behind a translucent screen cage to protect its branches from disease, insects, and greedy hands. I found myself standing before it on a bright morning in January during California's peak orange season. Inside the cage, ripe fruit hung from the tree's branches, each orange marked by its eponymous navel. I circled the tree's breadth slowly, taking in its peeling trunk and evergreen leaves which brushed the cage top. It was by far the biggest orange tree I had seen. Outside the screen, a plaque, fringed with green hedge like a war memorial, declared that the Washington navel orange tree had "proved the most valuable fruit introduction yet made by the United States Department of Agriculture."

I was in town to visit the University of California, Riverside's Citrus Variety Collection, one of the most extensive citrus collections in the world. I had been emailing its curator, Dr. Tracy Kahn, for a few months and she had agreed to show me around the collection. I had taken an early morning train from LA to Riverside, rattling past hills and freeways into the rising sun. My inability to find orange trees in LA had unsettled me. I had thought that I was travelling to the land of sun, citrus, and sea, and so far, only the sun was making good on the promise of Southern California. Outside Riverside's small station, I waited for Tracy. An abandoned plastic bag spilled its insides—tiny easy-peel oranges—across the sidewalk. A good omen, I hoped, in the city that had been deemed the "home of the orange" in 1902.[167]

A small car pulled up beside me, and a woman waved enthusiastically from behind its window. I climbed inside and met Tracy with a handshake and smile. She was slight, in her sixties, and wore a purple coat that matched the purple arms of her spectacles. She apologised for my wait, and I told her I had been more than happy to wait in the sun. She chuckled and told me this was Riverside at its coldest. She laughed again when I told her I wasn't driving in LA and, with concern that was both faux and genuine, asked me how on earth I was moving around the city.

"Now," she said as she signalled right to leave the station's parking lot. "Tell me why you're here again."

As she drove, I explained that I was writing a book about oranges and my research had led me to the Citrus Variety Collection. She seemed amused that a writer—and one who was adamantly *not* a science writer—had travelled all the way from Scotland to Southern California to visit orange trees. Even though I had only asked if I could see the collection, Tracy decided that I should get the full tour of Riverside's citrus history for the bother of travelling so far. We had started with Eliza's tree.

"Look down there." Tracy pointed to the tree's base. Rather than a single trunk, multiple thick branches curved from its base into the earth. It looked not dissimilar to a banyan tree. Tracy explained that this was caused by inarching. In 1903, one of

Eliza's trees was transplanted to downtown Riverside as a living memorial to the city's citrus history. But in 1918, the tree became ill, suffering from *Phytophthora* root rot. Inarching—a process in which rootstocks from other citrus trees are grafted to the recipient tree to create a new root system—was carried out by three scientists, so that no single person could be blamed if the operation failed and Riverside's beloved tree died.[168] Lemon and orange seedlings were inarched successfully by the three scientists, with several more grafted in 1951. Eliza's other tree had died after it was transplanted elsewhere in Riverside, so this one was now the only survivor.

I circled the tree one last time. It wore its age in its pummelled knots of wood and its tough, scarred skin. In a grove in Bahia in the 1800s, it had mutated spontaneously as a bud sport on a Selecta variety orange tree.[169] Its fruit had been tasted by a missionary who had sent word of her discovery to the Department of Agriculture. The sapling had left Brazil to eventually be rooted here in Riverside. It had stood witness through the boom and bust of California's citrus industry. It had outlived most of its own descendants, which had been culled in the twentieth century to make way for highways and housing. Now Southern California's great citrus ancestor stands alone, breathing in car fumes from behind a screen and rooted between two slabs of pavement. It is a sickly tree kept alive by grafted roots. And yet this 150-year-old Brazilian immigrant tree still grows oranges every January. The people who maintain the tree pick some of its fruit to take home, but mostly it piles up behind the safety screen. Each orange ripens until it falls from its branch and begins to rot.

TO MAKE AN INDUSTRY of the orange is a precarious business. Never mind the possibilities of strange mutations, insurgent seedlings, and freak weather; the seven years it takes for a seed to bear ripe fruit is too long to wait for profit. So, to reduce risk, you'll want to tighten your grip on nature. Control, curtail, cull if necessary.

By the twentieth century, Riverside is the epicentre of California's orange industry. Its infrastructure has been adapted for its citrus groves: an entire irrigation system is built in the 1880s to redirect water from the San Gabriel Mountains.[170] Across California, the landscape changes as agriculture becomes the dominant industry. By 1890, pipes and canals run from dams and reservoirs to water one million acres of land, ready for new trees and crops.[171] Railroad tracks criss-cross the desert, waiting to carry millions of ripe oranges out of California in fleets of the Southern Pacific Transportation Company's refrigerated cars to eastern markets.

Irrigation and distribution are ready. Now it is the fruit's turn. Before California's orange boom in the late nineteenth century, only a small percentage of Americans had seen an orange—never mind tasted one. The orange must be saleable. The product must be perfect. Each orange needs to taste, feel, and smell the same. The consumer should not be able to differentiate one fruit from the other. There is no margin for idiosyncratic textures, blemishes, or flavours. The skin of each orange needs to be smooth enough to shine under lights in any store throughout the US.

To create perfection, the grove becomes a factory. Oranges do not ripen all at once. Instead, the fruit growing on the sunniest side of a tree is ready to be picked first, while the shaded branches act as a natural incubator for the rest of the crop. It can take nine weeks for a single tree to ripen all its fruit. But when it does, the race against rot begins.

Each picker is assigned a tree, and they ascend wooden ladders, each equipped with cotton gloves, clippers, and an empty sack. Early in California's orange rush, pickers are paid by the weight of their harvests, but when oranges arrive at sorting stations bruised and broken, an hourly rate is established. A perfect orange cannot be yanked from its stem. Patience, skilled hands, and a sharp pair of clippers are required to collect the harvest.

When the picker has filled a sack of fresh fruit, he descends the ladder and opens a flap at the bottom of the sack, encouraging a gentle tumble of oranges into a crate. If the foreman—the manager of pickers in the field—hears the fruit thump into the container, the picker's job is on the line. Once picked, an orange is a product with a price tag and must be handled with care.

Crates arrive at packing houses that are built close to the groves so that the production line can move quickly. The fruit is checked, weighed, washed, dried, and waxed by the packers, who tend to be women. Orange production is organised into a gender binary: men work outside, cultivating the trees, while women labour inside, preparing the fruit. The image of women handling the fruit will eventually become a marketing ploy by orange sellers. While both Mexican and white women work in packing houses, a romance is sold to shoppers: California oranges grown from the fertile land and prepared by gentle, white, feminine hands.[172] However, the labour itself is no romance. One report from inside a packing house is horrified by "pale and worn looking, almost wilting" women. "Hour after hour their flying hands repeat a monotonously mechanical movement."[173]

Once polished to a satisfactory shine, the oranges are sorted by grade, wrapped in tissue paper, and sealed in boxes stamped with branding. Hundreds of these boxes leave California every day, travelling by refrigerated trains on tracks that span the continent. Their destinations are stores where the oranges will be unboxed and stacked in pyramids, each fruit identical and promising a bite of West Coast paradise.

By 1901, California's citrus industry comprises over four and a half million trees.[174] Growers seek new varieties, new methods of cultivation, and new means of production as the industry continues to boom. In 1905, the California Fruit Growers Exchange controls 40 percent of the state's citrus,[175] and the collective of growers appeals to the state's legislature for an official research station. Already considered the home of the orange industry with its navel trees, the city of Riverside is chosen as the location for the Citrus Experiment Station. The station opens a year later on the slopes of Riverside's Mount Rubidoux. The scientists look for ways to improve fertilisation, irrigation, and pest control, so that growers can increase their harvest yields—and their profits—each year.

As the station grows, research focuses on citrus varieties and hybridisation. In 1910, the Citrus Variety Collection is initiated as part of the station's experimental work, and seven years later, five acres of Riverside are dedicated to collecting different varieties of citrus.[176] The historian Douglas Sackman draws a direct correlation between the Riverside station's work and the passage of the Plant Patent Act by Congress in 1930, which enables scientists to claim varieties as their own inventions. "Plant patents, under which living organisms could be stamped as 'property,' enabled a corporate colonization of nature," writes Sackman. "Instead of providing the liberation from nature that the rhetoric of improvement had promised, nature would now more efficiently be incorporated into the growth machine."[177]

California's orange industry is the prototype for modern agriculture in which control of production has been moved from individual farmers to corporations which oversee every step of the "farm to fork" process, from genetics to marketing. Although citrus has been cultivated and cross-bred throughout history, in California, the modern orange as a product is invented.

The work of scientists in experimental stations gets a mention in John Steinbeck's novel *The Grapes of Wrath*. "Behind the fruitfulness are men of understanding and knowledge and skill, men who experiment with seed, endlessly developing the techniques for greater crops of plants whose roots will resist the million enemies of the earth," Steinbeck writes. "And always they work, selecting, grafting, changing, driving themselves, driving the earth to produce."[178]

THE CITRUS VARIETY COLLECTION was fenced in from the freeway in southeast Riverside. As Tracy drove us into the compound, one sign announced that we were on the University of California, Riverside's property, while another, temporary sign warned against bringing in or removing citrus from the collection. As Tracy drove along a dirt path, she explained that the state was seeing a resurgence of the oriental fruit fly, a pest which lays its eggs in fruit, and as a precaution, the collection was under quarantine from foreign citrus. In Riverside's neighbouring county, San Bernardino, trees were being stripped of their fruit in an escalating war between the fruit fly and the California Department of Food and Agriculture. An invasion into the collection would be devastating, said Tracy. It was already wreaking havoc for the mass production groves.

Tracy parked her car, and we stepped out and into the collection. Trees of every size and shape—tall and short, heavy and thin—ran in twenty-two acres of perfect parallel lines, one after the other, in every direction. Oranges grew in their thousands. I had never seen so much citrus. After the dearth in LA, I felt giddy.

"How many trees are there?" I asked Tracy.

"Over a thousand varieties—we call them accessions—are in the collection," she answered as she rummaged around the back seat of her car. "And there are two trees for each variety."

Tracy found what she was looking for: a heavy blue binder. She began wrestling with its pages, which were flapping in the wind. It was the first morning that was truly windy during my trip to Southern California, and I commented on the sudden gusts.

"That's the Santa Ana winds," Tracy explained as she flipped through the documents. The winds, and the forest fires they incite, have swept through the region and shaped the landscape for thousands of years, and have become famous for disrupting the pleasant, sunny lifestyles of Angelenos. When the Santa Ana winds arrive, they bring chaos. "The wind shows us how close to the edge we are," wrote Joan Didion.[179]

"Right! Here it is." Tracy laid the folder flat on the car hood to show me what looked like school timetables. She explained that the numbers and lines were, in fact, a map of the collection.

"What first?" Tracy muttered to herself as she ran a finger along one column. "I suppose the beginning. . . ."

Then she was off, moving fast through the rows of trees. I stumbled after her over the uneven brown earth that was littered with rotting citrus peel and empty snail shells.

Tracy stopped suddenly at a tree, its branches laden with heavy oranges, and I nearly walked into her. It had been grafted from one of Eliza Tibbets's Washington navels, Tracy explained as she took a pocketknife from her pocket. She reached up for one of the oranges and pulled the fruit from the tree's branches.

"See the navel?" She turned the orange over to show me the bump that resembled a belly button. The species' unique feature is caused by an embryonic orange growing inside another, larger fruit. She quartered the orange with her knife and handed me a segment. I bit into the fruit and it became sweet juice and stringy flesh between my teeth. It would have tasted good anywhere, but pulled fresh from its tree and ripened in a grove that grew under the California sun, it was a mouthful of pure pleasure.

"Delicious," I declared, and Tracy handed me another quarter in approval. She tossed the rind at the base of the tree, and I followed suit. I shook juice from my fingers and hurried after Tracy, who was already striding on to the next tree, following her map of citrus.

Tracy was keen for me to sample as much as I could eat. We stopped and started along the rows of trees, Tracy slicing into different fruit and sometimes joining me in the sampling. I bit into an acidless Vaniglia Sanguigno that tasted like candy and then nibbled at a Boukhobza that made my lips and eyes sting with its bitter flesh. The juice from a Moro—a Sicilian blood orange hybrid—ran down my hands, and a sticky residue gelled under the rings on my fingers.

"This is a popular one," Tracy said as she pulled apart two citrus halves to reveal splotchy ruby flesh in a heart-shaped rind. "It's a cross between a Siamese acidless pomelo and a blood orange mandarin. It's called a Valentine."

I ate a slice of it and then one from a yellow yuzu from the Philippines and then another slice from a plump pomelo from Tahiti, and soon my lips had gone numb. When I mentioned this to Tracy, she laughed and reminded me that Sichuan peppers are a type of citrus.

As we walked—and ate—our way around the collection, Tracy recounted the history of the Citrus Variety Collection and the Citrus Experiment Station. I asked how she had become involved with the collection. She had become interested in citrus after taking a class at the University of California, Riverside taught by the then curator of the collection, Dr. W. P. Bitters. ("Yes," said Tracy. "His real name.") Bitters retired in 1982, and Tracy took over the collection's curatorship while also teaching a course on human sexuality. When I asked her if there was any overlap between her two fields of study, she paused and then answered, "Well, sex!"

In 2006, the collection formed a partnership with the fragrance and flavour company Givaudan. Tracy pointed her finger into the distance.

"Do you see that structure over there?"

What looked like an enormous white tent stood on an empty plot of land. Givaudan had contributed $3.5 million to the construction of a Citrus Under Protective Screen (CUPS) to protect the collection. Once it is completed, a nearly three-acre-long structure will function as a bigger version of the screen which guards Eliza's navel tree in downtown Riverside. Researchers will be able to safely grow one of each variety in the collection behind the mesh, protected from the bacterium that causes huanglongbing, a citrus infection which turns the skin of an orange green and stunts the fruit's ripening. The CUPS structure will be a Noah's ark, a living archive dedicated to the preservation of over a thousand varieties of citrus.

Tracy stopped by a tree that had stubby evergreen leaves and thin fruit with brown wrinkly skin. It looked nothing like any of the other citrus trees we had visited so far. She sliced her knife into one of the fruits and squeezed the rind until tiny lime-coloured vesicles spilled out.

"They're Australian finger limes, or sometimes called citrus caviar," she explained. As well as preserving citrus, the Citrus Variety Collection still experiments with cross-breeding varieties, usually to find solutions to disease-susceptible varieties. The collection's researchers had discovered that the finger lime contains stable antimicrobial peptides that inhibit the spread of huanglongbing, which continues to jeopardise the industry. Researchers were experimenting with cross-breeding finger limes with other citrus varieties, with the hope that the peptides could bolster their resistance.[180] Tracy cut into a few more finger limes from neighbouring trees and passed me some. They were all filled with tiny balls, a different colour in each lime. I nibbled at the end of the strange fruit and its purple caviar popped between my incisors. They were surprisingly dry.

My mouth was now completely numb. My tongue throbbed like a heartbeat from all the acid. The last time I had eaten this much citrus had been in early 2021, when I had sat at the kitchen table and eaten what I know now to be navel oranges, one after another until my stomach ached. I had eaten those oranges as an act of desperation, a bid to fill and stupefy my sorrow after an act of violence unravelled me. The sting of citric acid brought me back to that morning, after a white man had murdered six Asian women. But it also reminded me of the journey from then to now. Here, in Riverside, I was eating to satiate my curiosity. I was here to learn the orange's history and discover its future.

Before this visit to Southern California, I had met the orange as theory, history, and concept. Now I felt like we were familiar. It was one thing to read a science paper about the taxonomy of citrus, and it was another to stand in a grove and pull an orange from its tree, slice into its flesh, and place a segment between my teeth. Each bite was an encounter with its past through my body.

I knew I would soon be reaching the end of the orange's journey. But right there and then, I found myself standing in a living archive of citrus a long way from home, my face warmed by the winter sun, and all I wanted was to surrender to the pleasure of eating ripe fruit.

"Can you stomach any more?" asked Tracy. Her purple coat was dotted from the spray of citrus. She held her pocketknife with its wet blade in one hand and another segmented fruit in the palm of her other hand.

"Yes," I answered and held my palm out for a slice. "Yes, I can stomach more."

"You'll be glowing in the dark later," Tracy replied with a smile. We pulled the flesh with our teeth and left the skin behind.

SOUTHERN CALIFORNIA'S CITRUS EMPIRE balloons until it bursts. During the Great Depression, food prices plummet and the US government intervenes to save the agricultural industry. President Franklin Roosevelt signs the Agricultural Adjustment Act of 1933, which attempts to stabilise the economy by authorising payment to food producers if they destroy surplus stock. While starving citizens go on hunger marches across the US, piglets are slaughtered, cotton crops razed, and oranges piled up and set on fire. In the years 1938 and 1939, it costs the US $600,000 to destroy its surplus citrus.[181]

"A million people hungry, needing the fruit—and kerosene sprayed over the golden mountains," writes John Steinbeck in

The Grapes of Wrath. "There is a crime here that goes beyond denunciation. There is a sorrow here that weeping cannot symbolize. There is a failure here that topples all our success. The fertile earth, the straight tree rows, the sturdy trunks, and the ripe fruit. And children dying of pellagra must die because a profit cannot be taken from an orange."[182]

Steinbeck's denouncement of ruined oranges is so damning that the anti-labour organisation the Associated Farmers of California tries to have *The Grapes of Wrath* banned upon its publication in 1939. Farmers in Kern County are so incensed by the book's descriptions of their industry that they gather and set copies of the book on fire.

But it is too late. The fantasy of a Californian Eden has gone up in smoke with the pyres of fruit destroyed in the Great Depression. The orange has a ruined reputation, and a reinvention is required.

Up until the 1930s, Americans squeeze their own oranges in their homes—unpasteurized fresh juice clots into a disastrous gloopy mess when it is shipped nationwide—then in 1945 a group of scientists working in Florida invent frozen concentrated orange juice while developing a vitamin C vehicle for soldiers fighting in World War II.[183] The process evaporates liquid from the juice to form a concentrate. A small dose of fresh orange juice is then added to restore the tangy taste of the orange. Concentrated orange juice travels farther and its composition is easily controlled to create one perfect, homogenous product. Unlike fresh orange juice with its diversity of flavour and texture, every bottle from concentrate tastes the same. Even though the war ends before the concentrated juice can be shipped to troops, the orange juice industry explodes.

No more tedious peeling and squeezing. Juice arrives pasteurised and concentrated in tiny tins on supermarket shelves, marketed to post-war housewives as natural and wholesome; a bright, fresh drink for families that evokes middle-class luxury.

Orange growers pivot to cultivating fruit for juicing, as raw material to be processed into another product.

Yet despite the pivot, California's citrus empire is coming to an end. In the 1930s, California produces 70 percent of America's oranges; by 1960, that number will fall to 15 percent.[184] After World War II, California's citrus industry moves north while Los Angeles and its surrounding counties are engulfed in infrastructure. Highways and houses prove more lucrative than citrus, and land is made profitable by covering it with concrete. In Anaheim, groves of Valencia oranges are uprooted to build Walt Disney's amusement park.[185] California's Eden is replaced by a paradise of entertainment, and orange trees are made redundant, reduced to set dressing like the palm trees which line Hollywood's boulevards.

Orange juice continues to grow in popularity, and from the mid-twentieth century onwards, Americans drink more oranges than they eat.[186] Despite being marketed as "natural," "real," and "pure," supermarket orange juice is a heavily processed product, and its manufacturers have been sued for their misleading labelling.[187]

From concentrate, not from concentrate, with pulp, without pulp; no matter the label, orange juice has become the most popular processed fruit drink in the world. "Drink an orange" was the famous advertising slogan run by Sunkist. Drink an orange and you drink in everything the fruit has come to embody— health, sunshine, nostalgia, luxury, California—even if its juice is nothing but sugar and invention.

BEFORE I RETURNED to Los Angeles, Tracy wanted me to visit California Citrus State Historic Park. The Santa Ana winds had discarded palm leaves across Riverside, and Tracy snaked round them as we drove the deserted road through two hundred acres of navel and Valencia oranges. The park's visitors' centre stayed closed throughout the week, and only one worker, who introduced himself as José, was loitering around near the parking lot. Tracy told him that she was a board member of the park and convinced him to let me in for a quick look around. She stayed by the front desk to speak with José while I walked the centre's perimeter. Placards on the wall outlined California's part in citrus's global history.

I already knew its journey, but I followed the path anyway. Hybrid fruit, offspring of pomelo and mandarin orange; cultivated in East Asia, carried to Europe and then onwards to the New World, to finally reach Riverside. The orange has a long history, and within it a multitude of other stories are contained, some remembered and some forgotten.

In the visitors' centre, black-and-white photographs had been enhanced and hung up on an exhibition wall to highlight the role of immigrants in California's orange industry. Faces of Chinese, Japanese, and Filipino workers stared out of the photographs, dated to the late nineteenth century. The men's eyes were shaded by wide-brimmed hats. I imagined they had been asked to pause in the middle of their day for a photographer to document their labour. They stood in lines, bored and impatient to return to the trees—after all, many groves were still paying their workers' wages by the pound at this time. Despite their agricultural skills, the men would not be allowed to buy land to start their own groves. In a few years their immigrant communities would be told that they were no longer welcome in California, and many of them would be driven out of the state. While the Washington navel orange that they harvested had been rechristened to become American, the men who picked the fruit remained foreign. The lives of the people who worked for the citrus industry, who helped build California's wealth, would be excluded from the story of oranges for decades.

And yet these photographs—and the faces that looked out from them—were no longer lost in an archive. Look, their presence said. Look at us in the groves. See what we created.

DECADES BEFORE ORANGES become big business in California, Karl Marx reflects that farming, as an industry under capitalism, threatens agriculture's original sources of wealth: "the soil and the worker."[188] As a capitalist industry grows, profits need to increase while labour stays cheap. In California in the late nineteenth century, cheap labour means a workforce of mostly East Asian immigrants. At the end of the first Opium War between Britain and China in 1842, a wave of people migrate from China, fleeing poverty to take advantage of the high demand for labour in European colonies on nearly every continent.[189] While many leave China willingly, others are taken overseas as part of the "coolie" trade. The US outlaws the importation of enslaved people in 1808, leaving a vacuum of labour in plantations. Consequently, thousands of indentured workers from East and South Asia leave their homelands to work in America in the nineteenth century, when the word "coolie" becomes a derogatory synonym for "Asian." "Coolie" labour builds the US's infrastructure: 90 percent of the workers on the nation's transcontinental railroad—the tracks that millions of oranges will soon rattle down—are Chinese. The remaining 10 percent are Irish.[190] While indentured labourers are traded into abysmal living conditions, free immigrants also arrive from China to take advantage of California's Gold Rush. Most of them come from Guangzhou, a region famous for its fruit and vegetable farming.[191] So, when the gold runs out, agriculture seems a good fit for them, and it's on farms where most Chinese immigrants earn their living.[192]

Orange groves provide seasonal work for Chinese immigrants, who are commended—if not fairly compensated—for their expert picking and packing skills.[193] Despite their role in laying America's foundational infrastructure—literally in the case of railroad workers—anti-Chinese sentiment and violence spreads throughout the US. Although they comprise less than 5 percent of the US's immigrant population in the 1870s, and less than 2 percent in the 1880s, Chinese foreigners are perceived as taking work from white Americans.[194] The number of Chinese orange pickers wanes when Congress passes the Chinese Exclusion Act in 1882, which bans Chinese people from immigrating to the US.

Chinese workers are replaced with Japanese immigrants, who are later replaced with Mexican and Filipino workers. In California's orange groves, a strict racial and class hierarchy is established. Immigrant, indigenous, and poor people do the heavy labour, while a small crop of upper-class white men manage the production lines, own the groves, and grow rich from citrus. To the wealthy white grove owners who build mansions for themselves amongst the orange trees, this racist hierarchy is the correct order of nature. Sunkist's president Charles Collins Teague describes Mexican orange pickers as "naturally adapted for agricultural work," while another grower compares his Filipino workers to "monkeys on these ladders."[195] California's citrus paradise is a paradise of prejudice. White owners wield pseudoscientific language to argue that a hierarchy of race is simply evolution, all while ignoring the poor wages and legal barriers to citizenship that prevent immigrants from buying land for their own groves.

Foreign labour enables California's orange empire to thrive, yet it is all too easy for consumers never to learn who is picking their fruit. The orange industry is wrapped up in branding that conjures a fantasy of whiteness. On crate labels and painted billboards, smiling white women pose with orange crates and fresh fruit in front of flowering groves. On others, white American men wearing straw hats and dungarees stand atop ladders to collect oranges fresh off the trees. One label advertising Chapman's Old Mission Brand oranges shows three friars admiring fruit beside an Orange County grove empty of workers.[196] Gone from these painted advertisements are the labourers and factories, the foreign and indigenous faces and hands that work the groves. Instead, orange growing is conjured as wholesome, pure, and white, a gift from sunny California to the rest of the nation, who are sold a bite of this paradise.

Like Eve's apple and Persephone's pomegranate, California's oranges are as much myth as they are fruit. They tell a story of an Eden at the end of the Wild West, of a paradise of empty land waiting to be cultivated into groves of ripe fruit by a new generation of Anglo-Americans. But that myth holds a multitude of other stories: of indigenous genocide, of forgotten foreign hands, of land reshaped, of orange barons, of capitalism, of manifest destiny. Oranges created California, and California agriculture bolstered the US's industrial growth. Once you start to pull the fruit apart, you start to pull apart a nation's self-mythology.

In an 1846 letter, the US explorer and governor William Gilpin describes his vision for America. "The *untransacted* destiny of the American people is to subdue the continent," he writes, "to rush over this vast field to the Pacific Ocean . . . to establish a new order in human affairs . . . to teach old nations a new civilization—to confirm the destiny of the human race—to carry the career of mankind to its culminating point . . . to perfect science . . . to shed a new and resplendent glory upon mankind."[197]

I wonder if Gilpin would have been proud to know that science was in fact perfected by pomologists in the US. Fruit breeding, in California's and Florida's citrus industries and beyond, becomes about perfecting nature. One of the most famous plant breeders at the turn of the century is a man called Luther Burbank. He sees plants as products of their lineage, and he cross-breeds "parent" species with desirable traits to create perfect hybrid children. Burbank's obsession with selective breeding is not limited to plant life. To him, the US is "the grandest opportunity ever presented of developing the finest race the world has ever known."[198] In his book *The Training of the Human Plant*, Burbank advocates for breeding people like his plants to perfect the species. "During the course of many years of investigation into the plant life of the world, creating new forms, modifying old ones, adapting others to new conditions, and blending still others," he writes, "I have constantly been impressed with the similarity between the organization and development of plant and human life."[199]

Burbank is active in the American eugenics movement, as are several other renowned plant and animal scientists, including the biologist Charles Davenport—who holds contempt for mixed-race "hybridized people"—and the ichthyologist David Starr Jordan—who advocates for the sterilisation of the societal "unfit." By evolving their research in plant or animal breeding into ideologies for perfecting human society, these great men of science give eugenics legitimacy in the public eye. Thirty-two states in the US pass eugenics legislation. From 1909 to 1979, California sterilises twenty thousand people deemed "unfit to produce" without their knowledge or consent, targeting Latinos, Native Americans, and people with disabilities.[200] The eugenics movement is so successful in the US that it is adopted in Nazi Germany as the guiding philosophy of the Third Reich, thanks to the sharing of ideology and methodology between scientists in the two countries.

I don't know whether this legacy was the desired outcome of William Gilpin's dream of manifest destiny. He died in 1894 and didn't live to witness the height of the American eugenics movement. But to me there is an undeniable thread that runs between subduing a continent, perfecting nature, and establishing a new order of humans. Control, curtail, cull.

TWO YEARS BEFORE Eliza Tibbets plants her Washington navel orange trees, a night of violence descends on Southern California. It is a long time coming. By 1871, Los Angeles' Chinese community has grown to 179 people, around 3 percent of the city's population. Sixty-six Chinese immigrants stay on Calle de los Negros (named for the dark-skinned Californios who were its original tenants), the city's first Chinatown.[201] It is cramped and derelict, a small street lined with windowless, one-storey adobes—but it is a refuge in this new land where Chinese immigrants are unwelcome, pelted with rocks and chased by mobs.[202]

As in the orange groves, Chinese people are accused of taking jobs from white people and they are attacked, robbed, killed, and expelled. The historian Beth Lew-Williams suggests that while white Americans were hostile to all non-white races, the Chinese were perceived as "racially incapable of becoming American" because of their assumed loyalty to their homeland. Lew-Williams argues that the anti-Asian attitude was a case of "yellow peril": "While white citizens worried that Native Americans and African Americans would contaminate the nation, they feared the Chinese would conquer it."[203]

First-hand accounts from Chinese immigrants of this time are rare, but decades later, in 1924, the Survey of Race Relations collects memories from those who lived in the American West in the late nineteenth century. "Oh, it was terrible, terrible," one man, Andrew Kan, testifies. "The hoodlums, rough-necks and young boys pull your queue, slap your face, [throw] all kind of old vegetables and rotten eggs at you. All you could do was to run." Another Chinese immigrant, Law Yow, recalls: "I think we gonna get killed. They stand on side, throw rock, club, say God Damn Chinaman."[204]

Then, on a cool October evening in 1871 in Los Angeles, rage and resentment ripen.

The massacre begins at dinnertime. A small police force arrives in Chinatown to contain an escalating shoot-out between two warring Chinese factions. A white police officer is killed when he shoots blindly into a room of Chinese men and one of them shoots back.[205] The police and Chinese gunmen open fire on each other. While the residents of Chinatown panic, unsure whether they should stay or flee, the commotion draws a crowd of over five hundred white and Latino locals, many of them criminals who are eager for a fight.[206] As night comes to Los Angeles, a Chinese man, Ah Wing, attempts to escape the gunfire. He leaves his building and tries to slip unnoticed down the streets, but instead he falls into the hands of the mob, which has swelled to one hundred people. They begin to beat Ah Wing with canes, until two officers take custody of the Chinese man, hurrying him towards the jail. They are followed by shouts of "Hang him!"[207]

A frenzy breaks out in the crowd, and they surge forward, overpowering the policemen and capturing Ah Wing. He is dragged through the streets to a high gateway. A rope is thrown over the beam—fastened in place by a boy—and looped around Ah Wing's neck. He wails as he is lifted. When Ah Wing's neck doesn't break immediately, one of the mob climbs the gate and jumps onto the man's back, shattering his bones and breaking his body.[208]

"The mob was now fairly maddened, and raved for more victims," a first-hand witness will write in the next morning's *New York Times*.

The violence continues as dusk falls on Los Angeles. The streets are dark; only the major thoroughfares are lit with gas lamps. But Calle de los Negros sounds like the gates of hell have opened. The mob arms itself with weapons and years of pent-up hatred towards the Chinese immigrants. "Clean the Chinese out of the city" is yelled. So is "All the Chinamen in the country ought to be hung."[209] They surround Chinatown until they grow impatient waiting for the terrified residents to emerge from their homes. Firebombs are thrown into doorways to burn the people out, until parts of the mob protest against the fire in case it catches and burns down the city. Hoses are used next; first to put out the fires, and then to flush the Chinese residents out of their homes. When neither fire nor water works, the mob storms the buildings.

"Trembling, moaning, and in some instances wounded Chinese were hauled from their hiding-places and forced into the street," the *New York Times* will report. Makeshift gallows are created from a wooden awning and a covered wagon.[210] Chinese men are dragged through the street to be lynched, some dying on their way to be hanged, others strangled slowly by noose. Some are shot and some are stabbed until their blood pools in the street. They are tortured. Chinatown's physician, Dr. Chee Long Tong—also called Gene—speaks fluent English and begs for his life when he is captured. One of the mob shoots him through the mouth with a pistol. While Dr. Tong's housemate, a man called Chang Wan, is being lynched, his murderers lift him to bang his head on the cross-beam. One witness, a teenage boy, says that the men "took a special delight" in their actions, "the blow each time resounding like the breaking of a water-melon."[211]

Children participate in the massacre. So do women. A local landlady cuts down her clothesline to make a rope.[212] The youngest victim is Ah Loo, a fifteen-year-old boy who arrived from China a week earlier. He is lynched. Two cooks are lynched. So is a shopkeeper. Now that the adobes of Chinatown stand empty, looters raid the buildings, stealing an estimated $40,000 in cash, gold, and jewels.[213] The bodies of the dead are also plundered. Dr. Tong is stripped of clothes while he hangs from the beam. Other dead Chinese men are ransacked with such impatient ferocity that the thieves "[lacerate] the flesh" while they cut off pockets with knives.[214] A finger is sliced off a hanging victim for a diamond ring.[215] Long braids of hair are clutched in fists as trophies.

The massacre lasts three hours. By eleven o'clock that night, nineteen Chinese men and boys will be dead, and the mob will have dispersed. The streets will be quiet again. The next morning, eastern newspapers will call the evening's events "one of the most horrible tragedies that ever disgraced any civilized community,"[216] while a local paper will praise the massacre as "a victory of the patriots over the heathens."[217]

The days after the massacre will see Los Angeles' Chinese immigrants rebuild their community, although the feelings of resentment and anger from locals do not dissipate. The hostility will, in fact, worsen and it will spread farther. The Chinese will be chased out of western towns, and lynchings will continue. Another mob will kill twenty-eight Chinese miners in Rock Springs, Wyoming, fourteen years after the LA massacre. Labour unions will promote the boycotting of Chinese businesses, and Chinese-picked fruit and vegetables will go unsold and uneaten.[218] The Chinese will not become American. Instead, they will remain foreign aliens in a country that despises them. In 1882, the US Congress will pass its first anti-immigration law, the Chinese Exclusion Act, to keep them out. Some of them will stay and struggle and survive in a land that does not want to see them thrive upon it. But many will leave California and return to China, cast out of an Eden that reserves its bounty for a privileged few.

This is all coming for the Chinese people who hide from the angry mob on the streets of Los Angeles in 1871. Fearing for their lives, some of Chinatown's residents flee the city, leaving the open roads to seek refuge in the orange and lemon groves which surround LA.[219] It is October and the branches are covered in green fruit. In a few months they will ripen to gold, but right now the trees have nothing to offer the scared, shivering people who hide beneath their branches.

The mob disappears, spent from its bloody frenzy. Silence falls in LA. Its streets are spoiled with blood, gore, and broken bodies. The dead hang. The Chinese who survived the massacre wait. How many of them are dead? Have their homes been destroyed? Will the mob kill them if they return to Chinatown? Perhaps they ask if they can survive this city, this place that seeks to break their bodies and their spirits. Perhaps they promise themselves that they will leave, or perhaps they promise themselves that they will stay to endure this hostile land. Perhaps—

Branches fork away from each other, each offering a different path forward.

I hesitate over the blank page. My role in this narrative is to fill it—with stories, memories, histories. The future must atone for the past, but there is sudden reluctance in my body. It will not comply. The hand which holds the pen refuses to write on.

To exorcise the past is to make choices. How many of the violent details should I include? How much should be glossed over and sanitised? Am I re-creating violence by preserving it on the page? Is this an archive or entertainment? What is the purpose of this remembrance? Is it to say, "Look at what they did to us"? Or is it to say, "Look at what we did to them"?

The dead have been appearing to me in my dreams. Sometimes, they wear the faces of my loved ones. Sometimes they die in the ways I have been reading about in history books. Rope around neck. Flesh over stone. Bone through muscle.

Worse, though, is when they come to me as the mob, with twisted mouths and faces like thunder. Sometimes I am the crowd too, and I feel how hatred fires up the soul. Other times I am pulled into the swarm of bodies by familiar hands.

It is the names of the dead that keep me writing. I read them and the slim details of their lives cut short. Dr. Tong, still young in his thirties, a married man who keeps himself to himself. Ah Loo, a fifteen-year-old boy newly arrived in LA. Tong Won, a musician new in town from San Francisco. Ah Won, a cook. Ah Long, a cigar maker. Leong Quai, who runs the laundry.[220] They are only six of the nineteen who were murdered. It is not enough to only remember. But I think it is better than forgetting.

On the night of the massacre, in the orange grove, the survivors wait. When the sun rises, they will leave the safety of the trees and walk back into the city, where they will begin to sort through the ruins of the dead.

THE WHISTLE OF THE FREEWAY was getting closer. I had returned to Los Angeles from Riverside and was attempting to align my body on the sidewalk with the map rotating on my phone. I passed Plaza de Los Ángeles, California's oldest plaza, where old men sleep on benches and rows of pink and yellow papel picado bunting flutter in the breeze. I followed the sound of rushing cars and found my destination: Southern California's oldest surviving Chinese building, the red-brick Garnier Building. It is also where the Chinatown massacre began in 1871.

I walked the length of the Garnier Building's exterior to the freeway, where lanes of traffic rushed past. This was where nineteen Chinese men and boys were lynched, where LA's Chinatown residents were chased from their homes by a mob, and yet there was nothing on the street to commemorate the dead. In the sun, the passing cars were mirrors, their flashes of white light unbearable to look at for long. I walked back to the Garnier Building. Part of the building is now the Chinese American Museum, which opened in 2003 after a long, hard-won campaign from local historians, educators, and Chinese American community leaders.[221]

I stepped from the sun into the darkness of the museum. Inside, rooms chronicled the story of Chinese immigration in the US. As in the visitors' centre at Citrus State Historic Park in Riverside, the museum's placards began with a place of origin—China—and ended where I stood—in California. Memories were recorded and artefacts were displayed. One room had been transformed into the general store that opened in 1891 to provide Chinatown residents with imported goods like furniture, silk, porcelain, and umbrellas from China. Another wall had been dressed to look like a Chinese herb shop, stocked with tiny bottles, steel jars, and neon yellow boxes of medicinal supplies.

In 1952, what remained of LA's original Chinatown was destroyed to make way for the freeway. Nothing remained to commemorate the history of Chinese immigrants. There was nowhere to visit and remember the beginnings of LA's Chinese community. Instead, the city rushed through its past, concrete hiding a story of suffering and survival that was just one story amongst many of its kind which make up the history of the US.

It is a privilege to forget the past. Sometimes I do, too, until it confronts me when I least expect it.

One morning in LA, I stood on the Metro platform waiting for a train. A man walking along the other side of the tracks was speaking loudly, gesturing wildly while holding his phone up to his face, I thought to live stream his tangent. As he approached, I caught words in his Southern California accent: "Russia," "Ukraine," "Israel," "Korea." When he was directly opposite me, he turned to face where I stood across the tracks. Still looking through his phone, he shouted, "You'll see! When we invade Taiwan!" Then he kept walking down the platform.

I looked around me and the only other person standing on my side of the station was a young woman of East Asian heritage. Through his phone screen, I think he saw empty ciphers to be filled with meaning, instead of people. I wonder now what the man meant by "you." You, Chinese. You, Taiwanese. You, Asian. You, easy targets. You, who are facing me. You, who are not on my side. You, who are different, who are foreign to me. You, who are not me and who are not us.

People of colour are confronted with history every time we step across the threshold to enter the public world. Our bodies are read like books, to be interpreted, judged, and evaluated. The past, and its memories of violence, never goes away, but I think for people whose bodies cannot be so easily seized by the imaginations of others, it is easier to forget this. Spaces of commemoration, like the Chinese American Museum with its rooms that are dressed with the past, push back against the amnesia of a city. Step inside and remember what has been done on this land—which is your land too now—and how it remains in each of us who live upon it.

In 2021, 150 years after it happened, the city's Department of Cultural Affairs announced plans for a public memorial to remember the victims of the 1871 Chinatown massacre. Searching online for the site of the massacre before my trip to California, I had come across the design for the planned memorial, by artist Sze Tsung Nicolás Leong and writer Judy Chui-Hua Chung. Silver trees will be sculpted and placed along the sidewalk outside the Garnier Building, where I would pace up and down unable to find anything that marked the massacre's site.[222] The trees will be shrunken, their branches cut off at their trunks—future growth curtailed too early. They will be gathered close to one another to create a grove of memory. But farther along the street, there will be one fully grown tree. It will stand alone, and its long branches will reach high so that its silver skin can shine in the California sun.

After I left the Chinese American Museum, I stood on the street and imagined what would be there in the years to come. It gave me hope to think about the site of remembrance that would grow in place of this empty concrete. Benches engraved with the names of the dead will be placed so that people can spend time amongst the sculptures. I looked forward to returning one day and sitting under the silver trees.

THE DAY BEFORE I left Los Angeles, I went to the ocean. Keeping the water to the west, I walked from Venice to Santa Monica, along the stretch of sand and the palm trees, past the buskers and the Muscle Beach bros. It was evening by the time I reached the pier, where Route 66 ends. I sat on the cold sand and watched night come to California. The sun set and the sky ripened: pale lemon, grapefruit, blood orange. Above the Pacific Ocean's green waves, a crescent moon surfaced. Down the beach, the Santa Monica Pier's Ferris wheel flashed its neon whirl. The colours were beautiful, and like the other gathered tourists I took insipid photographs of the horizon with my phone. It reminded me of the woman who had sat across the aisle from me on the flight to LA. I had watched her attempt to capture the city at night as our plane descended. She took photograph after photograph. Through the window, the golden lights were so bright it looked like LA was on fire. But on the woman's screen, they were transformed into lifeless white streaks. Still, it didn't hinder her attempts. She didn't stop photographing until the plane had landed and the only view from the oval window was LAX's grey hangars.

I scrolled through my recent messages from family and friends for someone to send my photographs to. Although Ireland, Britain, and Malaysia were all asleep, I sent a photograph anyway, so that they would wake up and see the sunset.

I walked down the beach to the Pacific Ocean to put my feet in. The cold wet sand slid between my toes. If it had been warmer, I would have swum, but standing in the water would do for a January evening. I stood looking west, my body pointing towards Asia, and then I turned east back towards the shore, facing Europe. I knew I could orient myself like this anywhere on earth, but the ocean let me imagine myself standing on a world map, like the blue-and-red one that came with my DNA results. That map had made me feel like a prisoner of geography, split in half as two perfect semicircles, two colours, and two lands. But while maps keep us inside or outside borders, they do not detail life inside their black lines. The complexity of moving through the world cannot be so neatly segmented.

I had come to California to find orange trees, and I had found enough for a lifetime. But in the groves, I had also discovered the intertwining histories of a citrus industry and a nation which grew from roots of supremacy, exclusion, and sorrow. The fruit it offered dangled like fool's gold: beautiful and tempting, empty and worthless.

SEVEN

· · · · · · · · · · ·

KUALA LUMPUR

IN A WEEK IT WOULD BE THE YEAR OF THE RABBIT AND preparations for the celebrations were well under way. Kuala Lumpur was swathed in red. In the airport, malls, and banks, cutouts of glittering Chinese characters and cartoon rabbits clung to the walls. Enormous billboard screens posted Happy New Year wishes from tech and skin care companies. Paper lanterns swayed in the doorways of nearly every business. And everywhere there were oranges. Supermarkets sold them individually wrapped in plastic, in red netting, and in Lunar New Year baskets. Potted bushes with tiny mandarins dangling like baubles decorated doorways, windows, and the lobby of my aunt's building. Inside the apartment, a green pomelo sat beside a bowl of oranges waiting to be distributed for luck in the new year.

Our family had descended on my aunt's apartment to celebrate the new year together. Even though most of my cousins, my brother, and I were all thirty or nearing thirty, we were still segregated from the real adults. At the many extended family dinners we attended over the week leading up to the first day of the new year, we sat at the cramped plastic kids' table of our youth. We received ang pows, red envelopes of small cash, from aunts and uncles. Marriage is the boundary between childhood and adulthood for many Chinese families, and ours was no different. When my recently married cousin threatened to give me a red envelope, I told her not to dare. As we departed each relative's home, aunts and uncles placed oranges into my hand. Many of them had been bought specially for the holiday: each individual fruit was wrapped in plastic that was stamped with red Chinese characters for good luck. Soon there were more oranges than we could eat in the apartment. Ah Ma piled them up in bowls and baskets in different rooms, the bright peel and shiny plastic catching the sun and scattering rainbows on the walls.

During Lunar New Year, oranges are little flames of hope in the winter darkness. One morning, while we walked through a mall, a blaze caught my eye. A wall of glossy oranges, piled one on top of another, waited at a shop front. As I got closer, the fruit became too brilliant, too shiny, too lively. I reached my hand out for an orange. It was formed of a plastic so thin that when I held it up to the fluorescent light, I could see clean through its body. Plastic fruit has become popular in East and Southeast Asia during festivities in lieu of real citrus. Instead of decaying, the artificial peel of a plastic orange holds its hollow centre for eternity.

When it was time to sleep, my cousins, brother, and I searched for floor space to lay our mattresses on, debating over who would get the coveted spot under the whirling ceiling fan. The mattresses are still the same as when we were children, and their patterns—the baby-blue and yellow paisley swirls, the teddy bear and clown characters, the fading pink-and-white gingham—are the colours of my nostalgia. At night, alert yet exhausted from jet lag, I tossed and turned on the soft memory of my childhood.

Everything reminded me of the past. Mandarin blasting from the television because Ah Kong still refused to wear his hearing aids at home, garlic and ginger and smoke sizzling around metal woks, video game music chirping from my youngest cousin's phone, smoke wafting in from the balcony as my father and uncles sneaked cigarettes; to me, these were the sounds, the smells, the sights of being a kid. By the time New Year's Eve arrived, the layers of adulthood I had grown over the previous decade had peeled away, leaving me tender.

Like millions of families, in Malaysia, in China, across the world, we ate a reunion dinner to usher in the Lunar New Year. Three generations crowded around the table. In its centre was the yee sang, a large dish of cold, shredded salad that is arranged by ingredient in segments: pink pomelo, pale beansprouts, white daikon, green onion, ground peanuts. Sliced sausages and fish cakes were set aside to keep the yee sang meat-free for me. Auntie Sian sprinkled a layer of dry crackers over the vegetables, and Ah Ma poured a viscous sauce of hoisin, plum jam, and honey across the top. Then each of us took a pair of chopsticks and on the count of three dug them into the salad and began tossing the pomelo, vegetables, and crackers.

"The higher you go, the more prosperity you get!" my uncle Boon said, and we started throwing the food into the air. When all the ingredients had been thoroughly mixed and everyone was satisfied that they had accumulated enough prosperity for the new year, we sat down to eat.

We ate the yee sang with dishes of noodles, chilli prawns, stir-fried greens, chicken legs, and a whole fish, its eye lolling back towards the ceiling. After the plates were cleared, Auntie Sian produced a jelly coconut cake decorated with silver rabbits and blooming flowers. We washed down our slices with sake and beer and talked into the night. My father, uncle, and aunt get together only a few times a year now and they were reminiscing about old family friends when loud bangs interrupted the conversation. Outside the window, fireworks were lighting up KL's sky. I rushed onto the balcony with my cousins. Over the patch of rainforest near my aunt's apartment, fireworks whizzed skywards, just about reaching the twentieth floor where we stood, and exploded in a shower of pink and red light.

"Do you see where they park their cars?" My aunt appeared beside me. She pointed down to the lane illuminated with streetlights. "They walk from there into the forest and set off fireworks for New Year and Diwali."

All around Kuala Lumpur, fireworks careened across the sky to celebrate the Year of the Rabbit. We watched the light show until well past midnight. When I lay down on my mattress they were still letting them off, and I fell asleep to the echoes of celebration reverberating across the city.

IT IS 1949 and Mao Zedong, chairman of the Chinese Communist Party, stands in Tiananmen Square. He is here to proclaim the liberation of his countrymen. It is the first day in October and Beijing is finally turning cool after a long summer. Mao reads from the piece of paper in his hand and declares that "the Central People's Government of the People's Republic of China was established today." With those words, black ink written on white paper, China's future is set. It is an announcement that brings with it uncertainty and relief after the decades of turmoil and civil war which followed the fall of China's last dynasty. The opposing political party has fled to Taiwan. Some citizens have migrated to neighbouring countries. My grandmother, then twelve years old, has left Longyan and boarded a junk ship with her mother and uncle to begin a new life in British Malaya.

Four days after the foundation of the People's Republic of China is Mid-Autumn Festival. Families gather to light lanterns, eat cakes, and give thanks to the moon for its waxing and waning that bring about the seasons. Each household buys a pomelo, its round globe a harvest moon and its Chinese name, 柚子 (yòuzi), a homophone for "blessing." The fruit's heft signifies good fortune, its circumference a full belly after the next harvest. 1949 is the Year of the Ox. The People's Republic of China is born under an auspicious animal: hard labour will bring rich returns. It is time to get to work to create a new nation.

China has historically been an agricultural society. Up until 1949, it has also been a poor country. Farmland is privately owned, worked by people and oxen, and lacking in the west's technological advancements of tractors and combine harvesters. Mao's vision is to transform this China by introducing socialist agricultural collectivisation, which will feed the nation and eliminate poverty, freeing more workers for steel production. Despite Stalin's similar bid for collectivisation in the Soviet Union that ended in disaster in the 1920s, Mao wants change and he wants it now. The programme of rapid collectivisation, agricultural reform, and focus on steel is called the Great Leap Forward. It will cause the worst famine in human history.[223]

In the decade following the birth of the People's Republic of China, Mao becomes a student of pseudo-botany. He learns from the Soviet Union's best: the agricultural scientist Trofim Denisovich Lysenko, who believes he can make lemons flourish in Siberia's icy winters. Lysenko sees the US's evolving understanding of hereditary genetics—and the rise of eugenics—as evidence of the "degradation of bourgeois culture."[224] Turning his back on modern developments, Lysenko instead proposes his own theory of genetics, a hybrid of Darwinian evolution and Communist ideology. He argues that it is a plant or an animal's environment that decides its nature, and that crops can learn to survive unnatural climates. Even when his agricultural experiments fail—when "educated" wheat seeds refuse to germinate and sugar beet plants rot in the desert—Lysenko ascends the Soviet ranks, imprisoning his critics and detractors, while the government-controlled press heralds his mastery over nature as a success.[225]

Totalitarianism does not stop at controlling a nation's people. Everything must bend to the will of the centre. Mao, like Stalin, sees the natural world as subordinate to and separate from human life. "There is a new war," the chairman declares on the cusp of the Great Leap Forward. "We should open fire on nature."[226] China's land, its forests and its mountains, its plains and its rivers, are to be bent to one man's vision. Mao bases his agricultural policies on Soviet collectivisation. Grain is prioritised over all other crops, and farmers are instructed to practice "close planting" sowing to increase the harvest yield per plot. Perfectly good farmland is ripped up so that crops can be crushed together and, as Lysenko purports, learn to change their nature. As happened in the Soviet Union in 1930, and which caused a three-year-long famine there, the majority of China's crops will fail to germinate.[227]

Private property, including land, is redistributed to the state, and families are organised into communes. Pots, pans, even sewing needles are smelted for steel, so that China's peasants are reliant on commune kitchens to boil water for tea. Houses and temples are torn down for cement to create fertiliser. Burial grounds are flattened into fields of sweet potatoes.[228] In Mao's vision for China, there is no place for frivolous cash crops like fruit, tea, and sugarcane. Orchards and plantations are razed. In Fujian, tea bushes are yanked from the ground and replaced with ill-suited grain fields, while in Gansu, almost half the province's tea-oil trees are felled.[229]

While China's landscape and social order are being remade, the autumn harvest is rotting. The peasant farmers are no longer tending to their fields. Instead, their communes have reallocated labour to smelting in steel factories, constructing irrigation systems, and burning the forest to generate more farmland. Women and the elderly generation are left to bring in the harvest, but there are too few of them, and besides, the scythes and sickles have been melted down for steel.[230] The crops die before they can be collected.

Although a catastrophe is being inscribed into the future, Mao is celebrating. Fabricated reports from local officials arrive and proclaim that the new agricultural policies are a success. The Great Leap Forward is working. China's luck is changing. This will no longer be the land of frequent famine. Food will be abundant in the republic. Mao encourages his countrymen to eat as much as they can, and they are more than happy to oblige. By the winter, the granaries are empty, and the seeds, sown in tight, compact fields, refuse to change their nature to suit Mao's agenda.

As Lunar New Year approaches in 1959, people are starving. There are no homecoming feasts or citrus fruit to see in the Year of the Pig. Instead, grain and livestock quotas are set, so that 40 percent of an expected yield is seized by state officials. The "close planting" policy is such a disaster that in some provinces, like Fujian, 40 percent is almost the entire harvest, leaving nothing behind after the quota is taken.[231] Peasants are accused of hiding food, and party representatives begin searching villages, beating, torturing, and killing people to maintain an illusion of control. Dissidents are removed from society, and over four million people are imprisoned in forced labour camps where most of them will die.[232]

Soon the villages fall silent. There is no birdsong in the morning, no dogs barking in the distance. Even the rats and mice are gone. Bark, blossom, and leaves have been stripped from trees, so that it looks like the land is caught in an infinite winter. No babies have been born for years. At first anyone caught picking wild fruit or herbs is beaten, but soon people are eating the earth. The dead lie where they fall, by the sides of roads and in barren fields. At night, people steal into the darkness with knives to cut flesh from stiff corpses. There is no new harvest to hope for; in desperation, the farmers have dug up the seeds from the earth to eat raw.[233] And in the distance in this wasteland, the furnaces keep belching smoke.

While they still have strength, people attempt to flee. The tens of thousands of refugees who make it to the borders of British-governed Burma and Hong Kong are returned to China; and Taiwan, the US, and Canada refuse to extend their quotas for refugees.[234] The world does not even know that there is a man-made famine in China; the republic will not acknowledge what is happening to its own people. From 1959 to 1961, tens of millions of Chinese people will die from starvation, torture, and forced labour.

Historians date the famine as ending in 1961, but recovering from three years of agricultural disaster, economic mismanagement, and mass starvation takes decades. Rural peasants go without basic food commodities, like oil, meat, and tea, for years.[235] Fresh fruit disappears for decades. A doctor from Guiyang, whose first child was born in 1963, remembers the years after the famine. "My kids never saw any apples or oranges while they were growing up," he tells a researcher. "They only learned about these fruits from their primary school textbooks later on. I often went out to look for some apples or oranges for my kids, but it was impossible to find them. These were the most ordinary fruits."[236]

During the famine, citrus cultivation never stops in China. Production plummets: most groves are destroyed and converted into flat farmland for grain. The agricultural reports for 1959 and 1961 show citrus production halving, but some groves survive.[237] In those years of suffering, scattered around different provinces, oranges and pomelos and tangerines ripen. When they are picked from their trees, they are seized by party officials and exported to China's Communist allies, the Soviet Union, North Korea, and North Vietnam, alongside shipments of pork, poultry, and cotton. The CCP exchanges its resources for the machinery to engineer Mao's Great Leap Forward, while millions of its people starve.[238]

The Great Leap Forward is declared finished in 1962. The commune kitchens are disbanded, food packages arrive from

Taiwan and overseas relatives in Hong Kong, Malaysia, and Singapore, and people begin to piece together what is left of their lives. Gradually harvest seasons return in China. By 1972, citrus production returns to pre-famine levels, and by 1978, rural peasants finally eat as much as they did before the Great Leap Forward.[239]

For twenty years, no one is sure if the famine even happened. Then in the 1980s, American demographers gain access to China's census data after the country begins opening itself to the rest of the world. The records are astounding. The first calculations put the death toll between 16.5 and 23 million. This number later rises to between 23 and 30 million deaths. When Chinese officials speak out after Mao's death, the number of dead increases to 40 million.[240] The true death toll still remains unknown because the Chinese government has never publicly investigated the famine. There has never been an official acknowledgment of the deaths caused by Mao's Great Leap Forward. In the Cultural Revolution, documents about the famine are lost and destroyed. There are no statues or museums, no books or documentaries in the country. There is no official memory of the millions of people who have disappeared. Instead, the nationwide catastrophe of 1959–61 is remembered as the "three years of difficulty" and blamed on natural disasters. The truth of what happened in those years is collaged together by historians from the memories of those who survived and those who are willing to risk breaking the silence.

I have no doubt that if my grandmother had stayed in Longyan, she would have died in the famine. In 1959, she is a twenty-two-year-old woman. In the famine years, young women's food portions are given to their brothers, and, after the old, they are the first to be allowed to die. They toil in fields until they fall down dead, and they are worked to the bone in steel plantations. They are raped and killed when they are left the only survivors of their family. Their menstrual cycles stop and they lose their babies. In 1959 my grandmother is in Malaya, which has just thrown off its British colonisers. She is pregnant with her first child, my father. My story is about to begin, while across the South China Sea millions are ending. The doors of history slide closed, yet the question of *What if?* lingers.

I remember our village in Fujian and the lady, married to my grandfather's uncle, who had the smallest hands I've ever held. I could have wrapped one hand around both of hers. I remember her slender fingers reaching through the dark room to pet the fabric cat. She survived the famine. I wonder how much she lost in those years. I wonder how long it was until she tasted an orange again.

ON THE FIRST DAY of the new year, we did a round of house calls. When we returned to my aunt's apartment that evening, I was full; from the never-ending dishes of delicious food and from a day spent with family and their many well-meaning, if nosy, questions. I emptied my pockets of oranges and ang pows and slumped down on the sofa.

Ah Kong flicked on the television to a blast of CNN. An American newscaster's voice punctured the apartment. In a city in Southern California, a man had walked into a Chinese-owned dance studio and opened fire. The death toll was still being confirmed, but corpses and injured people had been reported. I listened to the news and my body reacted before I could think. My neck tensed. My shoulders hunched. My jaw began to ache. A bitterness flooded my mouth. And then my brain caught up. *Not again*, I thought. I sat on the sofa, every muscle of my body on alert, and listened to the television. The city had a majority Asian American population. The dance studio was popular with older Asian Americans who had been celebrating a New Year count-down before the shooting began. A few blocks over, thousands of people had been celebrating the Year of the Rabbit on the streets. It had taken a few minutes for joy to turn to sorrow. The newscasters moved on to another segment and my uncle, who had been listening with me, stood up. "America," he muttered.

From where I was sitting, I could see into the kitchen. On the counter, a bowl of oranges sat, each fruit wrapped in plastic luck. *Not again* reverberated around my head. And yet, again, violence had happened. It had happened and it happens and it will keep happening. Unstoppable; one boulder after another thundering down a mountain.

Later that night, I lay on my childhood mattress on the floor and scrolled through my phone in the dark. The man who had fired with blind abandon into the dance studio had killed eleven Asian people.[241] The murderer himself was an elderly Asian man, from the same demographic as his victims. He had turned his weapon on himself before he could be captured. I stopped scrolling on a photograph of the man. His face was blurry, caught on CCTV footage. He wore glasses and a tall knitted hat. He looked like any other uncle I would have passed by in an Asian supermarket. What would motivate a person to turn on his own community? How much hate do you have to hold against the world to do something so terrible? How much hate do you have to hold for yourself that it would express itself in such a violent outburst?

From the corners of my eyes, tears rolled over my cheekbones and caught in my hair. I felt so much anger and sorrow for this man and for the world that had created him and allowed him to do this. I don't believe that people are born with an innate desire to hurt and destroy and ruin, but rather it is the weight of our circumstances that cultivates this nature. Each of us inherits the past and we have to choose what to do with it. Some of us ignore it and some of us are motivated by it. Some of us wield the weight of history as a weapon. Others paint it into still lifes, each brushstroke a desire for revelation.

And then, an interruption to my thoughts and tears. Outside the apartment, a bouquet of fireworks was erupting. I wiped my face and left the mattress to walk over to the balcony.

My uncle Boon was sitting at the table, reading on his tablet. "They're still going," he said and kept flicking through the news.

I stepped out onto the balcony and leaned on the railings to watch. Sparks whizzed from the shadows of trees to just reach my eye level. An explosion of green and red and gold rained down into the patch of rainforest below. My uncle and cousin joined me on the balcony.

Fireworks are launched to chase away ghosts and evil spirits. They light up the night skies on Lunar New Year's Eve to celebrate the chance for a fresh start, free from the hauntings of the past year. But it was New Year's Day now. The year had already begun, but perhaps the people setting off the fireworks felt that today needed to be chased away, too.

I feared fireworks as a child. I still dislike them. The sound of explosions reverberating around cities makes me think of war zones. When I see the trails of smoke left behind as they take flight, I am reminded of images of bombings. I want to cower away with the scared cats and dogs. But despite my fear, I can never stop watching them. There is so much beauty that erupts from their violence. Even the small fireworks launched outside my aunt's apartment awed me when they lit up the treetops. I wondered how something so small—something that could fit in a fist—could contain all those colours and sounds and shapes that rippled through the night sky. It is strange to find celebration in explosives, little weapons invented with the intention to cause damage. And yet we gaze and we gape and we cry out in joy, awed by the spectacle. Maybe we light up the night sky because it makes us a crowd, all sharing in the same thrill of the sublime. Maybe we do it so that we feel connected to a vast fleeting feeling, one that makes us a little less lonely.

We watched the fireworks until the last burst of red fell like a bolt from heaven into the haze rising from the trees.

ORANGES RETURNED HOME. Today, California's citrus continues to travel west to China, where the US is one of the country's major citrus suppliers. In stores, white stickers stamped with the Sunkist logo mark the imported fruit as items of luxury for China's rising middle class. But orange production in China is also increasing with each passing year; a 2023 report by the US Department of Agriculture projected that it would exceed seven million metric tonnes of fruit in the following year.[242] In the warm southern provinces of Guangxi, Hunan, Fujian, and Sichuan, citrus hybrids are cultivated to reach fruit bowls throughout China. Foreign varieties, like the navel orange, arrived in the twentieth century, and, generations later, they still flourish.

And yet oranges remain a point of contention. In the geopolitical minefield that is China's military aggression in the South China Sea, citrus has become a pawn. In August 2022, Nancy Pelosi, then speaker of the United States House of Representatives, arrived in Taipei in what was perceived as a show of support for Taiwan, the democratic, self-governing island the CCP claims as a province. Later that day, China banned the importation of Taiwanese citrus fruits, just as the Mid-Autumn Festival approached and Taiwan's farmers were preparing to sell their pomelo harvest to China.[243] It was a move seen as punishment for Pelosi's welcome in Taiwan, as pomelos, oranges, and tangerines joined a list of two thousand other types of food banned from importation to China from Taiwan. Farmers were left with boxes of pomelos that would rot before they could all be sold and eaten. Finally, in 2024, Chinese officials said the citrus ban would be lifted.[244] Yet the island's reliance on the Chinese market has forced Taiwanese growers to diversify their agricultural produce, threatening the abundant pomelo groves that were once their livelihood.

Fruit grown on lands that are the sites of expulsion, occupation, and violence become an embodiment of expulsion, occupation, and violence themselves—as well as possible resistance. When the Palestinian author Ghassan Kanafani was a child, he was removed, along with his family, from Akka by Israeli militia during the 1948 Arab-Israeli War, which saw eight hundred thousand Palestinian people expelled from their homelands.[245] In Kanafani's story "The Land of Sad Oranges," a child reflects on his loss of innocence after his family is expelled from their home, passing Palestinian orange grove after Palestinian orange grove: "You were huddled there, as far from your childhood as you were from the land of the oranges–the oranges which, according to a peasant who used to cultivate them until he left, would shrivel up if a change occurred and they were watered by a strange hand."[246] The child's father weeps at the sight of the "big, clean fruit . . . beloved objects in our eyes," cultivated by generations of Palestinian people who have been severed from their land, their trees, and their livelihoods.

Since the first day of the war in 1948—which Palestinians call the Nakba—oranges, olives, and watermelons have become the embodiment of Palestinian resistance. Since Israel's occupation of the West Bank and Gaza in 1967, settlers have uprooted an estimated eight hundred thousand olive trees, robbing Palestinian growers of their livelihoods and devastating the land.[247] During the Israeli siege on Gaza in the winter of 2023–24, Palestinians were forced to choose between their trees and fuel, culling their decades-old olive, orange, and lemon trees to stay warm while being bombarded by Israeli forces.[248] The watermelon—with its green rind, red flesh, and black seeds, the same colours as the Palestinian flag—became a symbol of resistance. The fruit flooded social media feeds and soared high on flags at protests calling for the US, the UK, and European nations to cease supplying Israel with its armoury of destruction, and for an end to the genocide that has killed tens of thousands of Palestinian people.[249]

The future of the orange is as hazy as its origins. Now, there are too many paths for us to follow. In refrigerated ships and planes, fruit can travel the span of the globe in hours, reaching every continent. Oranges are everywhere. Their existence in supermarkets is a mundane affair. We peel them absent-mindedly at our desks, munching them between meetings. We drop them into our children's lunchboxes, and we forget them as they rot at the bottom of our bags.

But if we run our hands along the supply chains that deliver us our daily oranges, we find that there is a cost to our mundane fruit. Orange picking is a laborious task. In Calabria, Italy's southern region, thousands of migrants from Niger, Gambia, Ghana, and Somalia arrive to work the winter orange harvest. Most of Calabria's orange groves are on Mafia-owned land. Migrants are recruited to pick oranges all day—some earning a euro per crate of fruit—before the Mafia takes a cut of their wages.[250] At night, the pickers stay in cramped and dangerous slum towns, without drinking water or sewage systems. When the orange season finishes, they move north for the tomato, asparagus, and artichoke summer harvests, where the working conditions are no less harsh.[251]

For the Moroccan citrus industry, which specialises in clementines and mandarins, the European Union is its biggest export market. Research, published by Oxfam in 2020, into the Swedish grocery chain Coop and their Moroccan citrus supplier chains found that nearly 50 percent of farm workers received less than minimum wage.[252]

In Brazil, the world's largest orange juice producer, the citrus sector employs hundreds of thousands of workers. The state of São Paulo produces 80 percent of Brazil's oranges, which are picked by approximately fifty thousand workers. Most of that fruit is exported to other countries for juicing.[253] An investigation in 2020 by the nongovernmental organization Public Eye found that the Louis Dreyfus Company (LDC), the third-biggest orange juice producer in the world, had committed nearly two hundred violations of labour law on its Brazilian orange plantations since 2010.[254] One LDC orange picker told journalists that he had worked for eleven months, collecting one hundred boxes of oranges each day in the scorching heat, before quitting because of unsafe conditions.[255]

The modern orange is a commodity that is squeezed through a system of exploitation and profit-making before reaching our fruit bowls at home. How we treat food, the workers who pick it for us, and the land from which it is grown is a disaster. In the UK, an estimated 9.5 million tonnes of food are wasted each year, while 4.7 million of the country's citizens—including 12 percent of the UK's children—live in food poverty.[256] Consumers have been severed from production, and our expectations of what food should even look like—shiny, symmetrical, spotless—have become so warped that supermarkets will dispose of any misshapen fruit, knowing we will reject it. The orange has been reinvented by the romance of marketing and cultivated to be a perfect product: uniform, homogenous, immaculate. Scientists graft the hybrids that will appeal to our pleasure. Commercial groves are sprayed with pesticides and fertilisers that run off the land, polluting rivers, lakes, and oceans. Our seasonless appetite has turned the orange into a globe-trotting, fuel-guzzling tourist that leaves a wake of havoc and suffering behind it. Is the cost worth the convenience of being able to walk into any supermarket anywhere in the world, in the summer or in the winter, and pick up a bundle of oranges? The answer to that question depends on whom you ask: the shopper, the supermarket CEO, or the picker in the grove.

I BEGAN WRITING THIS BOOK while sitting at my parents' kitchen table, the same table where I had eaten five oranges the morning after a white man murdered six Asian women. I traced the fruit's origins to China, which recalled to me my first and only trip to the land of my ancestors: the time in Longyan and the day in our ancestral village all those years ago. I left the kitchen table and went upstairs to hunt out my old sketchbooks from school—I had sorted through them during the first lockdown, when I had lost and rediscovered meaning and creativity and a connection to the world around me. I flicked through the crinkled pages of watercolour paintings and still life drawings and found the photographs from the trip to Longyan. There were the statues from the temple, the hectic streets of Longyan, and the circular building we had visited—a tulou, I remembered. But I couldn't find any photographs of our ancestral village in the sketchbooks of my art project. I couldn't even remember the village's name. I messaged my auntie Suan, asking her what it was called.

She was online and responded immediately.

I found the village on Google Maps. With a finger on my laptop screen, I traced the road from the city of Longyan. It began thick, growing from the roots of the city, before splitting in two and then two again until it became a canopy of lines branching across Fujian. Finally, at the end of a thin grey line, the lane where the dogs had chased our van, my finger arrived at the village. I clicked its name, but no photographs appeared. Street View was not an option; China refuses to allow Google to survey its roads. I couldn't return to the village that way.

But there were photographs. I found the file buried on my father's computer. I opened the folder and began to click through the images. I was surprised by how young my aunts and uncles looked. We posed for the camera outside the tulou and inside the wet market and beside my grandmother's cousin's house in Longyan. Near the end of the file were the photographs from the village. I paused at one of my teenage self: in it, I stood, not looking at the camera but staring at something else beyond the borders of the frame.

As I looked at this person created from pixels and trapped in the past, I felt nothing but affection for her. She was so determined to find meaning in everything. I finished clicking through the images and saved them to my hard drive.

When I was younger, I thought that one day I would find a sense of belonging, like it was an object on a supermarket shelf that I could buy and take home. I thought that being a person was a project of self-actualisation that I could finish one day in the future. I thought that identity was a single story, a narrative in which I would contain my sprawling existence. I thought that inheritance was bequeathed, not chosen, and that the past was a foreign country. I thought a self was something that could be invented, over and over again, torn down and rebuilt again without consequence, for whatever purpose I saw fit. I thought that time was linear, only ever moving away from the stories we call history. And then a bowl of oranges unravelled me.

The morning after a white man murdered six Asian women, I ate five oranges—and then I left the rinds behind. So many of us are taught to crush, to repress, to look away from difficult, complex, painful feelings. In school, history is blinkered, and a nation's complicity in the suffering of entire continents becomes yet another story to be regurgitated in exams, mythologised as glorious, and celebrated as inevitable. I grew up on a continent where the past is severed from the present and preserved behind glass; where the lived experiences of millions of people are denied, contested, and refused. We are told to swallow our feelings and keep moving forward with the promise of a better tomorrow.

The morning after a white man murdered six Asian women, the fragile glasshouse that had once housed my understanding of being in the world finally shattered. The weight of the past crashed into my present. A hostile, bitter wind threatened to wither me. Instead of letting it in, I chose to uproot myself and begin a journey to seek a place where I might thrive. I slipped the orange—a talisman, a compass, an anchor, a map—into my pocket and left.

I had thought that the orange was a single story with a past, a present, and a future; a beginning, a middle, and an ending that I could shape my own life around. I craved narrative satisfaction, and I was sure this fruit, with its point of origin and its journey from east to west, would offer me structure, meaning, discipline. But by tracing the lineage of a foreign fruit and my foreign self, I have discovered how various a story can be as it moves through the world. From east to west and west to east, the orange's meaning has waxed and waned across time. It has, at once, been a creation of nature and of the laboratory, a symbol of Islam and Christianity, a luxury of European kings and Chinese emperors, an artificial commodity, a holy vessel, a ripe metaphor, a simple fruit.

After I left school, I lost my love for drawing. I feared my creations lacked authenticity when compared to the real world. But now I relish the space between representation and imagination, memory and myth, real and unreal, organic and artificial. Perhaps it is there, in the cracks that run amongst singular, fixed positions, where we can cultivate our meanings, rather than forcing ourselves to choose a single story and, by doing so, exile all other possibilities. After all these years I find that I am still preoccupied with still life. In front of a fruit bowl and a blank page, I escape into the act of creation and my sketching hand continues to rescue oranges from the haze.

THEAN HOU TEMPLE sits atop a small peak, overlooking the sprawl of skyscrapers, highways, and condominium blocks that makes up Kuala Lumpur. I went there alone in the first days of the new year. The temple's neat gardens had been decorated with orange trees for the occasion and a few visitors took photographs with the twelve statues of the zodiac animals. Thean Hou Temple was built in the 1980s, in dedication to the sea goddess Mazu. In the temple's garden, I crossed the bridge that led to a statue of the goddess, standing tall and proud in white and pink robes in a small pond. Coins glittered between her toes. By the water's edge and around her skirts, gardeners had left pots of shrubs covered in golden fruit.

By the temple stairs a pair of rabbits held a basket of coins between them. I passed their greedy eyes and ascended the steps, beneath a canopy of hanging red lanterns, each fringed with yellow tassels. I climbed the stairs, which wrapped around the insides of the temple building, until I was back outside, standing high above the garden. In front of me was KL's skyline, its grey and white buildings in shadows as an afternoon storm passed over the city. I turned and approached the stairs to the altar. Sandals, sneakers, and flip-flops were arranged in neat pairs on the steps. I slipped my own sandals off as I climbed up. Stone dragons danced around the white pillars which supported the ornate roof sweeping up towards the sky. More dragons—this time painted matte blues and reds—stood on constant guard on the sharp eaves. Another canopy of red lanterns, all arranged in perfect straight lines, guided visitors to the altar.

At the top of the stairs, enormous pots of burning joss sticks dropped their embers into pillows of ash. Beside them was a long table waiting for offerings. Arranged on it were red plates overflowing with oranges, apples, and Starburst sweets, and porcelain vases holding bouquets of pale lilies and pink chrysanthemums, their stems still stiff despite the humidity. A fat Buddha grinned from the centre of the table. I passed the table and crossed the threshold into the altar room. Footsteps, chatter, and the din of distant traffic died away. Inside, a few people were in silent prayer, either kneeling on pillows or standing with clasped hands. Before us, a statue of Mazu sat gazing ahead. Below her were offerings: green pomelos, pyramids of small oranges, and gourds belted with golden ribbons. Placed beside them were soft rabbits and gift baskets of cosmetics. Overhead, the wooden dougong brackets holding the roof were painted with intricate details: golden dragons flying over fields of emerald greens and seas of midnight blues, free-floating pink lotus flowers, waves buoyed amongst stars.

I stood before Mazu in the midst of silent prayers. I wished I had the conviction of the faithful; the knowledge that if I stepped inside a temple or a church or a mosque, I would be connected to a vastness that existed beyond the limitations of my own self. But those have never been the sites of my devotion. I left the altar room, passed the table of offerings and the burning joss, and took a seat on a stone bench. I closed my eyes, stilled my breathing and listened to the garden beneath the temple. There was the wind rushing through the leaves and the grass. There was the whine of insects buzzing through the flower beds. There was the heat of the sun on the back of my arms as it began its evening descent. I looked down to the temple floor and there, running between the white tiles and past the soles of my sandals, was a line of ants. The scent of the citrus and flower offerings drew them from a crack in the temple wall towards the altar. I wondered how many oranges they would gorge themselves on before they were caught. I watched the trail of ants as the sun set.

After some time had passed, I checked my phone. I would be late to meet my family for dinner. I followed the ants across the temple floor to the table of offerings. From my bag I unearthed the oranges I had taken from the new year's stash that morning. I took one of the red, round dishes and arranged the fruit on it, careful to still them so they wouldn't topple from their perch. I stepped back and watched them for a moment. Then I turned and began to make the journey back down the hill.

EPILOGUE

. . . .

FOLLOW THE SOUND OF RUSHING WATER.

In a valley far away from here lives a grove of trees. It grows for the sun and against the planet's gravitational pull, and it has forgotten where it came from, having first spread its roots in this patch of earth a long time ago. The trees' pale tendrils now run far and deep and their branches are peeling, grey, and brittle, revealing a soft brown core. Wind dashes through their canopies, which convulse and shudder, an evergreen hymn. Something has been forgotten here.

Origins have been lost, but the grove continues to create itself. A buried seed becomes a small green alien head pushing through the earth. New life takes its time and a tree grows inch by inch as the seasons change. Overhead, cirrus clouds drift across the blue expanse, from east to west and back again. They are in the midst of their own journey.

A tree grows until there are two directions it can go. Why should it limit itself to only one way when there is so much light and air to reach? Its trunk splits itself and then splits itself again and again as it spreads and multiplies and twists in new directions. Leaves unfurl, silken and chaste, to greet the light. Possibilities are endless under the earth, too. In the valley, there are no borders yet; no concrete walls, no planted fences, no obstacles to bypass. Beneath a sea of grass, roots are free to roam the darkness. The farther they explore, the more stable the tree becomes, and soon tangled webs of lateral roots move through and around and alongside one another. Above the soil line, the tree stands alone, a solitary obelisk, built from time, light, and inheritance. But hidden away from the light, beneath the earth there is a network that connects the grove as one creature.

The grove has become a world unto itself. Parasites run amok on branches and roots. Teams of ants arrive to collect leaves, and bees set themselves down between petals. Birds make their nests in the folds of branches, and little mammals curl themselves into the bases of trunks. Flowers bloom and fruit falls. A cycle of rot and resurrection rotates with the seasons of the planet.

The grove has settled in the valley, but it is not fixed here. Gales that blow from desert storms and streams that run from mountain glaciers flow through the valley and carry away vessels of flesh. The seeds of the grove leave to enter the world, where they are transformed into a fruit of paradise, of empire, of capital, of meaning. As it travels across new lands, the fruit leaves a wake of groves behind it, and time begins to spiral. History is an infinite ribbon of peel and it keeps unravelling, even after the groves are razed, the gods are dead, the villages are abandoned, and the books are written.

The fruit continues on its journey until the world is circumnavigated and its seeds can return home. The valley is different now—the mountains have moved and the rivers have changed direction—but so, too, are the seeds. They have been cultivated and changed by their dissemination. Fruit is crushed and pips are spat into the dirt. Now, there is an opportunity for an alternative future. A seed can be the successor of its parent tree, follow its genetic coding and continue its species. Or it can surrender to its hybrid nature and create something altogether new.

What happens next is lost to time. Until, one day, a person arrives in the valley. There, they will discover a ripe fruit, hanging alone on a tree. It will be chosen, plucked from its branch, and carried in human hands, out of the valley and into the world. The cycle begins again. There are new myths to be made from its flesh.

Acknowledgments

EARLY VERSIONS OF, and ideas in, *Foreign Fruit* were first published in *Extra Teeth*, *Port*, *Gutter* and *gal-dem*. I am deeply grateful to Heather Parry, Samir Chadha, Malachy Tallack and Suyin Haynes for being my editors on these pieces. Thank you to the Anne Brown Essay Prize for twice-shortlisting essays that would become parts of *Foreign Fruit*.

Thank you to my agent Matt Turner for his faith from the beginning, and to my editors Helena Gonda and Masie Cochran for understanding this book and shaping it with me. I could not have written *Foreign Fruit* without the three of you.

My thanks to Jamie Byng, Claire Reiderman, Lucy Zhou, Caitriona Horne, Leila Cruickshank, Hannah Watson, Stephen Parker, Charlie Tooke, Jess Neale and Phyllis Armstrong, Jo Lord, Sasha Cox, Mel Tombere and everyone at Canongate. Thank you to Ed Wall for copywriting and Jo Dingley for illustrating my words.

My thanks to Win McCormack, Becky Kraemer, Jacqui Reiko Teruya, Beth Steidle, Nanci McCloskey, Dassi Zeidel, Anne Horowitz, Alyssa Ogi, Elizabeth DeMeo and Isabel Lemus Kristensen and everyone at Tin House, as well as Deborah Sun de la Cruz and her colleagues at Penguin Canada, for shepherding this book into the world on the other side of the Atlantic.

My deep thanks to Creative Scotland and the Society of Authors for grants that supported the writing of this book. Thank you to Alan Bett for supporting my writing over the years and for commissioning my first ever printed piece in *The Skinny*.

I am grateful to staff at the University of Edinburgh libraries, the National Library of Scotland and the Huntington for assisting my research. My heartfelt thanks to the researchers, scientists, historians and writers in *Foreign Fruit*'s notes and bibliography for helping me to better understand the world.

Thank you to Dr. Tracy Kahn at the University of California, Riverside for my tour of the Givaudan Citrus Variety Collection and Riverside, and for answering my questions.

For their early guidance, my thanks to Amy Key and Eli Goldstone, and for their collective support, my thanks to my Arvon 2022 essay-writing cohort. Thank you to Paul Maddern for my stay, and the cakes, at The River Mill.

Thank you Amy Key, Jessica Gaitán Johannesson and Angela Hui for reading and lending their support to *Foreign Fruit* when it was in its earliest stages.

I am deeply grateful to the many authors in Scotland who have supported and encouraged me while writing this book. Special thanks to Heather Parry, Andrés N. Ordorica and Malachy Tallack for their assurance and advice all the way through. And thank you to Candice Chung for being my writing partner and literary therapist throughout this project. Thank you to my actual therapists, past and present, and to LGBT Health and Wellbeing.

Thank you to my friends for putting up with me talking about oranges, oranges, oranges for three plus years. Thank you to Rachel Arthur for celebrating with me, in our Scottish kitchen and in a KL bar. Thank you to Deborah Chu for being an early reader and for encouraging me when I needed it most. Special thanks to Riyoko Shibe, Katie Hawthorne, Tara Shields and Rhona Kappler for their support during and beyond this project, and for bringing so much sweetness into my life. Thank you to Jon Place for loving me through it all.

This book is about and for my family. I am deeply grateful to my aunts Sian and Suan for their patience with my questions, for housing me in Malaysia and for sharing my heritage with me. Thank you to my uncle Boon and my cousin Claire in Singapore, and to my sprawling family in Malaysia, Singapore, Ireland and throughout the world. I am very lucky to know you all. Thank you always to my grandparents, my parents and my brothers for loving me, and for encouraging me to read and write and think.

Bibliography

Addison, Joseph, *The Spectator* no. 69, May 19, 1711

Alestig, Mira and Banerji, Sabita, *The Workers Behind the Citrus Fruits: A Focused Human Rights Impact Assessment of Coop Sweden's Moroccan Citrus Fruit Supply Chains* (Cowley, Oxford: Oxfam, April 2022)

Alsadir, Nuar, *Animal Joy* (London: Fitzcarraldo, 2022)

Amer, Ruwaida, 'The Olive Tree, Symbol of Palestine and Mute Victim of Israel's War on Gaza', Al Jazeera, January 22, 2024

Backhouse, Fid, et al., 'plague of Justinian', *Encyclopedia Britannica*

Barthes, Roland, *Mythologies*, trans. Annette Lavers (New York: Farrar, Straus and Giroux, 1991)

Barthes, Roland, 'The World as Object', *Critical Essays*, trans. Richard Howard (Evanston: Northwestern University Press, 1972)

Becker, Jasper, *Hungry Ghosts: China's Secret Famine* (London: John Murray, 1996)

Beckett, Lois and Luscombe, Richard, 'Monterey Park shooting death toll rises to 11, including dance hall manager', *Guardian*, January 24, 2023

Benn, Charles, *Daily Life in Traditional China: The Tang Dynasty* (Westport, Conn.; London: Greenwood Press, 2002)

Benton, Gregor, Gomez, Edmund Terence, *The Chinese in Britain, 1800–present: Economy, Transnationalism, Identity* (Basingstoke: Palgrave Macmillan, 2008)

Blakemore, Erin, 'California's Little-Known Genocide', History, November 16, 2017

Bonynge, Francis, 'The Future Wealth of America: Being a Glance at the Resources of the United States and the Commercial and Agricultural Advantages of Cultivating Tea, Coffee, and Indigo, the Date, Mango, Jack, Leechee, Guava, and Orange Trees, etc; with a Review of the China Trade' (New York, 1852)

Borinskaya, Svetlana A., Ermolaev, Andrei I., and Kolchinsky, Eduard I., 'Lysen-koism against Genetics: The Meeting of the Lenin All-Union Academy of Agricultural Sciences of August 1948, Its Background, Causes, and After-math', *Genetics* 212, no. 1 (May 2019)

Bowman, Kim D. and Gmitter Jr, Frederick G., 'Forbidden Fruit (*Citrus* Sp., Rutaceae) Rediscovered in Saint Lucia', *Economic Botany* 44, no. 2 (April–June, 1990)

Bown, Stephen R., *Scurvy: How a Surgeon, a Mariner and a Gentleman Solved the Greatest Medical Mystery of the Age of Sail* (Chichester, West Sussex: Summersdale, 2003)

Brain, Stephen, 'The Great Stalin Plan for the Transformation of Nature', *Environmental History* 15, no. 4 (2010)

Broberg, Gunnar, 'The Dragonslayer', *TijdSchrift voor Skandinavistiek* 29, no. 1 & 2 (2008)

Broberg, Gunnar, *The Man Who Organized Nature: The Life of Linnaeus*, trans. Anna Paterson (Princeton: Princeton University Press, 2023)

Bulley, Victoria Adukwei, 'Interview with Saidiya Hartman', *The White Review* No. 26, September 2019

Burbank, Luther, *The Training of the Human Plant* (New York: The Century Co., 1909)

Burge, Daniel J., *A Failed Vision of Empire: The Collapse of Manifest Destiny 1845–1872* (Lincoln: University of Nebraska Press, 2022)

Bryson, Norman, *Looking at the Overlooked: Four Essays on Still Life Painting* (London: Reaktion Books, 1990)

Camões, Luís De, *The Lusiad; Or, The Discovery of India*, 5th ed., trans. William Julius Mickle (London: George Bell and Sons, 1889)

Cantor, Norman F., *In the Wake of the Plague: The Black Death and the World It Made* (London: Pocket Books, 2002)

Carbó, Adrià Budry, 'Bitter Oranges: The Reality That the Industry Does Not Want You to See', Public Eye, June 2020

Casid, Jill, *Sowing Empire: Landscape and Colonization* (Minneapolis; London: University of Minnesota Press, 2005)

Chalutz, Edo and Roessler, Yorum, 'Israel', in *Fresh Citrus Fruits*, ed. Wilfred F. Wardowski, Steven Nagy and William Grierson (London: Macmillan, 1986)

Chan, Sucheng, *This Bittersweet Soil: The Chinese in California Agriculture 1860–1910* (Berkeley: University of California Press, 1986)

Chang, Hsiung-feng, Lu Chia-jung, and Lee Hsin-Yin, 'China to Lift Ban on Taiwan Fish, Citrus Fruit: Chinese Official', Focus Taiwan, April 28, 2024

Chen, Hauiyu, 'Religion and Society on the Silk Road: The inscriptional Evidence from Turfan' in *Early Medieval China: A Sourcebook* edited by Wendy Swartz, Robert Ford Campany, Yang Lu and Jessey J. C. Choo (New York: Columbia University Press, 2014)

Christian, David, 'Silk Roads or Steppe Roads? The Silk Roads in World History', *Journal of World History* 11, no. 1 (spring 2000)

Collingham, Lizzie, *The Hungry Empire: How Britain's Quest for Food Shaped the Modern World* (London: Vintage, 2018)

Collins, David, *An Account of the English Colony in New South Wales* (London: T. Cadell Jr and W. Davies, 1798)

Cooper, Lina Orman, 'Oranges: "The Poor Man's Fruit"', *The Girl's Own Paper* 18, Christmas issue (December, 1897)

Crook, Frederick, *Agricultural Statistics of the People's Republic of China 1949–86* (Washington, DC: Agricultural and Trade Analysis Division, Economic Research Service, US Department of Agriculture, April 1988)

Curtis, Mark, 'Britain's Forgotten War for Rubber', *Declassified UK*, September 13, 2022

Davies, Frederick S., Albrigo, L. Gene, *Citrus* (Wallingford: CAB International, 1994)

De Waal, Edmund, *The White Road: A Pilgrimage of Sorts* (London: Chatto & Windus, 2015)

Deleuze, Gilles and Guattari, Félix, *A Thousand Plateaus: Capitalism and Schizophrenia*, trans. Brian Massumi (London: Continuum, 1988)

Didion, Joan, *Slouching Towards Bethlehem* (New York: Farrar, Straus and Giroux, 1968)

Dikötter, Frank, *Mao's Great Famine: The History of China's Most Devastating Catastrophe, 1958–62* (London: Bloomsbury, 2010)

Dikötter, Frank, 'The Disappeared', *Foreign Policy*, no. 198 (2013)

Doherty, Jack, *Porcelain* (London: A&C Black Publishers, 2002)

Dols, Michael Walters, *The Black Death in the Middle East* (Princeton: Princeton University Press, 1977)

Drayton, Richard, *Nature's Government: Science, Imperial Britain, and the 'Improvement' of the World* (New Haven: Yale University Press, 2000)

Eldridge, Ellen, 'Police: Suspect Charged in Massage Parlor Deaths Planned to Kill More,' Georgia Public Broadcasting, March 17, 2021

Farge, Emma, et al., 'Gaza Death Toll: How Many Palestinians Has Israel's Campaign Killed', Reuters, July 10, 2024

Foucault, Michel, *The Order of Things: An Archaeology of the Human Sciences* (London: Tavistock Publications, 1971; London: Routledge, 2005)

Francis-Devine, Brigid, Danechi, Shadi, and Malik, Xameerah, 'Food Poverty: Households, Food Banks and Free School Meals', report no. 9209 (House of Commons Library, August 24, 2023)

Freedberg, David, Baldini, Enrico, Continella, Giovanni, *Citrus Fruit* (London: Harvey Miller, 1997)

Freedman, Paul, *Out of the East: Spices and the Medieval Imagination* (New Haven: Yale University Press, 2008)

Frykberg, Mel, 'Environmental Terrorism Cripples Palestinian Farmers,' IPS, April 6, 2015

Fuller, Dorian Q., et al., 'Charred Pummelo Peel, Historical Linguistics and Other Tree Crops: Approaches to Framing the Historical Context of Early *Citrus* Cultivation in East, South and Southeast Asia', in *AGRUMED: Archaeology and History of Citrus Fruit in the Mediterranean*, ed. Véronique Zech-Matterne and Girolamo Fiorentino (Naples: Publications du Centre Jean Bérard, 2017)

Gabriel, Sharmani Patricia, 'Postcolonialising Heritage and the Idea of "Malaysia"', in *Making Heritage in Malaysia: Sites, Histories, Identities*, ed. Sharmani Patricia Gabriel (Singapore: Springer Singapore, 2020)

Gandhi, Lakshmi, 'A History of Indentured Labor Gives "Coolie" Its Sting', *Code Switch*, NPR, November 25, 2013

Garey, Thomas A., *Orange Culture in California* (San Francisco: Pacific Rural Press, 1882)

Gaskell, Elizabeth, *Cranford* (London: Chapman and Hall, 1853; London: Collector's Library, 2008)

Geisseler, Daniel and Horwath, William R., *Citrus Production in California* (University of California, Davis, June 2016)

Gmitter Jr, Frederick and Hu, Xulan, 'The Possible Role of Yunnan, China, in the Origin of Contemporary *Citrus* Species (Rutaceae),' *Economic Botany* 44, no. 2 (April–June 1990)

Goody, Jack, *The Culture of Flowers* (Cambridge: Cambridge University Press, 1993)

Gonzalez, Gilbert G., *Labor and Community: Mexican Citrus Worker Villages in a Southern California County, 1900–1950* (Champaign: University of Illinois Press, 1994)

Grad, Shelby, 'The Racist Massacre That Killed 10% of L.A.'s Chinese Population and Brought Shame to the City', *Los Angeles Times*, March 18, 2021

Grootenboer, Hanneke, *The Pensive Image: Art as a Form of Thinking* (Chicago : The University of Chicago Press, 2021)

Hale, Erin, 'The Farmers Caught Up in Taiwan's Tensions with China', BBC News, October 5, 2022

Hansen, Valerie, *The Silk Road: A New History* (Oxford, England; New York, N.Y.: Oxford University Press, 2012)

Harper, T.N., *The End of Empire and the Making of Malaya* (Cambridge: Cambridge University Press, 1998)

Hartman, Saidiya, *Lose Your Mother: A Journey Along the Atlantic Slave Route* (London: Serpent's Tail, 2021)

Hepper, F. Nigel, *Royal Botanic Gardens Kew: Gardens for Science & Pleasure* (London: H.M.S.O., 1982)

Heussler, Robert, *British Rule in Malaya: The Malayan Civil Service and Its Predecessors, 1867–1942* (Oxford: Clio Press, 1981)

Hochstrasser, Julie Berger, *Still Life and Trade in the Dutch Golden Age* (New Haven: Yale University Press, 2007)

Hochstrasser, Julie Berger, 'The Conquest of Spice and the Dutch Colonial Imaginary: Seen and Unseen in the Visual Culture of Trade', in *Colonial Botany: Science, Commerce, and Politics in the Early Modern World*, ed. Londa Schiebinger and Claudia Swan (Philadelphia: University of Pennsylvania, 2005)

Hong, Cathy Park, *Minor Feelings: A Reckoning on Race and the Asian Condition* (London: Profile, 2021)

Hornung, Tabea C. and Biesalski, Hans-Konrad, 'Glut-1 explains the evolutionary advantage of the loss of endogenous vitamin C-synthesis: The electron transfer hypothesis', *Evolution, Medicine, and Public Health* 2019, no. 1 (August 2019)

Hobhouse, Penelope, Taylor, Patrick, The Gardens of Europe (London: G. Philip, 1990)

Hu, Zhaoling, 'China', in *Fresh Citrus Fruits*, ed. Wilfred F. Wardowski, Steven Nagy and William Grierson (London: Macmillan, 1986)

Huang, Josie, 'Here's the Winning Design for LA's Memorial to the 1871 Chinese Massacre', *LAist*, May 4, 2023

Hyde, Elizabeth, *Cultivated Power: Flowers, Culture, and Politics in the Reign of Louis XIV* (Philadelphia: University of Pennsylvania Press, 2005)

Hyman, Clarissa, *Oranges: A Global History* (London: Reaktion Books, 2013)

Jenkins, Benjamin T., *California's Citrus Heritage* (Charleston, South Carolina: Arcadia, 2021)

Jindia, Shilpa, 'Belly of the Beast: California's Dark History of Forced Sterilizations', *Guardian*, June 30, 2020

Jones, Tobias and Awokoya, Ayo, 'Are Your Tinned Tomatoes Picked by Slave Labour?', *Guardian*, June 20, 2019

Joy, Mark S., *American Expansion, 1783–1860: A Manifest Destiny?* (London: Taylor & Francis, 2003)

Kanafani, Ghassan, *Men in the Sun and Other Palestinian Stories*, trans. Hilary Kilpatrick (Boulder, Colorado: Lynne Rienner Publishers, 1999)

Kenyon-Flatt, Brittany, 'How Scientific Taxonomy Constructed the Myth of Race', *Sapiens*, March 19, 2021

Khaldûn, Ibn, *The Muqaddimah: An Introduction to History*, trans. Franz Rosenthal (Princeton: Princeton University Press, 1967)

Khansari, Mehdi, Moghtader, M. Reza and Yavari, Minouch, *The Persian Garden: Echoes of Paradise* (Washington, DC: Mage Publishers, 1998)

Klein, Shana, *The Fruits of Empire: Art, Food, and the Politics of Race in the Age of American Expansionism* (Oakland, California: University of California Press, 2020)

Kumamoto, J., et al., 'Mystery of the Forbidden Fruit: Historical Epilogue on the Origin of the Grapefruit, *Citrus paradisi* (Rutaceae)', *Economic Botany* 41, no. 1 (January–March 1987)

La Force, Thessaly, 'The European Obsession with Porcelain', *New Yorker*, November 11, 2015

Lamb, Jonathan, *Scurvy: The Disease of Discovery* (Oxford: Princeton University Press, 2017)

Laszlo, Pierre, *Citrus: A History* (Chicago: University of Chicago, 2007)

Lew-Williams, Beth, *The Chinese Must Go: Violence, Exclusion, and the Making of the Alien in America* (Cambridge: Harvard University Press, 2018)

Lewis, Mark Edward, *China's Cosmopolitan Empire: The Tang Dynasty* (Cambridge, Massachusetts: Harvard University Press, 2009)

Lind, James, *A Treatise of the Scurvy: In Three Parts, Containing an Inquiry into the Nature, Causes, and Cure, of That Disease: Together with a Critical and Chronological View of What Has Been Published on the Subject*, 2nd ed. (London: A. Millar, 1757)

Liu, May, *China: Citrus Annual*, report no. CH2023-0192 (Foreign Agricultural Service, United States Department of Agriculture, December 27, 2023)

Liu, Xinru, *The Silk Road in World History* (Oxford: Oxford University Press, 2010)

Lo, Kevin, 'The World's Oldest Botanical Gardens', Atlas Obscura, October 15, 2014

Locke, John, *Two Treatises of Government* (1689), ed. Peter Laslett Cambridge: Cambridge University Press, 1988)

Mabberley, D.J., 'A Classification for Edible *Citrus* (Rutaceae)', *Telopea: Journal of Plant Systematics* 7, no. 2 (July 1997)

Mac Sweeney, Naoíse, *The West: A New History of an Old Idea* (London: WH Allen, 2023)

MacNeice, Louis, 'Snow', *The Collected Poems of Louis MacNeice* (Oxford: Oxford University Press, 1967)

Marx, Karl, *Capital: A Critique of Political Economy*, trans. Ben Fowkes, vol. 1 (Harmondsworth, England: Penguin Books in association with New Left Review, 1976)

Masters, Nathan, 'A Brief History of Palm Trees in Southern California', PBS SoCal, December 7, 2011

McClung, William Alexander, *Landscapes of Desire: Anglo Mythologies of Los Angeles* (Berkeley: University of California Press, 2000)

McCracken, Donal P., *Gardens of Empire: Botanical Institutions of the Victorian British Empire* (London: Leicester University Press, 1997)

McPhee, John, *Oranges* (London: Daunt, 2016)

Meng, Xin, Qian, Nancy, Yared, Pierre, *The institutional causes of China's great famine, 1959–61* (London: Centre for Economic Policy Research, 2010)

Morton, A.G., *History of Botanical Science: An Account of the Development of Botany from Ancient Times to the Present Day* (London: Academic Press, 1981)

Nanji, Azim and Niyozov, Sarfaroz, 'The Silk Road: Crossroads and Encounters of Faiths', Smithsonian Institution

Naphy, William and Spicer, Andrew, *The Black Death: A History of Plagues 1345–1730* (Stroud, Gloucestershire: Tempus, 2001)

Nylan, Michael, *The Five 'Confucian' Classics* (New Haven: Yale University Press, 2001)

Oddone, Elisa, 'Exploited, Hated, Killed: The Lives of African Fruit Pickers', Al Jazeera, July 22, 2018

Pearson, Andrew and Jeffs, Ben, 'Lemon Valley, St Helena: An East India Company and British Colonial Landscape in the South Atlantic', *Post-Medieval Archaeology* 57, no. 1 (January 2023)

Pollack, Susan L., Lin, Biing-Hwan, and Allshouse, Jane, *Characteristics of U.S. Orange Consumption*, Electronic Outlook Report from the Economic Research Service (United States Department of Agriculture, August 2003)

Porter, Eduardo, 'In Florida Groves, Cheap Labor Means Machines', *New York Times*, March 22, 2004

Price, Catherine, 'The Age of Scurvy', *Science History Institute*, August 14 2017

Purcell, Victor, *Malaysia* (London: Thames and Hudson, 1965)

Rasmussen, Cecilia, 'A Forgotten Hero from a Night of Disgrace', *Los Angeles Times*, May 16, 1999

Regalado, Antonio, 'More Than 26 Million People Have Taken an At-Home Ancestry Test', *MIT Technology Review*, February 11, 2019

Reitz, Herman J. and Embleton, Tom W., 'Production Practices That Influence Fresh Fruit Quality', in *Fresh Citrus Fruits*, ed. Wilfred F. Wardowski, Steven Nagy and William Grierson (London: Macmillan, 1986)

Ricklefs, M.C., *A History of Modern Indonesia since c.1300*, 2nd ed. (London: Macmillan, 1993)

Rogers, Ford, *Citrus: A Cookbook* (London: Greenwich Editions, 1997)

Rude, Emelyn, 'The Surprising Link Between World War II and Frozen Orange Juice', *Time*, August 31, 2017

Sackman, Douglas C., '"Nature's Workshop": The Work Environment and Workers' Bodies in California's Citrus Industry, 1900–1940', *Environmental History* 5, no. 1 (January 2000)

Sackman, Douglas Cazaux, *Orange Empire: California and the Fruits of Eden* (Berkeley: University of California Press, 2005)

Sandoval-Velasco, Marcela, et al., 'The Ancestry and Geographical Origins of St Helena's Liberated Africans', *American Journal of Human Genetics* 110, no. 9 (September 2023)

Schafer, Edward H., *The Golden Peaches of Samarkand: A Study of T'ang Exotics* (Berkeley: University of California Press, 1963)

Schama, Simon, *Landscape and Memory* (London: Fontana, 1996)

Schama, Simon, *The Embarrassment of Riches: An Interpretation of Dutch Culture in the Golden Age* (Berkeley: University of California Press, 1988)

Schneider, Norbert, *Still Life: Still Life Painting in the Early Modern Period*, translated by Hugh Beyer (Köln: B. Taschen, 1994)

Scora, R.W., et al., 'Contribution to the Origin of the Grapefruit, *Citrus paradisi* (Rutaceae)', *Systematic Botany* 7, no. 2 (April–June 1982)

Scora, Rainer W., 'On the History and Origin of Citrus', *Bulletin of the Torrey Botanical Club* 102, no. 6 (1975)

Shapiro, Emily, 'Georgia sheriff's department under fire after official says spa shootings suspect had "really bad day",' ABC News, March 19, 2021

Sheehan, Dan, 'A Brief Remembrance of Ghassan Kanafani', Literary Hub, April 8, 2024

Siddique, Haroon, 'St Helena Urged to Return Remains of 325 Formerly Enslaved People to Africa', *Guardian*, March 27, 2024,

Simard, Suzanne W., 'Mycorrhizal Networks Facilitate Tree Communication, Learning, and Memory', in *Memory and Learning in Plants*, ed. Frantisek Baluska, Monica Gagliano, and Guenther Witzany (Cham, Switzerland: Springer, 2018)

Sinn, Elizabeth, *Pacific Crossing: California Gold, Chinese Migration, and the Making of Hong Kong* (Hong Kong : Hong Kong University Press; 2013)

Slive, Seymour, 'Realism and Symbolism in Seventeenth-Century Dutch Painting', *Daedalus* 91, no. 3 (summer 1962): 484

Smith, Henry Nash, *Virgin Land: The American West as Symbol and Myth* (Cambridge: Harvard University Press, 1995)

Smith, Nigel J.H., et al., *Tropical Forests and Their Crops* (Ithaca: Cornell University Press, 1992)

Solnit, Rebecca, *Orwell's Roses* (London: Granta, 2021)

Sontag, Susan, *Illness as Metaphor and AIDS and Its Metaphors* (New York: Picador, 1977, 1978)

Sörlin, Sverker, 'Ordering the World for Europe: Science as Intelligence and Information as Seen from the Northern Periphery', in 'Nature and Empire: Science and the Colonial Enterprise', ed. Roy MacLeod, *Osiris* 15 (2000)

Soule, James and Grierson, William, 'Anatomy and Physiology', in *Fresh Citrus Fruits*, ed. Wilfred F. Wardowski, Steven Nagy and William Grierson (London: Macmillan, 1986)

Soule, James and Grierson, William, 'Maturity and Grade Standards', in *Fresh Citrus Fruits*, ed. Wilfred F. Wardowski, Steven Nagy and William Grierson (London: Macmillan, 1986)

Smil, Vaclav, 'China's Great Famine: 40 Years Later', *BMJ* 319, no. 7225 (December 1999)

Spengler III, Robert N., *Fruit from the Sands: The Silk Road Origins of the Foods We Eat* (Oakland: University of California Press, 2019)

Spiegel-Roy, Pinhas and Goldschmidt, Eliezer E., *Biology of Citrus* (Cambridge: Cambridge University Press, 1996)

Spyrou, Maria A., et al., 'The source of the Black Death in fourteenth-century central Eurasia', *Nature* 606 (June 2022)

Steinbeck, John, *The Grapes of Wrath* (New York: Viking, 1939; London: Penguin, 2017)

Steinhardt, Nancy Shatzman, *Chinese Architecture: A History* (Princeton: Princeton University Press, 2019)

Sterling, Charles, *Still Life Painting: From Antiquity to the Twentieth Century*, second revised edition (New York: Harper & Row, 1981)

Quay, James, 'Beyond Dreams and Disappointments: Defining California through Culture', *A Companion to California History*, eds. William Deverell and David Igler (Chichester, West Sussex: John Wiley & Sons, 2014)

Tan, Vincent, 'Malaysia's Indigenous Tribes Fight for Ancestral Land and Rights in a Modern World,' Channel News Asia, September 2, 2019

Thomas, Keith, *Man and the Natural World: Changing Attitudes in England 1500–1800* (London: Penguin, 1984)

Tobey, Ronald and Wetherell, Charles, 'The Citrus Industry and the Revolution of Corporate Capitalism in Southern California, 1887–1944', *California History* 74, no. 1 (April 1995)

Tolkowsky, Samuel, *Hesperides: A History of the Culture and Use of Citrus Fruits* (London: John Bale Sons, 1938)

Turnbull, C. Mary, *A History of Malaysia, Singapore, and Brunei*, rev. ed. (London: Allen & Unwin, 1989)

Vaid-Menon, Alok, 'Interview with Ocean Vuong', *The White Review* issue no. 32, 2022

Van Neel, Annina, 'Scraping Away Generations of Forgetting: My Fight to Honour the Africans Buried on St Helena', *Guardian*, March 27, 2024

Wallace, Kelly, 'Forgotten Los Angeles History: The Chinese Massacre of 1871', Los Angeles Public Library, May 19, 2017

Waltham, Clae, *Shu Ching: Book of History; A Modernized Edition of the Translations of James Legge* (London: George Allen & Unwin, 1972)

Walvin, James, *Fruits of Empire: Exotic Produce and British Taste, 1660-1800* (Basingstoke: Macmillan, 1997)

Wearn, James A. and Mabberley, David J., 'Citrus and Orangeries in Northern Europe', *Curtis's Botanical Magazine* 33, no. 1 (February 2016)

Weebers, Robert C.M. and Idris, Hanizah, 'Decisions Made on the Development of the Hill Station of Cameron Highlands from 1884 till Present Day', *Journal of Surveying, Construction and Property* 7, no. 1 (June 2016)

Wei, Clarissa, 'China's Massive Earthen Fortresses Once Housed Up to 800 People', *National Geographic*, January 10, 2018

Wemyss, Georgie, *The Invisible Empire: White Discourse, Tolerance and Belonging* (London: Routledge, 2016)

Whitfield, Susan, *Life Along the Silk Road*, rev. ed. (London: John Murray, 2004)

Wills, Clair, *Lovers and Strangers: An Immigrant History of Post-war Britain* (UK: Penguin Books, 2018)

Wood, Michael, *The Story of China* (New York: St Martin's Press, 2020)

Wright, Juwayriah, 'The Solemn History behind Nakba Day', *Time*, May 15, 2024

Wrobel, David M., *Promised Lands: Promotion, Memory, and the Creation of the American West* (Lawrence: University Press of Kansas, 2002)

Wu, Guohong Albert, et al., 'Genomics of the origin and evolution of *Citrus*', *Nature* 554, 311–316 (2018)

Xun, Zhou, *Forgotten Voices of Mao's Great Famine, 1958–1962: An Oral History* (New Haven: Yale University Press, 2013)

Xun, Zhou, *The Great Famine in China, 1958–1962: A Documentary History*, ed. Zhou Xun (New Haven: Yale University Press, 2012)

Yam, Kimmy, 'L.A. groups commemorate 1871 massacre that killed 10% of city's Chinese community', NBC News, October 22, 2021

Yang, Dali L., *Calamity and Reform in China: State, Rural Society, and Institutional Change Since the Great Leap Famine* (Redwood City, California: Stanford University Press, 1996)

Yang, Jisheng, *Tombstone: The Untold Story of Mao's Great Famine* (London: Penguin, 2013)

Yanagihara, Hanya, 'The Silk Road's Enduring Romance, and Eternal Influence', *The New York Times Style Magazine*, May 2020

Young, Roger H., 'Fresh Fruit Cultivars', in *Fresh Citrus Fruits*, ed. Wilfred F. Wardowski, Steven Nagy and William Grierson (London: Macmillan, 1986)

Yu, Jessica Zhan Mei, 'All the Stain is Tender: The Asian Delude and White Australia', *The White Review* issue no. 30, 2021

Zaragoza, Salvador and Hensz, Richard A., 'Spain', in *Fresh Citrus Fruits*, ed. Wilfred F. Wardowski, Steven Nagy and William Grierson (London: Macmillan, 1986)

Zesch, Scott, *The Chinatown War: Chinese Los Angeles and the Massacre of 1871* (Oxford: Oxford University Press, 2021)

Notes

1   Lina Orman Cooper, "Oranges: 'The Poor Man's Fruit,'" *The Girl's Own Paper* 18, Christmas issue (December 1897): 54–55, https://www.victorian-voices.net/ARTICLES/GOP/1897/1897-Oranges.pdf.

2   Elizabeth Gaskell, *Cranford* (London: Chapman and Hall, 1853; London: Collector's Library, 2008), 63.

3   Ellen Eldridge, "Police: Suspect Charged in Massage Parlor Deaths Planned to Kill More," Georgia Public Broadcasting, March 17, 2021, https://www.gpb.org/news/2021/03/17/police-suspect-charged-in-massage-parlor-deaths-planned-kill-more.

4   Emily Shapiro, "Georgia Sheriff's Department under Fire after Official Says Spa Shootings Suspect Had 'Really Bad Day,'" ABC News; March 19, 2021, https://abcnews.go.com/US/georgia-sheriffs-department-fire-official-spa-shootings-suspect/story?id=76533598.

5   Shapiro, "Georgia Sheriff's Department under Fire."

6   Data on the percentage change in reported hate crimes/incidents against East Asian and Southeast Asian people by police jurisdiction in the UK between 2019 and 2020 has been compiled by the ESEA Data Collective in a 2022 study. It can be found at "Quant Research," Voice ESEA, accessed June 20, 2024, www.voiceesea.com/quant-research.

7   *Northern Ireland Census 2001 Key Statistics Report* (Belfast: Northern Ireland Statistics and Research Agency, December 19, 2002), https://www.nisra.gov.uk/sites/nisra.gov.uk/files/publications/2001-census-results-key-statistics-report-press-release.pdf.

8   D. J. Mabberley, "A Classification for Edible *Citrus* (Rutaceae)," *Telopea: Journal of Plant Systematics* 7, no. 2 (July 1997): 167–72, http://dx.doi.org/10.7751/telopea19971007.

9   Guohong Albert Wu, Javier Terol, et al., "Genomics of the origin and evolution of *Citrus*," *Nature* 554, 311–16 (2018), https://doi.org/10.1038/nature25447.

10 Romans 11:17 (New Revised Standard Version).

11 Eduardo Porter, "In Florida Groves, Cheap Labor Means Machines," *New York Times*, March 22, 2004, https://www.nytimes.com/2004/03/22/business/in-florida-groves-cheap-labor-means-machines.html.

12 Herman J. Reitz and Tom W. Embleton, "Production Practices That Influence Fresh Fruit Quality," in *Fresh Citrus Fruits*, ed. Wilfred F. Wardowski, Steven Nagy, and William Grierson (London: Macmillan, 1986), 52.

13 "Fruit Consumption by Type, World, 1961 to 2021," Our World in Data, with data from the Food and Agriculture Organization of the United Nations, March 14, 2024, www.ourworldindata.org/grapher/fruit-consumption-by-fruit-type.

14 Pierre Laszlo, *Citrus: A History* (Chicago: University of Chicago, 2007), 119.

15 Dorian Q. Fuller et al., "Charred Pummelo Peel, Historical Linguistics and Other Tree Crops: Approaches to Framing the Historical Context of Early *Citrus* Cultivation in East, South and Southeast Asia," in AGRUMED: *Archaeology and History of Citrus Fruit in the Mediterranean*, ed. Véronique Zech-Matterne and Girolamo Fiorentino (Naples: Publications du Centre Jean Bérard, 2017), https://doi.org/10.4000/books.pcjb.2173.

16 John McPhee, *Oranges* (London: Daunt, 2016), 62–63.

17 Nigel J. H. Smith et al., *Tropical Forests and Their Crops* (Ithaca: Cornell University Press, 1992), 97.

18 Laszlo, *Citrus*, 135.

19 James A. Wearn and David J. Mabberley, "Citrus and Orangeries in Northern Europe," *Curtis's Botanical Magazine* 33, no. 1 (February 2016): 999, https://www.jstor.org/stable/48505679.

20 McPhee, *Oranges*, 58; Cooper, "Oranges: 'The Poor Man's Fruit,'" 54.

21 Laszlo, *Citrus*, 133.

22 David Collins, "An Account of the English Colony in New South Wales" (London, T. Cadell Jr. and W. Davies, 1798), https://gutenberg.net.au/ebooks/e00010.html.

23 "Slavery in the Caribbean," National Museums Liverpool, 2024, https://www.liverpoolmuseums.org.uk/archaeologyofslavery/slavery-caribbean.

24 Clarissa Hyman, *Oranges: A Global History* (London: Reaktion Books, 2013), 73.

25 John Steinbeck, *The Grapes of Wrath* (New York: Viking, 1939; London: Penguin, 2017), 533. Citations refer to the Penguin edition.

26 Louis MacNeice, "Snow," *The Collected Poems of Louis MacNeice* (Oxford: Oxford University Press, 1967), 30.

27 Wu and Terol et al., "Genomics of the origin and evolution of *Citrus*," https://doi.org/10.1038/nature25447.

28 Frederick Gmitter Jr. and Xulan Hu, "The Possible Role of Yunnan, China, in the Origin of Contemporary *Citrus* Species (Rutaceae)," *Economic Botany* 44, no. 2 (April–June 1990): 267–77, JSTOR, http://www.jstor.org/stable/4255233.

29 Hyman, *Oranges*, 8–9.

30 Michael Nylan, *The Five "Confucian" Classics* (New Haven: Yale University Press, 2001), 134.

31 Clae Waltham, *Shu Ching: Book of History; A Modernized Edition of the Translations of James Legge* (London: George Allen & Unwin, 1972), 45–46.

32 Hyman, *Oranges*, 8–9.

33 Hyman, *Oranges*, 8–9.

34 Giovanni Baptista Ferrari, *Hesperides, sive de Malorum Aureorum Cultura et Usu Libri Quatuor* (1646), quoted in Hyman, *Oranges*, 85.

35 "Fujian *Tulou*," UNESCO *World Heritage Convention,* https://whc.unesco.org/en/list/1113.

36 Clarissa Wei, "China's Massive Earthen Fortresses Once Housed Up to 800 People," *National Geographic*, January 10, 2018, https://www.nationalgeographic.com/travel/article/fujian-tulou-unesco-world-heritage-site.

37 Laszlo, *Citrus*, 23–24; "Algerian clementine *Citrus clementina hort. ex Tanaka* CRC 279," Givaudan Citrus Variety Collection, University of California, Riverside, accessed September 3 2024, https://citrusvariety.ucr.edu/crc0279.

38 Saidiya Hartman, *Lose Your Mother: A Journey along the Atlantic Slave Route* (London: Serpent's Tail, 2021), 98.

39 Mark Edward Lewis, *China's Cosmopolitan Empire: The Tang Dynasty* (Cambridge: Harvard University Press, 2009), 97.

40 Susan Whitfield, *Life along the Silk Road*, rev. ed. (London: John Murray, 2004), 51.

41 Lewis, *China's Cosmopolitan Past*, 137; Edward H. Schafer, *The Golden Peaches of Samarkand: A Study of T'ang Exotics* (Berkeley: University of California Press, 1963), 40.

42 Xinru Liu, *The Silk Road in World History*, (Oxford: Oxford University Press, 2010), 12.

43 David Christian, "Silk Roads or Steppe Roads? The Silk Roads in World History," *Journal of World History* 11, no. 1 (spring 2000): 3, https://dx.doi.org/10.1353/jwh.2000.0004.

44 Robert N. Spengler III, *Fruit from the Sands: The Silk Road Origins of the Foods We Eat* (Oakland: University of California Press, 2019), 5–6.

45 Schafer, *The Golden Peaches of Samarkand*, 20.

46 Azim Nanji and Sarfaroz Niyozov, "The Silk Road: Crossroads and Encounters of Faiths," Smithsonian Institution, https://festival.si.edu/2002/the-silk-road/the-silk-road-crossroads-and-encounters-of-faith/smithsonian. Published in conjunction with the 2002 Folklife Festival, *The Silk Road: Connecting Cultures, Creating Trust*.

47 Spengler, *Fruit from the Sands*, 248.

48 Susan Sontag, *Illness as Metaphor and AIDS and Its Metaphors* (New York: Picador, 1977, 1978), 3.

49 Gilles Deleuze and Félix Guattari, *A Thousand Plateaus: Capitalism and Schizophrenia*, trans. Brian Massumi (London: Continuum, 1988), 24.

50 Salvador Zaragoza and Richard A. Hensz, "Spain," in *Fresh Citrus Fruits*, 153–54.

51 Pinhas Spiegel-Roy and Eliezer E. Goldschmidt, *Biology of Citrus* (Cambridge: Cambridge University Press, 1996), 7.

52 Zaragoza and Hensz, "Spain," in *Fresh Citrus Fruit*, 153–54.

53 Hyman, *Oranges*, 11.

54 The Qur'an 6:100, trans. M. A. S. Abdel Haleem (Oxford: Oxford University Press, 2004), 87.

55 McPhee, *Oranges*, 60.

56 Hyman, *Oranges*, 78.

57   Zaragoza and Hensz, "Spain," in *Fresh Citrus Fruit*, 153–54.

58   Fid Backhouse and others, "plague of Justinian," *Encyclopedia Britannica*, March 1, 2024. https://www.britannica.com/event/plague-of-Justinian.

59   Michael Walters Dols, *The Black Death in the Middle East*, (Princeton: Princeton University Press, 1977), 18.

60   Maria A. Spyrou et al., "The Source of the Black Death in Fourteenth-Century Central Eurasia," *Nature* 606 (June 2022): 718–24, https://doi.org/10.1038/s41586-022-04800-3.

61   Primary sources quoted in Dols, *The Black Death in the Middle East*, 75.

62   Michael Wood, *The Story of China* (New York: St. Martin's Press, 2020), 259.

63   Dols, *The Black Death in the Middle East*, 40.

64   Wood, *The Story of China*, 260.

65   William Naphy and Andrew Spicer, *The Black Death: A History of Plagues 1345–1730* (Stroud, Gloucestershire: Tempus, 2001), 53.

66   McPhee, *Oranges*, 71.

67   Norman F. Cantor, *In the Wake of the Plague: The Black Death and the World It Made* (London: Pocket Books, 2002), 7; William Naphy and Andrew Spicer, *The Black Death: A History of Plagues 1345–1730* (Stroud, Gloucestershire: Tempus, 2001) 31–32.

68   Ibn Khaldûn, *The Muqaddimah: An Introduction to History*, trans. Franz Rosenthal (Princeton: Princeton University Press, 1967), 83.

69   Dols, *The Black Death in the Middle East*, 58–59.

70   Deleuze and Guattari, *A Thousand Plateaus*, 20.

71   Deleuze and Guattari, *A Thousand Plateaus*, 7, 10.

72   Deleuze and Guattari, *A Thousand Plateaus*, 16.

73   M. C. Ricklefs, *A History of Modern Indonesia since c.1300*, 2nd ed. (London: Macmillan, 1993), 20–21.

74   Julie Berger Hochstrasser, "The Conquest of Spice and the Dutch Colonial Imaginary: Seen and Unseen in the Visual Culture of Trade," in *Colonial Botany: Science, Commerce, and Politics in the Early Modern World*, ed. Londa Schiebinger and Claudia Swan (Philadelphia: University of Pennsylvania, 2005), 175.

75   Denis Diderot, "Voyage en Hollande," *Supplement aux Oeuvres de Diderot* (Paris, A Belin, 1818), quoted in Julie Berger Hochstrasser, *Still Life and Trade in the Dutch Golden Age* (New Haven: Yale University Press, 2007), 16.

76   Karl Marx, *Capital: A Critique of Political Economy*, trans. Ben Fowkes, vol. 1 (Harmondsworth, England: Penguin Books in association with New Left Review, 1976), 918.

77   Roland Barthes, "The World as Object," *Critical Essays*, trans. Richard Howard (Evanston: Northwestern University Press, 1972), 5.

78   Johann Wolfgang von Goethe, quoted in Norman Bryson, *Looking at the Overlooked: Four Essays on Still Life Painting* (London: Reaktion Books, 1990), 124–5.

79   "Still Lifes," Rijksmuseum," accessed June 20, 2024, https://www.rijksmuseum.nl/en/rijksstudio/works-of-art/still-lifes.

80   Jack Doherty, *Porcelain* (London: A&C Black Publishers, 2002), 9.

81   Thessaly La Force, "The European Obsession with Porcelain," *New Yorker*, November 11, 2015, https://www.newyorker.com/books/page-turner/the-european-obsession-with-porcelain.

82   La Force, "The European Obsession with Porcelain."

83   Letter quoted in Hochstrasser, *Still Life and Trade in the Dutch Golden Age*, 136.

84   Augustus II the Strong quoted in Edmund de Waal, *The White Road: A Pilgrimage of Sorts* (London: Chatto & Windus, 2015), 151.

85   "The Twenty Views of the European Palaces of the Yuanming Yuan," Victoria and Albert Museum, June 25 2009, https://collections.vam.ac.uk/item/O398684/the-twenty-views-of-the-print-yi-lantai; Nancy Shatzman Steinhardt, *Chinese Architecture: A History* (Princeton: Princeton University Press, 2019).

86   Seymour Slive, "Realism and Symbolism in Seventeenth-Century Dutch Painting," *Daedalus* 91, no. 3 (summer 1962): 484, http://www.jstor.org/stable/20026724.

87   The arts and culture industry contributes £10.8 billion a year to the UK economy. Centre for Economics and Business Research, *Contribution of the Arts and Culture Industry to the UK Economy*, April 17, 2019, https://www.artscouncil.org.uk/research-and-data/contribution-arts-and-culture-industry-uk-economy.

88   Roland Barthes, *Mythologies*, trans. Annette Lavers (New York: Farrar, Straus and Giroux, 1991), 143.

89   Stephen Bann, *The True Vine: On Visual Representation and the Western Tradition* (Cambridge: Cambridge University Press, 1989), 66–101, discussed in Bryson, *Looking at the Overlooked*, 79–80.

90   *Genesis* 1:29 and 2:8 (New Revised Standard Version).

91   Mehdi Khansari, M. Reza Moghtader, and Minouch Yavari, *The Persian Garden: Echoes of Paradise* (Washington, DC: Mage Publishers, 1998), 29–31.

92   *Genesis* 3:17 and 3:19 (New Revised Standard Version).

93   Paul Freedman, *Out of the East: Spices and the Medieval Imagination* (New Haven: Yale University Press, 2008), 88–89.

94   Kevin Lo, "The World's Oldest Botanical Gardens," Atlas Obscura, October 15, 2014, www.atlasobscura.com/articles/world-s-oldest-botanical-gardens.

95   P. Stephens and W. Browne, *Catalogus Horti Botanici Oxoniensis* (Oxford, 1658), quoted in Richard Drayton, *Nature's Government: Science, Imperial Britain, and the "Improvement" of the World* (New Haven: Yale University Press, 2000), 9.

96   Wearn and Mabberley, "Citrus and Orangeries in Northern Europe," 98.

97   A. G. Morton, *History of Botanical Science: An Account of the Development of Botany from Ancient Times to the Present Day* (London: Academic Press, 1981), 119.

98   Suzanne W. Simard, "Mycorrhizal Networks Facilitate Tree Communication, Learning, and Memory," in *Memory and Learning in Plants*, ed. Frantisek Baluska, Monica Gagliano, and Guenther Witzany (Cham, Switzerland: Springer, 2018), 191–213, https://doi.org/10.1007/978-3-319-75596-0_10.

99 Wearn and Mabberley, "Citrus and Orangeries in Northern Europe," 99.

100 Michel Foucault, *The Order of Things: An Archaeology of the Human Sciences* (London: Tavistock Publications, 1971; London: Routledge, 2005), 143. Citation refers to the Routledge edition.

101 *La culture des fleurs* (Bourge-en-Bresse: Joseph Ravoux, 1692), quoted in Elizabeth Hyde, *Cultivated Power: Flowers, Culture, and Politics in the Reign of Louis XIV* (Philadelphia: University of Pennsylvania Press, 2005), 43.

102 Olivier de Serres, *Théâtre d'Agriculture et Mésnage des Champs* (Vol II) (Paris 1805) 402–3, as quoted in Samuel Tolkowsky, *Hesperides: A History of the Culture and Use of Citrus Fruits* (London: John Bale Sons, 1938), 203.

103 Hyde, *Cultivated Power*, 171.

104 Hyde, *Cultivated Power*, 148.

105 Sverker Sörlin, "Ordering the World for Europe: Science as Intelligence and Information as Seen from the Northern Periphery," in "Nature and Empire: Science and the Colonial Enterprise," ed. Roy MacLeod, *Osiris* 15 (2000), 57, https://www.jstor.org/stable/301940.

106 Gunnar Broberg, "The Dragonslayer," *TijdSchrift voor Skandinavistiek* 29, no. 1 & 2 (2008): 36, https://ugp.rug.nl/tvs/article/view/10739/8310.

107 Linn Soc., Linnaeus pat. Introductions, no date. Trans. from Latin, as quoted in Gunnar Broberg, *The Man Who Organized Nature: The Life of Linnaeus*, trans. Anna Paterson (Princeton: Princeton University Press, 2023) 343.

108 Gunnar Broberg, *The Man Who Organized Nature: The Life of Linnaeus*, trans. Anna Paterson (Princeton: Princeton University Press, 2023) 343.

109 Sörlin, "Ordering the World for Europe," 69.

110 Brittany Kenyon-Flatt, "How Scientific Taxonomy Constructed the Myth of Race," *Sapiens*, March 19, 2021, https://www.sapiens.org/biology/race-scientific-taxonomy/.www.sapiens.org/biology/race-scientific-taxonomy/. Accessed 10 July 2024.

111 Drayton, *Nature's Government*, 16, 72.

112 Drayton, *Nature's Government*, 108.

113 John Locke, *Two Treatises of Government* (1689), ed. Peter Laslett (Cambridge: Cambridge University Press, 1988), 291–92

114 Magazine Monitor, "Christingle: The Christmas tradition that only got going in the 1960s," December 14 2014, accessed September 3 2024, https://www.bbc.co.uk/news/blogs-magazine-monitor-30186196.

115 Rebecca Solnit, *Orwell's Roses* (London: Granta, 2021), 144.

116 Drayton, *Nature's Government*, 73.

117 Joseph Addison, *The Spectator* no. 69, May 19, 1711, https://www.gutenberg.org/files/9334/9334-h/9334-h.htm#section69.

118 McPhee, *Oranges*, 71–72.

119 C. Mary Turnbull, *A History of Malaysia, Singapore, and Brunei*, rev. ed. (London: Allen & Unwin, 1989), 124–25.

120   Turnbull, *A History of Malaysia, Singapore, and Brunei*, 88–89.

121   Turnbull, *A History of Malaysia, Singapore, and Brunei*, 172.

122   Lord Milverton, HL Deb. (27 Feb. 1952) (175), cols. 333, quoted in Curtis, "Britain's Forgotten War for Rubber," September 13, 2022, Declassified UK, www.declassifieduk.org/britains-forgotten-war-for-rubber.

123   T. N. Harper, *The End of Empire and the Making of Malaya* (Cambridge: Cambridge University Press, 1998), 270.

124   Robert Heussler, *British Rule in Malaya: The Malayan Civil Service and Its Predecessors, 1867–1942* (Oxford: Clio Press, 1981), 144.

125   Sharmani Patricia Gabriel, "Postcolonialising Heritage and the Idea of 'Malaysia,'" in *Making Heritage in Malaysia: Sites, Histories, Identities*, ed. Sharmani Patricia Gabriel (Singapore: Springer Singapore, 2020), 14.

126   Hans Sloane, *A Voyage to the Islands of Madera, Barbados, Nieves, St. Christophers, and Jamaica* (London: British Museum, 1707), quoted in J. Kumamoto et al., "Mystery of the Forbidden Fruit: Historical Epilogue on the Origin of the Grapefruit, *Citrus paradisi* (Rutaceae)," *Economic Botany* 41, no. 1 (January–March 1987): 100, http://www.jstor.org/stable/4254944.

127   Hans Sloane, *A Voyage to the Islands*, quoted in R. W. Scora et al., "Contribution to the Origin of the Grapefruit, *Citrus paradisi* (Rutaceae)," *Systematic Botany* 7, no. 2 (April–June 1982): 170, https://doi.org/10.2307/2418325.

128   Kumamoto et al., "Mystery of the Forbidden Fruit," 98–105.

129   Kumamoto et al., "Mystery of the Forbidden Fruit," 100–102.

130   Kumamoto et al., "Mystery of the Forbidden Fruit," 100.

131   Kim D. Bowman and Frederick G. Gmitter Jr., "Forbidden Fruit (*Citrus* Sp., Rutaceae) Rediscovered in Saint Lucia," *Economic Botany* 44, no. 2 (April–June 1990): 170, http://www.jstor.org/stable/4255226.

132   Stephen R. Bown, *Scurvy: How a Surgeon, a Mariner, and a Gentleman Solved the Greatest Medical Mystery of the Age of Sail* (Chichester, West Sussex: Summersdale, 2003), 45.

133   Luís De Camões, *The Lusiad: Or, The Discovery of India*, 5th ed., trans. William Julius Mickle (London: George Bell and Sons,1889), 158.

134   Bown, *Scurvy*, 9.

135   James Lind, *A Treatise of the Scurvy: In Three Parts, Containing an Inquiry into the Nature, Causes, and Cure, of That Disease: Together with a Critical and Chronological View of What Has Been Published on the Subject*, 2nd ed. (London: A. Millar, 1757), v.

136   Catherine Price, "The Age of Scurvy," *Science History Institute*, August 14 2017, https://www.sciencehistory.org/stories/magazine/the-age-of-scurvy.

137   Bown, *Scurvy*, 49.

138   Tabea C. Hornung and Hans-Konrad Biesalski, "Glut-1 Explains the Evolutionary Advantage of the Loss of Endogenous Vitamin C-Synthesis: The Electron Transfer Hypothesis," *Evolution, Medicine, and Public Health* 2019, no. 1 (August 2019): 221–31, https://doi.org/10.1093/emph/eoz024.

139 Bown, *Scurvy*, 53; Laszlo, *Citrus*, 84.

140 Bown, *Scurvy*, 91.

141 Ford Rogers, *Citrus: A Cookbook* (London: Greenwich Editions, 1997), 11.

142 McPhee, *Oranges*, 72.

143 S. R. Dickman, "The Search for the Specific Factor in Scurvy," *Perspectives in Biology and Medicine*, Volume 24, 1981, 382-95, as quoted in Bown, *Scurvy*, 255.

144 Dutch sailor quoted in Andrew Pearson and Ben Jeffs, "Lemon Valley, St. Helena: An East India Company and British Colonial Landscape in the South Atlantic," *Post-Medieval Archaeology* 57, no. 1 (January 2023): 61. https://doi.org/10.1080/00794236.2022.2156835.

145 Pearson and Jeffs, "Lemon Valley," 60.

146 "Slavery," StHelenaIsland.Info, accessed July 10, 2024, https://sthelenaisland.info/slavery/.

147 Pearson and Jeffs, "Lemon Valley," 61.

148 Marcela Sandoval-Velasco et al., "The Ancestry and Geographical Origins of St. Helena's Liberated Africans," *American Journal of Human Genetics* 110, no. 9 (September 2023): 1590-99, https://www.ncbi.nlm.nih.gov/pmc/articles/PMC10502851/pdf/main.pdf.

149 Annina van Neel, "Scraping Away Generations of Forgetting: My Fight to Honour the Africans Buried on St. Helena," *Guardian*, March 27, 2024, www.theguardian.com/world/2024/mar/27/scraping-away-generations-of-forgetting-my-fight-to-honour-the-africans-buried-on-st-helena.

150 Haroon Siddique, "St. Helena Urged to Return Remains of 325 Formerly Enslaved People to Africa," *Guardian*, March 27, 2024, https://www.theguardian.com/world/2024/mar/27/st-helena-urged-to-return-remains-of-325-formerly-enslaved-people-to-africa.

151 "The People," StHelenaIsland.Info, accessed July 10, 2024, https://sthelenaisland.info/the-people/.

152 Robert C. M. Weebers and Hanizah Idris, "Decisions Made on the Development of the Hill Station of Cameron Highlands from 1884 till Present Day," *Journal of Surveying, Construction and Property* 7, no. 1 (June 2016): 2, https://doi.org/10.22452/jscp.vol7no1.1.

153 Vincent Tan, "Malaysia's Indigenous Tribes Fight for Ancestral Land and Rights in a Modern World," Channel News Asia, September 2, 2019, https://www.channelnewsasia.com/asia/malaysia-orang-asli-ancestral-land-rights-1317616.

154 "Our History," BOH Tea, accessed July 10, 2024, https://bohtea.com/about/our-history/.

155 Antonio Regalado, "More Than 26 Million People Have Taken an At-Home Ancestry Test," *MIT Technology Review*, February 11, 2019, https://www.technologyreview.com/2019/02/11/103446/more-than-26-million-people-have-taken-an-at-home-ancestry-test/.

156 "Heritage Travel on the Rise: Airbnb and 23andMe Team Up to Make It Even Easier," Airbbnb Newsroom, accessed July 11, 2024, https://news.airbnb.com/heritage-travel-on-the-rise/.

157 Nathan Masters, "A Brief History of Palm Trees in Southern California," PBS SoCal, December 7, 2011, https://www.pbssocal.org/shows/lost-la/a-brief-history-of-palm-trees-in-southern-california.

158 Douglas Cazaux Sackman, *Orange Empire: California and the Fruits of Eden* (Berkeley: University of California Press, 2005), 18.

159 James Quay, "Beyond Dreams and Disappointments: Defining California through Culture," *A Companion to California History*, eds. William Deverell and David Igler (Chichester, West Sussex: John Wiley & Sons, 2014), 6.

160 Mark S. Joy, *American Expansionism, 1783–1860: A Manifest Destiny?* (London: Taylor & Francis, 2003), 79.

161 Erin Blakemore, "California's Little-Known Genocide," History, November 16, 2017, https://www.history.com/news/californias-little-known-genocide.

162 *Democratic Review* (1856) quoted in Daniel J. Burge, *A Failed Vision of Empire: The Collapse of Manifest Destiny 1845–1872* (Lincoln: University of Nebraska Press, 2022), ii.

163 Gilbert G. Gonzalez, *Labor and Community: Mexican Citrus Worker Villages in a Southern California County, 1900–1950* (Champaign: University of Illinois Press, 1994), 6.

164 Thomas A. Garey, *Orange Culture in California* (San Francisco: Pacific Rural Press, 1882), 7–8.

165 It is disputed whether William Saunders sent two or three saplings to Eliza Tibbets. I have gone with three as described in "Parent Washington Navel Orange (CRC 1241B)," Givaudan Citrus Variety Collection, University of California, Riverside, accessed July 12, 2024, https://citrusvariety.ucr.edu/crc1241B.

166 Sackman, *Orange Empire*, 22.

167 Sackman, *Orange Empire*, 40.

168 Sackman, *Orange Empire*, 67.

169 "Parent Washington Navel Orange (CRC 1241B)," Givaudan Citrus Variety Collection.

170 Sackman, *Orange Empire*, 32–33.

171 Sackman, *Orange Empire*, 32–33.

172 Sackman, *Orange Empire*, 147.

173 F. C. Mills, "The Orange Industry of Central California" (typescript, Commission of Immigration and Housing, Simon J. Lubin Papers, Bancroft Library, University of California-Berkeley, 1914), quoted in Douglas C. Sackman, "'Nature's Workshop': The Work Environment and Workers' Bodies in California's Citrus Industry, 1900–1940," *Environmental History* 5, no. 1 (January 2000): 42, https://doi.org/10.2307/3985534.

174 Daniel Geisseler and William R. Horwath, *Citrus Production in California* (University of California, Davis, June 2016), 1, https://apps1.cdfa.ca.gov/FertilizerResearch/docs/Citrus_Production_CA.pdf.

175 Ronald Tobey and Charles Wetherell, "The Citrus Industry and the Revolution of Corporate Capitalism in Southern California, 1887–1944," *California History* 74, no. 1 (April 1995): 8, https://doi.org/10.2307/25177466.

176 "History and Scope," Givaudan Citrus Variety Collection, https://citrusvariety.ucr.edu/about/history-and-scope.

177 Sackman, *Orange Empire*, 54.

178 Steinbeck, *The Grapes of Wrath*, 529, 531.

179 Joan Didion, *Slouching Towards Bethlehem* (New York: Farrar, Straus and Giroux, 1968), 221.

180 "Research," Givaudan Citrus Variety Collection, https://citrusvariety.ucr.edu/research.

181 Sackman, *Orange Empire*, 262.

182 Steinbeck, *The Grapes of Wrath*, 533.

183 Emelyn Rude, "The Surprising Link Between World War II and Frozen Orange Juice," *Time*, August 31, 2017, https://time.com/4922457/wwii-orange-juice-history/.

184 Geisseler and Horwath, *Citrus Production in California*, 2.

185 Benjamin T. Jenkins, *California's Citrus Heritage*, Images of America (Charleston, South Carolina: Arcadia, 2021), 117.

186 Susan L. Pollack, Biing-Hwan Lin, and Jane Allshouse, *Characteristics of U.S. Orange Consumption*, Electronic Outlook Report from the Economic Research Service (United States Department of Agriculture, August 2003), 2, https://www.ers.usda.gov/webdocs/outlooks/37012/50262_fts30501.pdf.

187 "California Woman Sues OJ Giant Tropicana Over Flavor Packs" ABC News, December 14, 2011, https://abcnews.go.com/Health/california-woman-sues-pepsicos-tropicana-alleging-deceptive-advertising/story?id=15394357.

188 Marx, *Capital*, 638.

189 Sucheng Chan, *This Bittersweet Soil: The Chinese in California Agriculture 1860–1910* (Berkeley: University of California Press, 1986), 16.

190 Lakshmi Gandhi, "A History of Indentured Labor Gives 'Coolie' Its Sting," *Code Switch*, NPR, November 25, 2013, https://www.npr.org/sections/codeswitch/2013/11/25/247166284/a-history-of-indentured-labor-gives-coolie-its-sting.

191 Scott Zesch, *The Chinatown War: Chinese Los Angeles and the Massacre of 1871* (Oxford: Oxford University Press, 2021), 6.

192 Chan, *This Bittersweet Soil*, 1.

193 Sackman, *Orange Empire*, 137.

194 Chan, *This Bittersweet Soil*, 42.

195 Sackman, *Orange Empire*, 128–29.

196 Jenkins, *California's Citrus Heritage*, 86.

197 William Gilpin (1846), *Mission of the North American People, Geographical, Social, and Political* (Philadelphia, 1874), 130 (quoting a letter from 1846), quoted in Henry Nash Smith, *Virgin Land: The American West as Symbol and Myth* (Cambridge: Harvard University Press, 1995), 37.

198 Luther Burbank, *The Training of the Human Plant* (New York: The Century Co., 1909), 5.

199 Burbank, *The Training of the Human Plant*, 3.

200 Shilpa Jindia, "Belly of the Beast: California's Dark History of Forced Sterilizations," *Guardian*, June 30, 2020, https://www.theguardian.com/us-news/2020/jun/30/california-prisons-forced-sterilizations-belly-beast.

201 Kelly Wallace, "Forgotten Los Angeles History: The Chinese Massacre of 1871," Los Angeles Public Library, May 19, 2017, https://www.lapl.org/collections-resources/blogs/lapl/chinese-massacre-1871.

202 Beth Lew-Williams, *The Chinese Must Go: Violence, Exclusion, and the Making of the Alien in America* (Cambridge: Harvard University Press, 2018), 17.

203 Lew-Williams, *The Chinese Must Go*, 6.

204 Andrew Kan, interview by C. H. Burnett, August 22, 1924, box 27, no. 178, Survey of Race Relations, Hoover Institution Library and Archives, Stanford University; Law Yow, interview by C. H. Burnett, August 12, 1924, box 27, no. 191, Survey of Race Relations, Hoover Institution Library and Archives, Stanford University quoted in Lew-Williams, *The Chinese Must Go*, 19.

205 Zesch, *The Chinatown War*, 127.

206 Kimmy Yam, "L.A. groups commemorate 1871 massacre that killed 10% of city's Chinese community," NBC News, October 22 2021, https://www.nbcnews.com/news/asian-america/l-groups-commemorate-1871-massacre-killed-10-citys-chinese-community-rcna3617.

207 "The Los Angeles Massacre, Particulars of the Wholesale Lynching of Chinamen—An Eyewitness' Account," *New York Times*, November 10, 1871, https://timesmachine.nytimes.com/timesmachine/1871/11/10/79002807.pdf.

208 Zesch, *The Chinatown War*, 132.

209 Zesch, *The Chinatown War*, 133.

210 Cecilia Rasmussen, "A Forgotten Hero from a Night of Disgrace," *Los Angeles Times*, May 16, 1999, https://www.latimes.com/archives/la-xpm-1999-may-16-me-37851-story.html.

211 Joseph Mesmer quoted in Zesch, *The Chinatown War*, 140–41.

212 Zesch, *The Chinatown War*, 143.

213 Rasmussen, "A Forgotten Hero."

214 "The Los Angeles Massacre," *New York Times*.

215 Shelby Grad, "The Racist Massacre That Killed 10% of L.A.'s Chinese Population and Brought Shame to the City," *Los Angeles Times*, March 18, 2021, https://www.latimes.com/california/story/2021-03-18/reflecting-los-angeles-chinatown-massacre-after-atlanta-shootings.

216 "The Los Angeles Massacre," *New York Times.*

217 Local newspaper quoted in Rasmussen, "A Forgotten Hero."

218 Chan, *This Bittersweet Soil*, 376; "Affidavit and Flyers from the Chinese Boycott Case," The U.S. National Archives and Records Administration, October 11, 2017, https://www.archives.gov/education/lessons/chinese-boycott.

219 Zesch, *The Chinatown War*, 149.

220 Zesch, *The Chinatown War*, 137, 139, 141, 144.

221 "Mission and History," Chinese American Museum, accessed July 11, 2024, https://camla.org/mission-and-history/.

222 Josie Huang, "Here's the Winning Design for LA's Memorial to the 1871 Chinese Massacre," *LAist*, May 4, 2023, https://laist.com/news/la-history/chinese-massacre-1871-memorial-winning-design, https://culture.lacity.gov/programs-and-initiatives/1871-2/

223 Zhou Xun, *The Great Famine in China, 1958–1962: A Documentary History*, ed. Zhou Xun (New Haven: Yale University Press, 2012), x.

224 Lysenko quoted in Jasper Becker, *Hungry Ghosts: China's Secret Famine* (London: John Murray, 1996), 65.

225 Svetlana A. Borinskaya, Andrei I. Ermolaev, and Eduard I. Kolchinsky, "Lysenkoism against Genetics: The Meeting of the Lenin All-Union Academy of Agricultural Sciences of August 1948, Its Background, Causes, and Aftermath," *Genetics* 212, no. 1 (May 2019): 1–12, https://doi.org/10.1534/genetics.118.301413; Becker, *Hungry Ghosts*, 67.

226 Mao's speech at Supreme State Conference on January 28–30, 1958, Gansu, quoted in Frank Dikötter, *Mao's Great Famine: The History of China's Most Devastating Catastrophe, 1958–1962* (London: Bloomsbury, 2010), 174.

227 Zhou Xun, *Forgotten Voices of Mao's Great Famine, 1958–1962: An Oral History* (New Haven: Yale University Press, 2013), 106.

228 Zhou, *The Great Famine in China*, 95.

229 Dikötter, *Mao's Great Famine*, 176.

230 Becker, *Hungry Ghosts*, 85.

231 Jisheng Yang, *Tombstone: The Untold Story of Mao's Great Famine* (London: Penguin, 2013), 332; Dali L. Yang, *Calamity and Reform in China: State, Rural Society, and Institutional Change Since the Great Leap Famine* (Redwood City, California: Stanford University Press, 1996): 114; Zhou, *The Great Famine in China*, 86–87.

232 Zhou, *Forgotten Voices of Mao's Great Famine*, 18.

233 Dikötter, *Mao's Great Famine*, 138.

234 Dikötter, *Mao's Great Famine*, 241.

235 Becker, *Hungry Ghosts*, 257.

236 Quoted in Zhou, *Forgotten Voices of Mao's Great Famine*, 226.

237 Frederick Crook, *Agricultural Statistics of the People's Republic of China 1949–86* (Washington, DC: Agricultural and Trade Analysis Division, Economic Research Service, US Department of Agriculture, April 1988), 31, https://doi.org/10.22004/ag.econ.154654.

238 Becker, *Hungry Ghosts*, 248.

239 Crook, *Agricultural Statistics*, 31; Becker, *Hungry Ghosts*, 257.

240 Vaclav Smil, "China's Great Famine: 40 Years Later," *BMJ* 319, no. 7225 (December 1999): 1619–21, https://www.ncbi.nlm.nih.gov/pmc/articles/PMC1127087/.

241 Lois Beckett and Richard Luscombe, "Monterey Park shooting death toll rises to 11, including dance hall manager," *Guardian*, January 24 2023, https://www.theguardian.com/us-news/2023/jan/23/monterey-park-california-shooting-victims-motive.

242 May Liu, *China: Citrus Annual*, report no. CH2023-0192 (Foreign Agricultural Service, United States Department of Agriculture, December, 27, 2023), https://fas.usda.gov/data/china-citrus-annual-6.

243 "China Customs Suspends Imports of Citrus Fruits, Some Fish Products from Taiwan," Reuters, August 2, 2022, https://www.reuters.com/world/china/china-customs-suspends-imports-citrus-fruits-some-fish-products-taiwan-2022-08-03; Erin Hale, "The Farmers Caught Up in Taiwan's Tensions with China," BBC News, October 5, 2022, https://www.bbc.co.uk/news/business-63128392.

244 Hsiung-feng Chang, Lu Chia-jung, and Lee Hsin-Yin, "China to Lift Ban on Taiwan Fish, Citrus Fruit: Chinese Official," *Focus Taiwan*, I English News, April 28, 2024, https://focustaiwan.tw/cross-strait/202404280013.

245 Dan Sheehan, "A Brief Remembrance of Ghassan Kanafani," Literary Hub, April 8 2024, https://lithub.com/a-brief-remembrance-of-ghassan-kanafani/; Juwayriah Wright, "The Solemn History behind Nakba Day," *Time*, May 15, 2024, https://time.com/6978612/nakba-day-history/.

246 Ghassan Kanafani, *Men in the Sun and Other Palestinian Stories*, trans. Hilary Kilpatrick (Boulder, Colorado: Lynne Rienner Publishers, 1999), 80.

247 Mel Frykberg, "Environmental Terrorism Cripples Palestinian Farmers," IPS, April 6, 2015, https://reliefweb.int/report/occupied-palestinian-territory/environmental-terrorism-cripples-palestinian-farmers.

248 Ruwaida Amer, "The Olive Tree, Symbol of Palestine and Mute Victim of Israel's War on Gaza," Al Jazeera, January 22, 2024, https://www.aljazeera.com/features/2024/1/22/the-olive-tree-symbol-of-palestine-and-mute-victim-of-israels-war-on-gaza.

249 Emma Farge et al., "Gaza Death Toll: How Many Palestinians Has Israel's Campaign Killed," Reuters, July 10, 2024, https://www.reuters.com/world/middle-east/gaza-death-toll-how-many-palestinians-has-israels-campaign-killed-2024-05-14/.

250 Elisa Oddone, "Exploited, Hated, Killed: The Lives of African Fruit Pickers," Al Jazeera, July 22, 2018, https://www.aljazeera.com/features/2018/7/22/exploited-hated-killed-the-lives-of-african-fruit-pickers; Tobias Jones and Ayo Awokoya, "Are Your Tinned Tomatoes Picked by Slave Labour?" *Guardian*, June 20, 2019, https://www.theguardian.com/world/2019/jun/20/tomatoes-italy-mafia-migrant-labour-modern-slavery.

251 Oddone, "Exploited, Hated, Killed."

252 Mira Alestig and Sabita Banerji, *The Workers Behind the Citrus Fruits: A Focused Human Rights Impact Assessment of Coop Sweden's Moroccan Citrus Fruit Supply Chains* (Cowley, Oxford: Oxfam, April 2022), 42, https://oxfam .se/wp-content/uploads/2022/11/Oxfam.The-Workers-Behind-the-Citrus-Fruits.2022.pdf.

253 Adrià Budry Carbó, "Bitter Oranges: The Reality That the Industry Does Not Want You to See," Public Eye, June 2020, https://stories.publiceye.ch/oranges-brazil/.

254 Public Eye, "Bitter Oranges: How Brazilian Orange Pickers Do Hard Graft for Swiss Agricultural Trader LDC," press release, June 15, 2020, https://www .publiceye.ch/en/media-corner/press-releases/detail/bitter-oranges-how-brazilian-orange-pickers-do-hard-graft-for-swiss-agricultural-trader-ldc.

255 Carbó, "Bitter Oranges."

256 "Food Waste 2024—the Facts," BusinessWaste.co.uk, accessed July 11, 2024, https://www.businesswaste.co.uk/food-waste-the-facts; Brigid Francis-Devine, Nerys Roberts, and Xameerah Malik, *Food Poverty: Households, Food Banks and Free School Meals*, report no. 9209 (House of Commons Library, August 24, 2023), https://researchbriefings.files.parliament.uk/documents/CBP-9209/CBP-9209.pdf